AF324090

The Challenges of Explicit and Implicit Communication

Text – Meaning – Context:

Cracow Studies in English Language, Literature and Culture

Edited by
Elżbieta Chrzanowska-Kluczewska
Władysław Witalisz

Advisory Board:
Monika Coghen (Jagiellonian University, Cracow)
Hans-Jürgen Diller (Ruhr-University, Bochum)
Marta Gibińska-Marzec (Jagiellonian University, Cracow)
Irene Gilsenan Nordin (Dalarna University, Falun)
Christoph Houswitschka (University of Bamberg)
Zenón Luis Martínez (University of Huelva)
Elżbieta Mańczak-Wohlfeld (Jagiellonian University, Cracow)
Terence McCarthy (University of Bourgogne, Dijon)
Andrzej Pawelec (Jagiellonian University, Cracow)
Hans Sauer (University of Munich)
Salvador Valera (University of Granada)
Olga Vorobyova (Kiev National Linguistic University)

Volume 11

Maria Jodłowiec

The Challenges of Explicit and Implicit Communication

A Relevance-Theoretic Approach

Bibliographic Information published by the Deutsche Nationalbibliothek
The Deutsche Nationalbibliothek lists this publicationin the
Deutsche Nationalbibliografie; detailed bibliographic data is
available in the internet at http://dnb.d-nb.de.

Reviewed by Anna Niżegorodcew and Magdalena Charzyńska-Wójcik

The publication was financially supported by the Faculty of Philology
and the Institute of English Studies of the Jagiellonian University in Kraków.

Library of Congress Cataloging-in-Publication Data
Jodłowiec, Maria, author.
  The challenges of explicit and implicit communication : a relevance-
theoretic approach / Maria Jodłowiec. – Peter Lang Edition.
      pages cm – (Text - Meaning - Context: Cracow Studies in English
Language, Literature and Culture; Volume 11)
  ISBN 978-3-631-65867-3 (Print) – ISBN 978-3-653-05190-2 (E-Book)
  1. Communication models. 2. Interpersonal communication. 3. Se-
mantics–Psychological aspects. I. Title.
  P93.55.J63 2015
  401'.45–dc23
                                                                  2014048514

ISSN 2191-1894
ISBN 978-3-631-65867-3 (Print)
E-ISBN 978-3-653-05190-2 (E-Book)
DOI 10.3726/ 978-3-653-05190-2

www.peterlang.com

To Bogusław and Kamil, with love

Table of Contents

Acknowledgements

This project would have never come to completion if I had not received invaluable feedback, intellectual stimulation and constant support over more than the last decade from Professor Deirdre Wilson. I owe a special debt of gratitude to Deidre Wilson for all her constructive advice, immense kindness and genuine concern she has not spared me over the years. Her insightful comments and improvements on chapter 2 were more than important.

I would like to thank the Institute of English Studies at the Jagiellonian University in Kraków for the financial assistance which made this publication possible.

My special thanks go to the two reviewers, Professor Anna Niżegorodcew and Professor Magdalena Charzyńska-Wójcik, for their critical remarks on the manuscript. Professor Anna Niżegorodcew helped in correcting some mistakes that even a native-speaker's eye did not notice. Professor Magdalena Charzyńska-Wójcik's perceptive comments, penetrating questions and interesting suggestions towards improvement are greatly appreciated. The responsibility for all the flaws remains my own, so the usual disclaimer holds.

I would like to extend heartfelt thanks to Professor Ewa Willim both in her capacity of the Head of the Institute of English Studies at the Jagiellonian University in Kraków and of a very close friend. Ewa's genuine concern, constant encouragement and spiritual support cannot be overestimated.

I received a lot of support from many colleagues at the Institute. Professor Elżbieta Chrzanowska-Kluczewska, Head of the Department of Applied Language and EFL Teaching, which I am part, of and one of the editors of the series within which this book is published, provided a lot of assistance and useful advice.

I would like to give my warm thanks to Professor Elżbieta Mańczak-Wohlfeld for her expert advice, generous help and consolation in times of crisis.

Professor Marta Dąbrowska shared with me invaluable insights about some technical procedures, which I am very grateful for.

Ramon Schindler proofread parts of the text.

I profited a lot from the discussions and work on some joint projects with Agnieszka Piskorska from Warsaw University – thanks Agnieszka!

Many friends kept their fingers crossed (for quite a long time) for me and provided lots of moral support. In particular, I would like to thank: Alicia Feitzinger, Laura and Maz Mazur, Per van der Wijst and Jerzy Wójcik – each of them helped in their own, very special and much appreciated way. I would like to thank also His Eminence Cardinal Marian Jaworski for his invaluable spiritual backing.

Last, but not least, I would like to thank my loving family, my husband Bogusław, my son Kamil and his girlfriend Ula, and my brother Józef. While it may sound strange to say that an academic book is written for anybody, there is a very real sense in which writing this book only made sense because of them and my late parents, Wanda and Julian, who were always there for me.

Introduction

The present research falls within the field of pragmatic studies. Despite various attempts at delineating the scope of pragmatics adequately, the dispute as to what pragmatic investigations embrace and what kind of division of labour there should be across such linguistic disciplines as grammar, semantics and pragmatics has been going on for decades now (cf. Ariel 2010, 2012; Bianchi 2004; Carston 2008; Horn 2006; Jaszczolt 2012, among others). It is not my intention to contribute to this dispute, as my aims are entirely different and much more modest. For the present purposes, a rather broad definition of pragmatics is adopted. It is treated as a study of general principles underlying the production and comprehension of utterances, that is, coded or non-coded signals intentionally used to convey meaning.

My major goal is to show how to account for various aspects of utterance interpretation within Relevance Theory, one of the leading pragmatic models of the present time. So this research is confined to verbal communication. There are three major focal points in the present study that have to do with: (a) how Relevance Theory accounts for explicature generation, (b) how it explains the implicit layer of communication, and (c) how the model rises to the challenge of elucidating the immense complexity and the extraordinary efficiency of human communication.

An in-depth investigation into the nature of explicatures, as envisaged in the relevance-theoretic framework, and certain doubts and controversies surrounding the so-called free enrichment mechanism, brought me to explore the nature of the processes involved. Fully endorsing the semantic underdeterminacy thesis, relevance theorists assume that bridging the gap between the decoded logical form and the speaker-intended meaning is accomplished via inferencing. Apart from such linguistically mandated pragmatic processes as saturation of contextual variables, resolution of ambiguities, reconstruction of the elliptical material, etc., Relevance Theory admits the process of free enrichment, which is not linguistically sanctioned. According to Carston (2004a: 819), free enrichment is "the incorporation of conceptual material that is wholly pragmatically inferred, on the basis of considerations of rational communicative behavior." Undeniably, getting the occasion-specific meaning may call for zeroing in on the precise content which is not linguistically licensed in any sense. However, if the process responsible for this adds conceptual elements to the representation, it appears suspicious. In the first place, if such a process is in operation, there may be different ways in which "gaps" in the decoded logical form can be filled in with supplementary concepts, so, in effect, potentially different explicatures will surface for exactly the same utterance with manifestly the same speaker-intended specific meaning. This is a problem for the theory. Besides, this type of conceptual enhancement of the decoded logical form is cognitively strenuous and creates an unnecessary cognitive burden for the interpreter. In an attempt to overcome these problems a new mechanism is put forward here. The contextual cognitive fix procedure, postulated as part of the relevance-oriented comprehension heuristic, appears to avoid these complications and makes explicature recovery more efficient and more appealing in my estimation. My aim in this book is to argue for this slight amendment to the model and suggest that Relevance Theory can benefit from replacing the controversial free enrichment procedure with the contextual cognitive fix mechanism.

At the level of implicit import, the most interesting and innovative idea in the relevance-theoretic framework is that of weak communication. This notion is original and unique to Relevance Theory and offers interesting insights into what happens when the communicator's goal is not so much to convey a determinate, explicit, well-defined and relatively precise meaning, but rather to affect the recipient's thought processes, as a result of which the latter will arrive at a complex and rich interpretation, not necessarily fully endorsed by the communicator's intention. Indeterminate intentions and impreciseness of the communicated content have their appeal, as will be shown in this book.

I have always been attracted by the challenge of the fundamental pragmatic question how human beings can communicate ever so efficiently. This is not a trivial query, considering the remote and putative nature of background information that needs to be brought to bear in the interpretation process, taking into account different degrees of familiarity (or complete unfamiliarity) of the interlocutors, thinking about idiosyncrasies in the linguistic competence of the speaker and the hearer, to mention just the most obvious factors that affect communication and prove insurmountable (at least as yet) for robots. Relevance Theory does suggest an answer to this question, but it somehow passes unnoticed. In asking and answering this Master Question (Neale forthcoming) I hope to bring to light the relevance-theoretic stance on the problem and demonstrate how it confronts the challenge.

The book has the following structure. In chapter 1, the relevance-theoretic model, its theoretical underpinnings and tenets are introduced. Basic conceptual apparatus of Relevance Theory is presented with a view to laying the foundation for the later discussion. In particular, The Cognitive and Communicative Principles of Relevance with the satellite notions are defined and briefly discussed. The cognitive bias of the theory is emphasized and its affinity with the modular view of the human mind is brought to the fore. Intentionality as approached in relevance-theoretic terms is highlighted and the inferential nature of comprehension processes is underscored. Because of its aim and subject matter, this introductory part amounts to a survey of the theoretical skeleton of the model. This chapter then is a useful synopsis for the reader familiar with the theory and a worthwhile read for those who may not be fully acquainted with the framework.

Chapter 2 focuses on the relevance-theoretic account of explicit meaning. The notion of explicature developed by Sperber and Wilson (1986/96; Wilson and Sperber 2002, 2004) is broader than the notion of what is said as conceived by Grice (1967/89). Relevance Theory views the process of explicature recovery as heavily inferential, with various types of semantic underdeterminacies getting resolved through inference, and the result is a fully-fledged proposition. Free enrichment, taken by many relevance theorists to be responsible for settling underdeterminacies, is critically approached in this chapter. In an attempt to eliminate some of its inadequacies, as hinted at above, the contextual cognitive fix mechanism is introduced. It is also argued that the relevance-driven search for the speaker-intended meaning may on certain occasions yield only a proposition schema and not necessarily a full proposition. Consequently, shallow interpretations at the level of explicature may frequently result – an effect predicted by the contextual cognitive fix construal postulated here.

The implicit layer of communication is the subject matter of chapter 3. Some vital concepts are discussed first, with the major focus on weak communication and poetic effects. To illustrate how the poetic effect is created, some examples of aphorisms are analysed. The main claim is that the role of poetic effects is to initiate the recipient on a certain interpretation path and he is encouraged to explore the meaning further on his own.

In chapter 4, the so-called miracle of communication problem is addressed from the perspective of Relevance Theory. The conception of the comprehension module with the in-built relevance-guided comprehension heuristic which ensures fast, frugal and automatic interpretation of ostensive stimuli is presented. It fits in with the massive modularity mental architecture, as is argued, and provides a plausible solution to the complexity vis-à-vis the efficiency of communication problem.

A summary of the major points raised in the study and suggestions for further research are presented in conclusion.

Chapter 1
Relevance Theory: a cognitive model of communication

1.1 Introduction

Sperber and Wilson's Relevance Theory (henceforth RT) is one of the most influential and important pragmatic models to date. It offers a full, thorough, stimulating and productive model of human communication, as shown by the vast relevance-theoretic research which has flourished over the last three decades.

The goal of this chapter is to describe the model and highlight its inherent cognitive motivation and bias. Essentially, the major underpinnings of RT derive from some fundamental observations about how human cognition works and the assumption that, in order to ensure its efficient functioning, there must be an in-built mechanism controlling the allocation of cognitive resources as well as the formatting and storage of information. Sperber and Wilson define this mechanism in terms of relevance. The principal claim that human cognition is relevance-driven will be focused on first (Ch.1.2). The Cognitive Principle of Relevance, providing a rationale for the mind's workings, not only fits in perfectly with, but also contributes to the modular view of the human mind, as argued in section 1.3. Relevance as the fundamental notion for the relevance-theoretic model of communication is defined next (Ch.1.4), In section 1.5 the prime and central conceptual tools of the theory are introduced, with the cornerstone of the relevance-theoretic framework in the form of the Communicative Principle of Relevance and its satellite, a presumption of optimal relevance. In the section that follows (1.6), the relevance-theoretic treatment of the communicator's intentions and their recognition by the addressee is presented: while considered pivotal in most pragmatic studies, intentionality in communication is largely taken for granted and left unexplained, so RT is a notable exception is this respect. The practical application of the relevance-based interpretation process is then demonstrated (Ch.1.7). The dynamic approach to context construction, one of the distinctive features of RT, and the overall non-demonstrative nature of comprehension processes are the subject matter of the penultimate section. Concluding remarks, which end the chapter, provide an overview of the major points made.

This chapter extensively draws on Sperber and Wilson writings, hence numerous references to their various publications will appear throughout.

1.2 Cognitive goals and relevance

Making psychological realism one of their primary tenets, Sperber and Wilson (1986/95) have anchored their theory of communication in certain basic observations about human cognition. By definition then, the relevance-theoretic framework fits in with the postulates of ecologism in linguistic studies (cf. Seuren 2009).[1]

Granted that human cognition is geared towards making sense of the reality around, the long-term cognitive goals that the mind pursues can be defined in terms of generating the most accurate representation of the world. As pointed out by Sperber and Wilson (1986/95: 47), "[t]his means adding more information, information that is more accurate, more easily retrievable, and more developed in areas of greater concern to the individual." It seems reasonable to assume that short-term cognitive aims, apart from monitoring the environment for possible hazards and risks in order to ensure that nothing threatens the organism's safety and well-being, will similarly be oriented towards inputs that are likely to help in achieving these life-long goals and to contribute to improving one's knowledge of the world. However, the problem is that at each moment of their being awake, individuals are bombarded with a great number of stimuli, and the conscious cognitive processes, with their limited capacity, cannot possibly attend to all of them. An attentional bottleneck results: "only a fraction of the monitored environmental information can be attentionally processed, and only a fraction of the memorised information can be brought to bear on it" (Sperber and Wilson 2002: 14). Hence it seems rational to postulate the existence of an in-built mechanism that will be responsible for filtering out some of the abundant available data and for allocating the processing

---

1   This does not mean that Seuren would accept or approve of RT as a viable model of language use. Just the opposite, Seuren (2009) is very critical of radical pragmatics, within which Sperber and Wilson's framework is commonly placed, as characterized by a strong aversion to formalism and, therefore, largely ignoring the prominent role that the constraints stemming from and imposed by the language system should be assigned. In Seuren's (2009: 37) own words, in radical pragmatic theories "[q]uestions about how precisely token interpretations are arrived at by humans are seldom taken up and never answered." This criticism appears grossly unfair with reference to RT, which not only makes context-specific utterance comprehension and elucidation of how interpreters arrive at speaker-intended token meanings its primary objective, but also provides conceptual apparatus designed to conduct such investigations (see the discussion below and the relevance-theoretic analyses in Ch. 2 and 3).

resources to information which is likely to be cognitively most beneficial (Sperber and Wilson 1986/95: 48).

Approaching cognition as a biological function and assuming that most (if not all) cognitive processes have evolved through natural selection as adaptations geared towards maximal efficiency, the originators of RT convincingly argue that

> [a]s a result of constant selection pressures toward increasing efficiency, the human cognitive system has developed in such a way that our perceptual mechanisms tend automatically to pick out potentially relevant stimuli, our memory retrieval mechanisms tend automatically to activate potentially relevant assumptions, and our inferential mechanisms tend spontaneously to process them in the most productive way. (Wilson and Sperber 2004: 610)

This kind of general cognitive orientation towards relevance, which is believed to permeate various levels of cognitive operations, from setting cognitive priorities to data configuration and storage to recall procedures, is believed to have developed in the course of phylogenesis (Sperber and Wilson 1986/95: 261-262) and to be related to the species' instinct for self-preservation (cf. Sperber 2000).[2]

The automatic tendency to orientate towards relevance and to capitalize on it for maximum cognitive outcomes is formalized in the model as the First Principle of Relevance (Wilson and Sperber 2004: 610):

> "*Cognitive Principle of Relevance*: Human cognition tends to be geared to the maximization of relevance."

Relevance is thus taken to be the key to cognitive efficiency, with inputs likely to yield most relevant information selected for inferential effort-demanding processing (cf. Sperber 1994b). It is recognized as an important property of mentally processed inputs, with a remarkable and principal role in human communication. Before relevance as conceived of in the pragmatic framework under scrutiny is characterized in some more detail, it seems useful to consider the architecture of the human mind that Sperber and Wilson's ideas accord with and support.

1.3 The mind's massive modularity

As indicated above, orientation towards stimuli, phenomena, objects, or in a more general sense, inputs that are potentially relevant, and processing them in the way that will maximize their relevance is postulated by Sperber and Wilson to be part of the human cognitive endowment (cf. Yus 2006: 512), which has evolved in the

---

2   This postulate is in line with the perspective characteristic of evolutionary psychology, according to which the mind is a cluster of mental devices, all developed as adaptations of the species repeatedly and systematically confronting major environmental problems of a certain kind (Sperber and Hirschfeld 1999: cxiv).

course of evolutionary adaptations (Sperber and Wilson 1986/95: 261-262).[3] This approach is fully compatible with a hypothesis about the computational model of the human mind (cf. Searle 1992, 1996), which started more than thirty years as the famous Fodor's (1983) modularity thesis and which has recently been developed into what is referred to as the massive modularity hypothesis (Carruthers 2006a; Sperber 1994b, 1996, 2001, 2005; Samuels 2000).

In very general terms, mental modularity assumes that the human mind is primarily an information processing device, developed in the process of natural selection (Cosmides and Tooby 1994), which – consisting of a set of highly specialized innate modules – works in a computer-like fashion.

Originally, the modules were conceived of by Fodor (1983) as input systems, mainly concerned with processing the data provided by the senses as well as the language module, and, roughly speaking, their task was to transform the signals received by the senses and the language parser into representations to be used in central processing at the level of conscious thought. Central processing units, non-modular in nature,[4] were posited to allow for the integration of information from the different systems in order to compute "'best hypotheses' about what the world is like" (Fodor 1983: 104).

Fodor (1983: 47-101) characterizes the modules in terms of special properties deemed essential to the mind's cognitive efficiency. Thus, among other qualities, the input systems are assumed to be: a) domain specific, which means that they are triggered by stimuli peculiar to their domains and have their own idiosyncratic computational principles; b) mandatory, so whenever perceptual processes can apply they must apply, with the system automatically set into action by a mere presence of a relevant stimulus; and c) inaccessible and encapsulated, owing to the fact that they allow only a very limited central access and have themselves

---

3   As Sperber and Wilson (2002) state, there are, roughly speaking, two types of evolutionary adaptations. On the one hand, there are those that have to do with a gradual modification of some feature of the organism, and therefore can be classified as continuous changes. On the other hand, there are discrete adaptations that involve "the gradual emergence of a new trait or property, such as eyes or wings" (Sperber and Wilson 2002: 13). Whereas the development of the tendency to maximize relevance at the level of cognitive processes can be seen as a gradual change, the emergence of a comprehension module (see Ch. 4) geared to the search for optimally relevant interpretations may have come about as a discreet adaptation.

4   As Fodor (1983: 119) forcefully puts it, "there are *no* content-specific central processes for the performance of which corresponding specific neutral structures have been identified. Everything we know now is compatible with the claim that central problem-solving is subserved by equipotential neural mechanisms. This is precisely what you would expect if you assume that the central cognitive processes are largely Quineian and isotropic" (original emphasis). Needless to say, Fodor (1983: 104-129) makes a strong case for a Quineian and isotropic thinking process.

virtually no access to information supplied by other systems, hence there is no across-input-systems information sharing. On top of all this, since they operate in a reflex-like, automatized and unintelligent fashion, they are extremely fast and relatively cheap (Fodor 1983: 64, 71).

On this original construal, the mind's modularity was very limited, with the (vertical) input systems being relatively few, principally peripheral[5] and subservient to the (horizontal) central processors, which could accommodate the information from the different input analysers and make use of it in the process of belief fixation. While Fodor's pioneering model has attracted a lot of criticism (see, e.g., Churchland 1988; Prinz 2006), it sparked off an intense and serious debate on mental modularity, which has led to what Carruthers and Chamberlain (2000: 2) refer to as liberalizing the notion. As a result, Fodor's "modest proposal" has developed into what now seems to flourish as the massive modularity thesis (see also Ch.4.4-4.5).

Fodor's picture of the mind, though fairly straightforward and clear, was definitely controversial, but more importantly, incompatible with a vast body of mounting evidence accumulated in various fields of science, in particular in biology (cf., e.g., Seely 1995 and Simon 1962, both in Carruthers 2006b), neuroscience, evolutionary psychology and anthropology. Additionally, his claims and assumptions have been found wanting in the face of persuasive arguments developed in the philosophical literature and artificial intelligence research (cf. Carruthers 2006b; Carruthers and Chamberlain 2000 and references therein).

Merely reporting, let alone elaborating on the various strands of the heated dispute about the structuring and functioning of the massively modular mind would go beyond the scope of the present discussion. The simple fact that there is a lot of controversy as to how the very notion of *module* should be defined and characterized (cf. Carruthers 2006a, 2006b; Sperber 2005) bears witness to the intense intellectual ferment surrounding the subject. As Samuels (2000) emphasizes, there are two major conceptions of what should count as the module within evolutionary psychology alone. One of them takes modules to be computational devices which, functioning in a domain specific way, manipulate symbols or representations. On the other hand, modules are viewed as mental representations, that is, systems of knowledge which underlie various kinds of human cognitive capacity, such as, for instance, systems of knowledge of physics, biology, mathematics, etc. The language faculty à la Chomsky is a paradigm case of the latter species of modules, called for this reason *Chomskian modules* by Samuels (2000). It is worth stressing that both conceptions are subject to debate (Samuels 2000), as are many other aspects of the massive modularity hypothesis of the human mind, like for instance, those related to control and flow of information

---

5   Sperber (1994b: 39) rightly points out that it is a bit of a paradox in the light of the fact that the title of Fodor's seminal book is The Modularity of Mind.

between modules, their hardwiring, computational tractability, etc. (cf. Carruthers 2006b; Samuels 2000, 2005; Sperber 1994b).

One crucial assumption shared across the different incarnations of the massive modularity view, which departs sharply from the Fodorian perspective, is that a number of central processing systems are in fact modular (cf. Carruthers 2006a, 2006b; Sperber 1994b). There is a lot of disagreement, though, as to which conceptual domains should be identified as "governed by domain-specific competences" (Sperber 1994b: 42) and hence assigned a modular status. There is no consensus either about whether it is fruitful to consider both micro- (with every concept potentially being a submodule; Sperber 1994b, 1996), and macro-modules (with metatemplates for specific cognitive domains; Sperber 1994b) at the conceptual level,[6] and there is a considerable diversity of opinion as to the feasibility and motivations behind possible networking across the different types of conceptual modules and their connections with perceptual systems (cf. Sperber 1994b), to mention but a few of the many themes of dissent.

Regardless of the turn that the modularity debate will take, it is crucial to emphasize that Sperber and Wilson's original model fits in perfectly with the modular outlook on the mind, whether in its modest version, that is, restricted to input modules and non-modular central processes (cf. Woodward and Cowie 2004), or the massively modular one, viz. embracing perceptual and a number of conceptual modules of a different kind (Sperber 1994b). Sperber (1994b, 1996) can be listed as one of the early advocates of massive mental modularity, but many other relevance theorists endorse the hypothesis (e.g., Carston 2010a, 2010c; Carston and Hall 2012; Wilson 2005, 2014). What is more, RT offers an important mechanism underlying the operation of cognitive systems, in accordance with which resources are allocated to inputs which are expected to be most relevant (Sperber 2001). As Sperber (2005: 68) explains,

> When an input meets the input condition of a given modular procedure, this gives this procedure some initial level of activation. Input-activated procedures are in competition for the energy resources that would allow them to follow their full course. What determines which of the procedures in competition get sufficient resources to trigger their full operation is the dynamics of their activation. These dynamics depend both on the prior degree of mobilization of a modular procedure and on the activation that propagates from other active modules. It is also quite conceivable that the mobilization of some procedures has inhibitory effects on some other procedures. The relevance-theoretic claim is that, at every instant, these dynamics of activation provide rough physiological indicators of expected relevance. The flow of energy in the system is locally regulated by these indicators. As a result, those input-procedure combinations that have the greatest expected relevance are the more likely ones to receive sufficient energy to follow their course. This is just a tendency, but it is strong

---

6   Tsimply and Smith (1998) express scepticism about such ideas.

enough to yield the kind of context-sensitivity that humans actually exhibit in their individual cognitive processes.[7]

It seems that the (massively) modular mind does need a mechanism responsible for managing the cognitive resources and computational procedures it uses in a principled and efficient way, and orientation towards maximizing relevance appears a worthwhile and feasible suggestion in this respect.

While, as Sperber (2005) himself admits, these claims are only speculative, and at this stage of research they cannot be anything more, the idea that relevance considerations affect people's performance on reasoning tasks has been empirically verified. Van der Henst et al. (2002) established that with reference to indeterminate relational problems, the subjects' reasoning was constrained by context-specific relevance judgements. Generally, in reasoning experiments participants are supposed to reason from the premises provided by the experimenters in order to answer questions about particular relations (of the type: *taller, better*, etc.) among the entities specified. For determinate problems, certain relations between the objects can be inferred from these premises. For indeterminate problems, there are some relations that are simply left unspecified by the premises, which makes conclusions about these relations based on the premises indeterminate, that is why they are referred to as indeterminate problems.[8] As is underscored by Van der Henst and Sperber (2004: 148-149), with reference to such problems it is always possible to infer a range of conclusions – usually of a trivial kind – from the delivered premises, but they can hardly be considered relevant. So, if in the case of indeterminate questions the subject's answer is: "Nothing follows", this is assumed to result from the fact that people invariably form specific expectations of relevance and when these are not met, they are inclined to conclude that nothing *relevant* follows. On the other hand, determinate problems lead to contextually relevant conclusions, which the subjects are ready to derive. As Van der Henst et al. (2002) show, a careful manipulation of the supplied contextual information increases or decreases expectations of relevance, which affects the subjects' readiness to draw or to abandon drawing a conclusion. It follows that both causes of reasoning that people are likely to engage in and the inferential procedures that they implement during reasoning tasks of this type appear to be relevance-driven. Thus Van der Henst et al.'s (2002) experimental findings provide support for the Cognitive Principle of Relevance (see also Van der Henst and Sperber 2004).[9]

---

7   For a fully-developed argument of what might be involved, see Sperber (2005).

8   For instance, from the premises like: "A is taller than B" and "A is taller than C" nothing non-trivial about the relation between B and C can be inferred (Van der Henst and Sperber 2004: 147).

9   Some further empirical evidence for relevance-guided reasoning in experimental tasks is available in Sperber et al. (1995) and Girotto et al. (2001).

Granted that human minds are essentially information processing devices, the existence of an in-built[10] tacit principle of cognitive economy, like the Cognitive Principle of Relevance, seems a well-grounded and reasonable assumption. This kind of principle seems essential to sanction "local arbitrations, aimed at incremental gains, between simultaneously available inputs competing for immediately available resources" (Sperber and Wilson 1986/95: 261).[11]

So far nothing has been said about relevance as such, so it is time to tackle the question: what exactly is relevance?

1.4 Cognitive effects and relevance

Attaining the long-term and short-term cognitive goals as defined above (see 1.2) is tantamount to enhancing the organism's "information state" (cf. Jaszczolt 2012: 2346), which in more practical terms can be expounded as accumulating true information about the world around. This suggests that delusions, false assumptions and incorrect conclusions, which do not yield a more accurate depiction of the reality, are not worth having (Sperber and Wilson 1986/95: 263-264): they distort the picture and are highly undesirable and "actually deleterious" (Floridi 2008: 84). Accordingly, the enhancement of knowledge is achieved only through what the originators of relevance theory call *positive cognitive effects*, that is, desirable cognitive gains (Sperber and Wilson 1986/95: 265).

Basically, positive cognitive effects, as Sperber and Wilson (1986/95: 108-117) argue, can be of three kinds, depending on how the currently accessed information interacts with the body of existing assumptions already present in the individual's mind. In the first place, thanks to the processing of a certain incoming stimulus together with some old information, a new piece of information may be acquired. This new information is neither derivable from the input nor from the existing knowledge alone, and as "a synthesis of old and new information" (Sperber and Wilson 1986/95: 108) has the status of a contextual implication. Second, the upshot of processing may be that an existing assumption entertained previously only as a weak one will be strengthened by becoming better evidenced. Third, it may happen that an existing assumption will be revised or even eliminated from

---

10   The term *in-built* should not be understood here in the Fodorian sense of being part of the mind's neural hard-wiring, but rather as a software mechanism.

11   Obviously, the potential existence of this kind of law aimed at high cognitive economy does not guarantee optimal functioning of the organism. Due to various factors, malfunctioning may occur, "many cognitive sub-mechanisms that fail to deliver enough effect for the effort they require, [and there may be] many occasions when the system's resources are poorly allocated" (Sperber and Wilson 1986/95: 262).

the individual's representation of the world as untrue when confronted with the newly presented input. As a rule, cognitive effects of whichever kind are taken to be modifications in the individual's belief state (Sperber and Wilson 1986/95: 265) and are hypothesized to contribute to achieving short-term as well as long-term cognitive goals.[12]

It needs to be added at this juncture that RT assumes that an individual's knowledge about the world is stored in memory in the form of assumptions, understood as "thoughts treated by the individual as representations of the actual world" (Sperber and Wilson 1986/95: 2).[13] These assumptions may come with different confirmation values, that is, various degrees of strength, depending on how well evidenced they appear to the individual.[14]

If we treat the body of assumptions with which the incoming information interacts as context, then the cognitive effects[15] obtained in any of the three types of manner characterized here also constitute contextual effects, and actually these two terms have been used side by side in relevance-theoretic literature, with a recent preference for the former term.[16] Moreover, whenever the incorporation of newly presented information into the context results in some contextual effects, technically, this information is *relevant in that context*, and conversely, if no such interaction takes place, the new information *fails to be relevant*.

Since recovering cognitive effects inevitably involves the expenditure of effort, cognitive efficiency – and consequently relevance – is viewed on this

---

12 In more epistemic terms, Sperber et al. (2010: 374-375) suggest that the three types of cognitive effects involve: "acceptance of contextually implied new beliefs, modification of strength of beliefs and revision of beliefs."

13 Assumptions are believed to be generated as "the output of cognitive processes of perception, recall, imagination or inference" (Sperber and Wilson 1986/95: 261), which suggests that their sources may be both external to the organism (e.g., perceptual) and internal (when assumptions arise through inferencing), but their status is invariably that of internal conceptual representations.

14 The strength of assumptions is not taken to be computed or represented in quantitative values, but rather gauged by the organism in terms of gross absolute judgements or in terms of comparative estimates. So the claim is that while some assumptions are entertained as strong, or certain, and others as quite weak, because they are poorly confirmed, still other assumptions may only feature in the mind as stronger, or more likely to be true when compared with some other assumptions. Evidently, strengthening some existing assumptions or eliminating those that get disconfirmed contributes to improving one's representation of the world.

15 In the light of the remarks above, only positive cognitive effects can count as genuine cognitive gains, so whenever the term *cognitive effect* is used from now on, it should be understood to refer to positive cognitive effects.

16 As Sperber and Wilson (1986/95) note in the "Postface", in their publications after 1986 they have used the term *cognitive effect* rather than *contextual effect*.

model in terms of the balance of effort and effect. Relevance then is "a positive function of cognitive effects and a negative function of the processing effort expended in deriving these effects" (Carston 2002: 44; see also Sperber and Wilson 2002: 13-14). This means that relevance is by definition a matter of degree: other things being equal, the bigger the cognitive effects derived in the processing of a given stimulus, the greater the relevance; on the other hand, other things being equal, the higher the effort required in recovering the cognitive effects, the lower the relevance (Wilson and Sperber 2004: 609). While relevance as a crucial property of inputs to cognitive processing can be defined in absolute terms, this kind of perspective appears psychologically unappealing. So a classificatory definition of relevance, in accordance with which an input will be relevant to an individual in a context at a given time if and only if processing it yields some positive cognitive effects in that context (cf. Sperber and Wilson 1986/95: 122), is possible, but much less interesting from the psychological point of view.[17] The problem is that the organism does not measure cognitive effect and effort in absolute terms, even though, as Sperber and Wilson (1986/95: 119) point out, people have intuitions about them. It is posited then that relevance, mental effort and cognitive effects are treated as non-representational mental properties, which as Sperber and Wilson (1986/95: 132) emphasize, "need not be represented, let alone computed, in order to be achieved" (see also Wilson and Sperber 2004: 610).

The inherent predisposition of human cognition towards securing cognitive effects, which, as indicated above, amounts to orientation towards relevant inputs and their relevance-guided processing constrained by optimal balancing of effect and effort, has significant consequences for human interactions and is the cornerstone of the relevance-theoretic account of communication.

1.5 Ostension, cognitive environment, manifestness and the Communicative Principle of Relevance

An insightful observation about human interaction that Sperber and Wilson make, which is fundamental for the model of human communication they have developed, has to do with the fact that communicative acts inevitably involve the communicator demanding the addressee's attention. Granted that cognition is

---

17   Strictly speaking then, having a contextual effect is a sufficient and necessary condition for being relevant, but comparative judgements of relevance in terms of effect-effort budgeting are much more important from the psychological point of view (Wilson and Sperber 2004: 610).

geared towards maximizing relevance, as the Cognitive Principle of Relevance posits (see 1.2), by overtly requiring the recipient's attention the communicator creates in the addressee an expectation that he will obtain some relevant information (Sperber and Wilson 1996/95: 49), and this tacit assumption in an important way provides the rationale underlying human communicative behaviours and helps to explain how it works.

Generally, expectations of relevance formed by an individual may arise internally or externally. In situations in which a person's attention is automatically directed towards alarming developments taking place in close proximity, or when someone chooses on their own to focus their attention on a given entity or event, the expectation of relevance has an internal source. This means that when our attention is automatically attracted by certain stimuli or phenomena, such as loud noises, flashes of light, salient fast moving objects in the vicinity, etc., we are reacting in a reflex-like fashion, precisely because we have been pre-programmed to treat such incidents as relevant, and our quick response may prove a life-saving action.[18] Such attention pre-empting stimuli are treated by the organism as relevant, as if by definition, so their relevance is taken for granted.[19] The situation is slightly different if a person chooses to attend to a certain phenomenon or stimulus in the environment of his own accord: then he may only cherish hopes that it will be relevant, but these hopes may be fulfilled or frustrated, so there is no guarantee of relevance whatsoever. However, when someone's attentional resources are openly and deliberately claimed by another person, the individual whose attention is demanded is entitled to expect adequate cognitive gains: there is a guarantee of relevance that external demands for attention of this kind come with. And in a relevance-theoretic framework a guarantee of relevance of this kind is assumed to have far-reaching consequences for how communication functions.

Notice that a guarantee of relevance comes only with attention-demanding acts that are overt and intentional. To be sure, not all kinds of communication meet this condition.[20] It must be explicitly stated that Sperber and Wilson do not aim at developing an all-embracing model of different possible kinds of communication. As they underline, they do not believe it is feasible to create such

---

18 Mercier and Sperber (2009: 156) claim that danger-detection modules "have an inbuilt expectation of relevance."

19 They may of course eventually turn out to be irrelevant, as, for example, is the case when the flashes of light and noises that we get alerted by happen to be just a birthday fireworks display in the neighbourhood.

20 For instance, there are different kinds of covert communication and accidental transmission of information that do not meet this criterion (see Wilson and Sperber 1993 and Ch.3.7 below).

a homogeneous and comprehensive theory that would elucidate unintentional communication, covert communication together with the intentional, fully overt type. Sperber and Wilson focus on the latter type, maintaining that some interesting and useful generalizations can be made about overt intentional communication, called *ostensive-inferential*. RT is designed as an explanatory account of precisely this type of communication. Before ostensive-inferential communication can be characterized in more detail, the notion of mutual cognitive environment and manifestness need to be introduced because they are fundamental for this sort of interaction.

In very general terms, on the relevance-theoretic model communication is approached as an interaction between two information-processing devices in which one modifies the cognitive environment of the other (Sperber and Wilson 1986/95: 1). The term *cognitive environment* refers to "a set of assumptions which the individual is capable of mentally representing and accepting as true" (Sperber and Wilson 1996/95: 46). In effect, one's cognitive environment comprises not only the assumptions that somebody actually holds, but also those that the person is potentially able to form and think of as true, even if mistakenly. As long as at a given time an individual is capable of representing a fact to himself and accepting it as true or probably true, in relevance-theoretic terms this fact is *manifest* to the individual.[21] "To be manifest, then, is to be perceptible or inferable" (Sperber and Wilson 1996/95: 39), though not necessarily known. Employing the notion of *manifestness*, we can redefine *cognitive environment* as "a set of assumptions that are manifest to" a given individual (Wilson and Sperber 1992: 71).

Manifestness, as relevance, is a matter of degree, so right now various assumptions may be more or less manifest to the reader of this book. It seems reasonable to assume that it is more manifest in this context, for instance, that the text being read is written in English and what time of day (or night) it is than, say, that Luanda is the capital of Angola. I do not want to suggest that any of these assumptions is actually relevant to the reader at this moment and therefore entertained, though potentially it may become so. For example, if their reading is interrupted by their partner's question: "Are you ready for supper?" or if the partner suddenly announces, "I'm flying to Luanda next Thursday", the assumption about the time of day or about the location of Luanda may become manifestly relevant and may surface in the reader's mind. The important thing is that in interactions certain assumptions become manifest or more manifest to the recipient.

---

21 As Sperber and Wilson (1986/95: 40) emphasize, "all the individual's actual assumptions are manifest to him, but many more assumptions which he has not actually made are manifest to him too."

If the same assumptions are manifest to certain individuals, then they share their cognitive environments with respect to these assumptions, or in other words, their "cognitive environments intersect, and their intersection is the cognitive environment that these (…) people share" (Sperber and Wilson 1986/95: 41). Furthermore, if in the "shared cognitive environment it is manifest which people share it", it is called a *mutual cognitive environment* (Sperber and Wilson 1996/95: 41). As Sperber and Wilson (1996/95: 45) proceed to explain,

> because we manifestly share cognitive environments with other people, we have direct evidence about what is manifest to them. When a cognitive environment we share with other people is mutual, we have evidence about what is mutually manifest to all of us. Note that this evidence can never be conclusive: the boundaries of cognitive environments cannot be precisely determined, if only because the threshold between very weakly manifest assumptions and inaccessible ones is unmarked.

In this way mutual manifestness makes it possible to establish what shared assumptions can be taken as mutual in that both the communicator and the addressee will be (even if only tacitly) aware they both have access to them and this (tacit) realization is mutually shared.[22]

If the individual's behaviour makes mutually manifest to another person an intention to make something manifest, this counts in relevance-theoretic terms as an act of *ostension* and the stimulus used (Sperber and Wilson 1986/95: 49), whether in a verbal and non-verbal form, is called *an ostensive stimulus* (Sperber

---

22 In this way mutual manifestness is a weaker but psychologically more plausible concept than the mutual knowledge requirement, critical for the code model of communication (cf. Perner and Garnham 1988). The mutual knowledge requirement, which is rooted in the assumption that successful communication ends with the speaker's thoughts being replicated in the hearer's mind, establishes that an identical range of contextual assumptions need to used by speakers and hearers. This can only happen if the speaker can identify the assumptions that she shares with the hearer and the hearer can identify those assumptions that the speaker might identify as those that he shares with her. As Sperber and Wilson (1987: 698) are quick to point out, this raises the question: "How are the speaker and hearer to distinguish the assumptions they share from those they do not? For that, they must make second-order assumptions about which first-order assumptions they share; but then they had better make sure that they share these second-order assumptions, which calls for third-order assumptions, and so on indefinitely." The infinite regress that this leads to makes proposals based on mutual knowledge psychologically unfeasible. The notion of mutual manifestness is a property of cognitive environments and not of mental processes of knowing, believing, etc., so it is not open to these objections (cf. Thomson's 2008 Graded Stance model, in accordance with which greater or lesser transparency of different speaker's intentions decides about whether the case will count as a better – or worse – case of meaning; and the recognition, or lack of recognition, of different speaker's intentions decides about whether the case will be regarded as a better – or worse – example of communication).

and Wilson 1986/95: 153). An *ostensive* behaviour then is a behaviour which makes mutually manifest an intention to make some assumption (or assumptions) manifest. By definition then, in ostension there are two layers of information that are conveyed: one has to do with the information that is brought to the recipient's attention, in the form of assumptions that a given ostensive act is designed to communicate, and the other is the information that it is intentional that this first layer of information is pointed out (Sperber and Wilson 1986/95: 50).

This suggests that ostensive acts are associated with two types of intention, that is, the informative and communicative intention, defined in RT in the following way:

> "*Informative intention:* to make manifest or more manifest to the audience a set of assumptions *I*." (Sperber and Wilson 1986/95: 58)

> "*Communicative intention:* to make it mutually manifest to audience and communicator that the communicator has this informative intention." (Sperber and Wilson 1986/95: 61)

On this approach, genuine communication is assumed to occur when direct evidence about the intention to convey some information is provided by the communicator (attributable as her informative intention) and when the intention to convey this content is made mutually manifest to both interactants (attributable as her communicative intention). Ostensive stimuli, which make the informative intention mutually manifest, are the *sine qua non* of overt communication. They are characterized by two properties, which are the key to explaining how communication works: first, ostensive stimuli openly claim the addressee's attention and, second, by bringing into focus the communicator's informative intention, they help to reveal it (Wilson and Sperber 2004: 611). Observe that if not treated as evidence about the communicator's intention, they would be totally irrelevant. Since the recipient's attention is overtly demanded, for reasons that have to do with how human cognition works, they *create expectations of relevance*. As already indicated above, these expectations provide the major driving force and guidance for the recipient in recovering what is being communicated. This is formalized in RT as the Communicative Principle of Relevance, with its corollary in the form of the presumption of optimal relevance:

> *The Communicative Principle of Relevance*: "Every act of ostensive communication communicates a presumption of its own optimal relevance." (Sperber and Wilson 1986/95: 158).
> "Presumption of optimal relevance:
> (a)   The ostensive stimulus is worth the audience's processing effort.
> (b)   It is the most relevant one compatible with communicator's abilities and preferences." (Wilson and Sperber 2004: 612)

As the creators of RT emphasize, each of the clauses in the presumption of optimal relevance significantly contributes to explicating how comprehension works (Wilson and Sperber 2004). Clause (a) suggests that the mental effort expended by the interpreter in the processing of a given ostensive stimulus is expected to be worth his while, which suggests that the stimulus should be taken as designed to yield satisfactory cognitive effects. This clause ensures then that the amount of effort necessary "to reconstruct the intended interpretation is treated as given, and the presumption is that the effect will be high enough for the overall relevance of the stimulus to be at or above the lower limit (below which the stimulus would not be worth processing). Clause (a) says, in essence, that the level of effect is at least sufficient" (Sperber and Wilson 1986/95: 267).

Now clause (b) indicates that the stimulus should be approached by the recipient as the most relevant one that the communicator was able and willing to produce (Wilson and Sperber 2004: 613), and this clause ensures that the first interpretation found relevant enough by the recipient can be identified as the intended interpretation, because if there were more competing intended interpretations, clause (b) of the presumption of optimal relevance would not be satisfied (Wilson and Sperber 2004: 614).[23] Basically, the whole idea behind engaging in interactions and producing ostensive stimuli has to do with making oneself understood (Sperber and Wilson 1986/95: 268), so it is judicious to assume that communicators, who are rational agents,[24] act accordingly. Actually, clause (b) above makes it reasonable to assume that in making sense of what is being communicated, the interpreter is entitled "to follow a path of least effort because the speaker is expected (within the limits of her abilities and preferences) to make her utterance as easy as possible to understand. Since relevance varies inversely with effort, the very fact that an interpretation is easily accessible gives it an initial degree of plausibility (an advantage specific to ostensive communication)" (Wilson and Sperber 2004: 613-614).[25] This should not be taken to mean that the ostensive stimulus is purposefully chosen to minimize the recipient's effort,

---

23 Obviously, intended ambiguities and puns manifestly do not conform to this; for a relevance-theoretic treatment of utterances intentionally yielding more than one interpretation, see Solska (2012a, 2012b, 2012c, 2012d), Tanaka (1992) and Yus (2003); for empirical evidence on how puns approached in relevance-theoretic terms can be seen to contribute to the appreciation of advertisements, see Van Mulken et al. (2005).

24 Just like for Grice, whose Cooperative Principle and conversational maxims assume that speakers function as rational agents and talking is "a special case or variety of purposive, indeed rational, behaviour" (Grice 1975/89: 28), rationality of interactants is an important consideration for relevance theorists (see also Ch. 3, footnote 44). For some critical comments on how rationality is allegedly idealized in RT, see Kalisz (1993: 86-87).

25 See Ch. 2.3 for the relevance-guided comprehension heuristic that the presumption of relevance motivates.

after deliberation over possible alternatives. Obviously, communicators have their own agenda: they frequently take action swiftly, they often act in an egocentric manner (cf. Kecskes 2013), they try to spare themselves extra effort in producing ostensive stimuli, and they may decide to follow some rules or social conventions that would be at odds with conveying their message in the easiest possible way (Sperber and Wilson 1986/95: 268-269). Clause (b) of the presumption of optimal relevance sanctions all that, indicating only that the recipient should treat a given ostensive stimulus as the most relevant one that the communicator could and was willing to use (see also Wilson and Sperber 1998).

1.6 RT and intentions

As emphasized above, the type of communication that relevance theorists are interested in involves, to express it in very simple terms, an overt manifestation of the intention to convey certain information, which is put into effect by producing stimuli overtly intended to communicate the intended meaning. This makes intentionality the backbone of the species of communication that RT is designed to account for.

Intentionality is a very important concept in language studies and there are at least two[26] different ways in which the notion is approached in the literature. On the one hand, intentionality is recognized as a pivotal aspect of human linguistic mental representations, since language – being the representation of the outside world – is assumed to be primarily *about* the reality around, and it is this *aboutness* that constitutes intentionality. In this sense, intentionality is related to mental states that are about objects, events, relations, etc., in the external world, so it stems from a basic assumption that language is the vehicle for thought (Barz 2008; Benga 2009; Davies 2006; Hacker 2001; Jaszczolt 2002; Lyons 1995). This kind of approach goes back to medieval scholasticism and the time-honoured distinction between *esse naturale*, that is, what exists naturally, and *esse intentionale*, that is, mental existence of entities in the human mind (Lyons 1995: 1). It is deeply rooted in the philosophy of language tradition, with Brentano's work (1874, in Hacker

---

26   Haugh and Jaszczolt (2012: 87) indicate that there are three ways of looking at speaker's intentions: apart from the *aboutness* understanding, they refer to "speaker intended effect of an act of communication" and speaker-intended meaning which goes beyond the truth-conditional content of the utterance to embrace the communicated implicit import. The latter ones are not treated separately in the present discussion, as the focus here is on intentions directly underlying the production and comprehension of an utterance. Haugh and Jaszczolt's (2012) comprehensive survey of different types of pragmatic intentions reaches well beyond the communicator's intentions whose recognition contributes to identifying the speaker-intended contextual meaning that RT concentrates on.

2001, Glock 2001 and many others) commonly credited (see, e.g., Glock 2001; Jaszczolt 2002; Segal 2005) with initiating its modern revival in philosophy, and Dennett's (1987, in Benga 2009, see also Lyons 1995) work on thought-to-world relations introducing the notion into the field of cognitive studies.

The other broad line of research on intentionality has taken a different, more pragmatic turn. It focuses on the speaker's intentions as an important parameter in communication, and it is primarily concerned with human communicative behaviour and the psycholinguistic reality underlying it. For this reason, it belongs to a wider scope of research into intentional action, the theoretical foundation for which was laid by Anscombe's (1957) monograph and more recently developed by Alvarez (2010). On this understanding, intentionality, as intrinsic to human purposeful behaviour, and in particular to acts of communication, is believed to contribute directly to how human endeavours are perceived and judged. What is most important for the goals of the present discussion, intentionality is recognized as a pivotal aspect of the production and comprehension of utterances. This is precisely how RT views it.

While there seems to be an almost unanimous consensus among researchers interested in language use that speaker intention recognition is an essential part of understanding what meaning she is conveying,[27] there is much less on offer in terms of explanations of how these intentions are actually identified by the interpreter.

Grice (1967/89), who can be credited with bringing the speaker's intentions into the limelight, does not attempt any explanation on how they are recognized.[28] He only suggests that in some, even though rather infrequent, communicative contexts the speaker's intention will be declared or made explicit (Grice 1957/89). In other cases "we would seem to rely on very much the same kind of criteria as we do in the case of non-linguistic intentions where there is a general usage. An utterer is held to intend to convey what is normally conveyed" (Grice 1957/89: 222). This view poses problems, but before these can be addressed, some other well-known approaches to intentionality in communication will be briefly considered.

---

27 See Arundale (2008) for an alternative view. For an overview of major cognitive-philosophical and socio-cultural interactional views on intentions, see Kecskes and Mey (2008).

28 Grice (1957/89, 1975/89) was not interested in psycholinguistic mechanisms involved, and he consistently maintained what Haugh and Jaszczolt (2012: 94) refer to as an "antipsychological stance." He was thus preoccupied with the principles underlying rational action and not with a psychologically plausible model of utterance production and processing. Principally, his theory accords with Frege's ideas that logic must shun psychologism in order to avoid dangerous contamination, duly attending to the difference between what is really true and what is only held to be true by an individual (Jaszczolt 2008). As Jaszczolt (2008) argues, sound psychologism is not only unavoidable but quite in place in pragmatic theorizing.

According to Searle (1969), linguistic conventions, and in particular semantic rules, help to bridge the gap between the speaker's intention and the hearer's recognition of this intention. It is the satisfaction conditions for different speech acts, posited by Searle (2007), that are supposed to provide the basis for identifying intentions (Searle 2007). Searle's ideas can be seen as an appealing and interesting philosophical argument, but not a psychologically relevant one.

Fully acknowledging the significance of speaker's intentions in discoursal contexts, and referring to their different kinds, Bach (1990) admits that they may elude a full, comprehensive and detailed explanation. That is why Bach and Harnish's (1979, in Bach 1990) Speech Act Schema (SAS), designed as a model of intentionality and inferencing, "gives no indication how certain mutual beliefs are activated or otherwise picked out as relevant, much less how the correct identification is made" (1979: 93, cited in Bach 1990: 393). Bach and Harnish's model of defeasible reasoning, based on a number of presumptions underlying conversational behaviours, as Bach (1990: 393) explicitly states, offers "no account of how particular explanations come to mind or of what makes a certain one seem good." The SAS is meant only to supply the ingredients for a model of the defeasible reasoning involved in understanding, with the communicative presumption driving "the hearer's inference to the speaker's intention (it implies that there is an inference to be made) but, of course, it does not give the directions" (Bach 1990: 393). The commitments and priorities of the creators of the SAS appear to favour conceptual accuracy and cohesion over psychological realism, as Bach (1990) himself implicitly concedes.

In his more recent publications, Bach's (2001, 2004, 2006b, 2012, 2014) general conception of the speaker's intentions, in particular the communicative ones,[29] and their recognition appear to converge with the relevance-theoretic views, though I am not sure he would be ready to subscribe to this comment. He underscores the importance of communicative presumptions that both speakers and hearers fall back on: the former in making their communicative intentions inferable, and the latter in recognizing these intentions (Bach 2004: 32). The explicit claims that he makes (Bach 2001, 2004, 2006b, 2012, 2014) seem to tie in with the relevance-theoretic approach to how the communicator's intentions are recognized. This

---

29   Bach's (1990, 2012) taxonomies of intentions, grouped into semantic, that is, determining "what she [the speaker] takes her words to mean as she is using them", and communicative, determining "how she intends her audience to take her act of uttering those words" (Bach 2012: 50), as well as illocutionary (roughly the same as communicative) and perclocutionary intentions ("to produce a perlocutionary effect, such as a belief or even an action, rather than the illocutionary effect of understanding"), do not coincide with the simple classification into informative and communicative intentions in RT.

is witnessed by the following citation in which, when characterizing utterances, Bach (2004: 30) writes,

> It is as an intentional act performed by a speaker that an utterance has a content distinct from that of the uttered sentence. But in this sense the content of an utterance is really the content of the speaker's communicative intention in making the utterance. So the only linguistic content relevant here is the semantic content of the sentence, and the only other relevant content is the content of the speaker's intention.

As he underscores, "mutually evident facts enable the speaker, at least when communication goes well, to make his intention evident and enable the hearer to identify it" (Bach 2004:38).[30]

The idea that recognizing the speaker's intentions has to do with recovering her intended speaker meaning is precisely the relevance-theoretic stance, as will presently be shown. The advantage of RT is that the fully-fledged model of communication that it offers, and in particular the two principles of relevance (unique to this framework), supplemented by the presumption of optimal relevance, provide a coherent conceptual apparatus which not only assigns a central role to intentionality, but also clarifies how communicators implement their intentions and how addressees are guided to recognize them.

This suggests that, in contrast to theorists who believe that intention attribution and recognition is vital for conveying and recovering the actually communicated meanings but do not deliver much explanation with regard to how interpreters go about identifying the relevant intentions, Sperber and Wilson rise to the challenge. Firstly, Sperber and Wilson (1986/95: 163) judiciously observe that, in contrast to Grice's (1957/89) proposal, recognizing the speaker's intentions cannot be done in the same manner in which intention identification proceeds in ordinary, everyday circumstances. In the latter case, intentions are usually inferred from the goal that the person engaged in a certain activity is evidently trying to achieve.[31] Thus the desired outcome and the predicted effects provide the basis for the identification of the agent's intentions in such contexts. Therefore, inserting the car key into the ignition will unequivocally reveal the intention of the person who has done it to

---

30 Does the phrase "mutually evident facts" not bring to mind the relevance-theoretic notion of mutual manifestness?

31 Bach (1990, 2004) emphasizes that intentions underlying communicative acts differ from intentions that underwrite other types of activities in that, unlike the latter, the former in a crucial way contribute to the very act performed: their recognition influences how interpreters recover communicators' meanings and hence they contribute to a potential communicative success. Intentions behind non-communicative actions do not have this role. "You won't succeed in standing on your head because someone recognizes your intention to do so" (Bach 2004: 469, 2006b: 153).

start the car, in the same manner in which turning on the coffee maker indicates that the agent wants to brew coffee.[32][33]

In the case of the informative intention, the intended effect is the outcome of the recognition of the intention, so the addressee cannot determine this effect prior to identifying the communicator's informative intention. In Sperber and Wilson's own words (1986/95: 163), "the informative intention cannot be inferred by observing its independently achieved effects" (see also Sperber 2000:130). So how is the informative intention behind an ostensive stimulus identified?

The process of recognizing the informative intention postulated in RT might seem elaborate, but in fact it is effortless and automatic. When the addressee's attention is overtly claimed, and the stimulus by which it is claimed can only be regarded as relevant if treated as evidence for the communicator's intentions, then the ostensive character of the stimulus becomes mutually manifest to the addressee and the communicator. As a result, it also becomes mutually manifest to both interactants that the communicator has an informative intention. Actually, making the informative intention mutually manifest is the ostensive act's raison d'être. Since, in accordance with the definition supplied earlier, the informative intention is the intention "to make manifest or more manifest to the audience a set of assumptions I" (Sperber and Wilson 1986/95: 58), identifying the informative intention is tantamount to identifying this set of assumptions I.

Granted that an ostensive stimulus comes with a guarantee of optimal relevance, the recipient expects sufficient cognitive effects to off-set his processing effort. In his search for an interpretation consistent with the Communicative Principle of Relevance, constrained furthermore by the presumption of relevance as described above, the addressee is entitled to follow a path of least effort and recover the cognitive effects that satisfy his expectations of relevance and can be treated as foreseeable and intended by the communicator (see Wilson 1998). As soon as the range of cognitive effects that the communicator might have intended to make

---

32 Of course, as it may happen, by inserting the key into the ignition someone may just want to turn on the car power supply in order to switch the car radio on, and the coffee machine may be switched on to show that the light indicator does not work. The point is that for a large number of intentional actions that we observe we have access to stereotypical scenarios about the intended outcomes, which enable us to hypothesize about the intentions behind these actions. Such stereotypical reasoning cannot be applied to identify the speaker's intentions.

33 It is a bit of an oversimplification to suggest that intention recognition is always so straightforward and unproblematic, as in such pedestrian cases. Philosophical analyses indicate that for an action to be intentional there must be at least foreknowledge, choice and subject's control involved. Moral considerations and norms often influence the ascription of intentionality and may make intentionality judgements difficult, complex and equivocal (cf. Cova et al. 2012).

mutually manifest is found satisfactory by the recipient, he can stop. In this way, the range of mutually manifest intended effects that meet the addressee's expectations of relevance is identified as the content of the communicator's informative intention. It is the guarantee of relevance, which is communicated by every ostensive stimulus in accordance with the Communicative Principle of Relevance, that "makes it possible for (…) [the recipient] to infer which of the newly manifest assumptions have been *intentionally* made manifest" (Sperber and Wilson 1986/95: 50; my emphasis). Thus, the tacit guarantee of relevance leads the audience to find out how the communicator has intended to make her ostension optimally relevant and, by recovering this interpretation, to identify the informative intention of the communicator, that is, the "set *I* the communicator had reason to think that it would confirm the presumption of relevance" (Sperber and Wilson 1986/95: 165). Once the informative intention is identified, the communicative intention – being a higher-order informative intention – is also realized (Sperber et al. 2010: 366).

As hinted at above, this may appear complex when described as a process, but it operates subconsciously and automatically in the recipient's mind.[34] The whole underlying mental procedure will certainly be easier to grasp on the basis of an example. Let us then proceed to more concrete considerations.

1.7 How ostensive-inferential communication works in practice

Here is an illustration how it all works in practice. Let us assume that Peter is having a mobile phone conversation with his close friend, Robert. After they have been talking for a long while, Peter's wife, Mary, enters the room and puts their wireless home phone receiver on the table in front of Peter. Peter immediately utters (1):

(1) Peter: "Does this connection cost you money, Robert? See, our flat rate calling plan gives us free mobile and landline calls, so let's hang up and I'll call back from our home number in a sec."

What has happened? Well, Mary has produced an ostensive gesture which turned out to be very meaningful to Peter, and affected his behaviour.

How does Peter identify what Mary has done as an ostensive gesture in the first place? By bringing the receiver, Mary produces a manifestly intentional stimulus which, on the one hand, overtly claims Peter's attention, and on the other, would be totally irrelevant unless Peter can recognize it as evidence for Mary's intentions to

---

34 As will be argued in Ch.4.6, intention-recognition is performed in an automatic way by the comprehension module.

communicate something. How can this gesture communicate anything? Recall that according to RT, an ostensive gesture comes with a guarantee of optimal relevance, that is, of worthwhile cognitive effects for the processing effort invested. So all that Peter needs to do is to treat Mary's ostensive behaviour as a piece of evidence for the informative intention that she has, and identify the range of assumptions that she has made mutually manifest by doing what she did. RT postulates that as soon as Peter's attention is demanded and he realizes an ostensive stimulus has been directed at him, his mind automatically searches for worthwhile cognitive effects that Mary's gesture can be taken to make mutually manifest. Seeing their home phone receiver, which Mary has ostensively put in front of Peter, makes a number of highly relevant assumptions immediately accessible to him. Among these, there is an assumption that Peter and Mary can make phone calls free of charge, which under the circumstances is highly relevant: if Robert's phone conversation with Peter adds to Robert's phone bill, then by calling back from the home number, Peter will help Robert eliminate unnecessary expenditure. This emerges as a worthwhile cognitive effect which Mary might have both foreseen and intended, so it is identified as the content of her informative intention.

The procedure is fast and frugal: Peter's reaction to Mary's signal is immediate. The assumptions retrieved in the interpretation process are "virtually instantaneously accessible, and more accessible than any alternative assumption likely to lead to an acceptable interpretation" (Wilson and Sperber 1991a: 388). The first interpretation of Mary's ostension that Peter – following a path of least effort – arrives at which returns a worthwhile range of cognitive effects is at once accepted as the intended interpretation. Needless to add, this interpretation follows from the tacit presumption of relevance that her ostension communicates, and involves relying precisely on the assumptions that become most salient as a result of Peter's processing of Mary's gesture.

This relatively straightforward analysis shows that there are two sides to the communication coin: ostension and inference. The communicator engages in ostension: by using a non-coded (as was the case in the example above), or coded (as is the case with linguistic utterances and coded non-verbal signals) stimulus, she makes manifest her informative intention.[35] The addressee engages in inferencing: treating the stimulus as evidence for the communicator's informative intention, he must infer the intended range of assumptions that her ostension makes mutually manifest, with the first hypothesis about the intended effects meeting the addressee's expectations of relevance and recognized as fulfilling the communicator's manifest intentions, identified as the intended interpretation.

---

35   The example worked out above was deliberately chosen to involve non-verbal communication; pivotal aspects of the relevance-theoretic approach to verbal communication are focused on in chapters 2 and 3 that follow.

For these reasons, this type of communication is called by Sperber and Wilson (1986/95) *ostensive-inferential*, or in short, *ostensive*.

While the ostensive nature of communication has been described in some detail, relatively little has been said so far about inferencing, so in order to complete the picture, it seems important to elaborate on its nature as well. Inferencing from ostensively provided evidence to the speaker-intended effect, as the illustration above shows, relies on accessing an adequate context. Pragmatic inferencing and context selection will be addressed in the next section.

1.8 Inference to the intended interpretation and context construction

As explicitly stated above (Ch.1.6) and illustrated by the example used (Ch.1.7), recovering the meaning conveyed through an act of ostension involves the addressee engaging in "the processes of pragmatic hypothesis formation and confirmation [which] are clearly context-dependent" (Wilson and Sperber 1991a: 391-392). These processes are posited to be global in character (pace the scepticism of Fodor 1983)[36] in that they have unrestrained access to background information of all sorts (Wilson and Sperber 1991a: 380). As Wilson and Sperber (1991a: 380) emphasize, "any item of information, however remote and unrelated to the information being processed, may legitimately be used" in comprehension. The majority of language users capable of the most rudimentary reflection on what happens in real-life communication, who are aware that they constantly context-shift and who intuitively feel the global nature of the processes involved, find the claim appealing, but it creates problems at the theoretical level, because the model must account for this kind of globality.

---

36 Fodor (1983: 128) starkly puts it that "global systems are per se bad domains for computational models" and, in consequence, for cognitive science, because any processes that involve the operation of global factors are virtually intractable. As Fodor (1983: 129) emphasizes, "nobody begins to understand how such factors have their effects." This amounts to claiming that "the more global a psychological process, the less chance anyone has of understanding it" (Wilson R. 2004: 409). The originators of RT do not share this pessimism (cf. their argumentation in, e.g., Sperber and Wilson 1986/95, 1987; Sperber 1994b; Wilson 2005; Wilson and Sperber 1991a). A strong case against Fodor's (1983, 2008) enduring scepticism concerning a possible creation of coherent, consistent and insightful theories of cognitive architecture, rooted in his thesis that cognitive processes are Quinean and isotropic, has recently been made by Fuller and Samuels (2014). See also Carruthers (2003) and Pinker (2005) for some other compelling reasons against Fodor's pessimism about the existence of cognitive science.

This brings us to the relevance-theoretic approach to context, which is assumed to be dynamically constructed in the process of interpretation, rather than predetermined by or confined to a set of certain elements or parameters.[37] In the relevance-theoretic framework, context is taken to be "a psychological construct, a subset of the hearer's assumptions about the world" (Sperber and Wilson 1986/95: 15) which constitute the premises for interpreting ostensive stimuli.

Thus recovering the speaker-intended meaning is taken to necessarily rely on the hearer accessing the right kind of context, basically the context envisaged by the speaker, as otherwise misinterpretation will result (Sperber and Wilson 1986/95: 16; see also Wilson and Sperber 1991b: 584-585). As argued by Sperber and Wilson (1986/95: 137-138), "a crucial step in the processing of new information, and in particular of verbally communicated information, is to combine it with an adequately selected set of background assumptions – which then constitutes the context." These background assumptions may come from various sources, the main ones being: short-term memory, long-term memory, and the environment (Sperber and Wilson 1986/95:138-139). In particular, the assumptions stored under the concepts accessed during the processing of a certain ostensive stimulus are crucial. As shown in the phone example discussed above, the expectations of relevance in terms of satisfying cognitive effects to be recovered for the processing effort expended, automatically lead the interpreter to access contextual assumptions that will yield such effects. In the case of verbal stimuli, the concepts stored under the encyclopaedic entries of the words decoded by the language parser processing a given utterance will become immediately accessible to the comprehender (Wilson and Sperber 1998: 14).

It should be added at this point that in the framework under discussion concepts evoked as a result of the processing of verbal stimuli consist of addresses in memory, or headings "under which various types of information can be stored and retrieved" (Sperber and Wilson 1986/95: 86). The information available at a given conceptual address is lexical, logical and encyclopaedic. The lexical entry for a concept embraces all the information about "the word or phrase of natural language which expresses it" (Sperber and Wilson 1986/95: 86). The logical entry contains the deductive rules "which apply to logical forms of which that concept is a constituent" (Sperber and Wilson 1986/95: 86). The encyclopaedic entry

---

37 Context used to be approached in this way prior to relevance-theoretic strong claims about context. A case on point is Montague semantics, in which, as pointed out by Roberts (2004: 203), context was conceived of "as a set of indices, or contextual parameters, attached to the interpretive apparatus for a given sentence. These were pointers to specified sorts of contextual information, used to feed the relevant information into the process of compositional interpretation that yielded the proposition expressed by the sentence in the specified context." This kind of approach is typical of index-based theories of context (Roberts 2004).

provides "information about the extension and/or denotation of the concept: that is, about the objects, events and/or properties which instantiate it" (Sperber and Wilson 1986/95: 86), which is stored as a set of background assumptions about the entities, activities, relations, etc. that the concept refers to.

The above clearly indicates that the concepts made available in the course of processing of an ostensive stimulus provide access to the assumptions stored in their encyclopaedic entries. It is assumed that those background assumptions which tie in with the incoming information to yield an interpretation consistent with the Communicative Principle of Relevance and backed up by the presumption of optimal relevance will be selected as the context for processing of a given stimulus. In effect, RT postulates that from a myriad of assumptions which the interpreter is capable of accessing, only those that contribute to optimizing relevance of the ostensive input will form the context for its interpretation. As Sperber and Wilson (1986/95: 144) argue, "[a]chieving maximal relevance involves selecting the best possible context in which to process an assumption: that is, the context enabling the best possible balance of effort against effect to be achieved. When such a balance is achieved, we will say that the assumption has been *optimally processed*" (original emphasis).

On this construal, context is not determined in advance: it is chosen and constructed in the course of interpretation (Sperber and Wilson 1986/95: 141). Context provides the basis for inferences aimed at the recovery of the range of cognitive effects satisfying the recipient's expectations of relevance and manifestly intended by the communicator. Since the presumption of optimal relevance entitles the addressee to follow an easiest interpretation route in recovering these effects, "a context which yields the least effort-consuming conceivable interpretation is chosen" (Sperber and Wilson 1986/95: 185), which places an important constraint on the scope of context actually used. This also means that the selected context provides the basis for inferences that lead to the final interpretation (see Jodłowiec 2009b).

These inferences are non-demonstrative in nature: as stated above more than once, what is involved is hypothesis formation and confirmation, which is not based on any rigid inference rules (Sperber and Wilson 1991a: 379). On this approach, non-demonstrative inferencing, which lies at the heart of the comprehension process, is taken to be a spontaneous "form of suitably constrained guesswork" (Sperber and Wilson 1986/95: 69).[38]

---

38 That is not to say that deduction is ruled out from human inferencing involved in the comprehension process. Deductive rules are admitted as a subpart of the non-demonstrative inferential process. Sperber and Wilson (1986/95: 69) contend that "[h]uman spontaneous non-demonstrative inference is not, overall, a logical process. Hypothesis formation involves the use of deductive rules, but is not totally governed by them; hypothesis confirmation is a non-logical cognitive phenomenon: it is a by-product of the way assumptions are processed, deductively or otherwise."

This guesswork, powered by the Principle of Relevance and its corollary, viz. a presumption of optimal relevance, is modelled as a relevance-theoretic comprehension heuristic, which in fact has been implicit throughout the above discussions on how interpretation proceeds. It will be given a more explicit treatment in chapter 2 devoted to some crucial aspects of explicitly communicated meanings.

1.9 Concluding remarks

The enormous potential of the human mind, with its amazing capacity to handle masses of data and its impressive efficiency in information processing, lends itself particularly well to a computational model of mental processes. The mind's inner architecture and composition is still a matter of dispute, but the hypothesis that it consists of a number of modular systems and subsystems showing sensitivity to data of specific types, with different specializations and networking potentials, appears very plausible.

Fully supporting the modular conception of the mind, RT articulates a cognitive economy principle which may contribute to understanding how the cognitive machinery works. RT postulates that information processing is controlled by a single underlying factor: achieving "maximal cognitive effect for minimal processing effort" (Sperber and Wilson 1991b: 544). This is the essence of relevance, which, on the one hand, is a property of cognitive inputs, and on the other, a factor constraining information processing in general, and the processes underpinning ostensive-inferential communication in particular. The existence of the relevance-oriented mechanisms underlying cognition and communication, formalized on this approach as two principles of relevance, affords a profound insight into human cognitive behaviour and is posited to be capitalized on in communicative contexts. Roughly, the idea is that the communicator can predict and manipulate certain mental states of the audience, and the audience is automatically led to follow a relevance-driven interpretation procedure to get the expected cognitive gains. The principles of relevance and the notions of cognitive effect, cognitive environment, manifestness, mutual manifestness and the informative and communicative intentions publicized in ostensive behaviour provide a solid basis for a cognitive theory of communication.

Over the last three decades the model has been used to account for various aspects of communication, which has led to various refinements and elaborations of the theory. The two successive chapters that follow are devoted to a relevance-theoretic account of explicit and implicit import. First, in chapter 2, explicature generation will be scrutinized and a minor amendment to the relevance-theoretic procedure will be suggested.

Chapter 2
Explicatures: how far do interpreters go?

2.1 Introduction

Any framework designed to provide a theoretically sound account of communication must explain what is communicated and how communication is accomplished (Sperber and Wilson 1986/95: 54).[1] There seems to be widespread agreement among pragmaticists of various persuasions that what is communicated in verbal exchanges should be viewed in terms of the speaker's meaning, but there is no agreement on how speaker meaning is to be analysed and accounted for (Orrigi and Sperber 2000:156). Most analyses assume that there are two distinct levels that need to be considered in elucidating what speaker meaning involves, that is, explicit and implicit import.[2] However, the issue of where the borderline between these two should be drawn and what processes underlie the recovery of each remains controversial and debatable (Carston 2004b).

RT is a fully inferential model of communication, in which the linguistic signal used by the communicator is assumed to constitute a piece of evidence for the meaning she intends to communicate. It is on the basis of this ostensive stimulus (see Ch.1.5-1.8) that the recipient *infers* the meaning expressed by the speaker (Sperber and Wilson 2008: 87-8; Wilson and Sperber 2004: 607). This means that on the relevance-theoretic approach, recovering the explicitly communicated meaning is taken to embrace decoding as well as inferential processes, with the former being an output of the workings of the language module and the latter involving hypothesizing from the decoded stimulus to the interpretation which would meet the recipient's expectations of relevance (Carston 2010c; Wilson and Sperber 2004).

The focus in this chapter is on how the relevance-theoretic model accounts for the comprehension process at the level of the explicitly conveyed meaning. First, the problem of setting the borderline between the explicit and implicit in verbal

---

1   I would like to thank Deirdre Wilson for her insightful and extensive comments on an earlier version of this chapter. All remaining faults are my responsibility alone.

2   There are different terms used to refer to the two levels of the speaker meaning: "said vs. implicated", "primary vs. secondary", "direct vs. indirect." For a useful discussion, see Carston (2009).

communication is briefly discussed (Ch.2.2). Then explicature as defined in RT is introduced and characterized. The description of various processes that contribute to explicature generation centres on free enrichment as the most controversial and debated mechanism that relevance theorists endorse (Ch.2.3). While a lot of the criticism levelled against free enrichment seems ill-founded, it still remains a controversial procedure, mainly because it appears a cognitively burdensome process and it may yield a range of propositions with different truth-conditions (Ch.2.4). A proposal to eliminate free enrichment is put forth in an attempt to avoid some of its pitfalls: it is argued that the procedure of pinning down the explicit meaning does not need to rely on adding conceptual material in order to arrive at the explicitly communicated meaning of an utterance (Ch.2.5 and Ch.2.6). The notion of a contextual cognitive fix posited to replace free enrichment, as is hopefully shown, follows from some fundamental assumptions of RT. It naturally fits in the relevance-theoretic utterance comprehension model, ties in with some empirical evidence that interpretations may sometimes be shallow and supports the basic claim about on-line communication that it is fast and frugal (Ch.2.7 and Ch.2.8). Some significant similarities and differences between the contextual cognitive fix mechanism and ad hoc concept construction are presented next (Ch.2.9). The chapter ends with concluding remarks (Ch.2.10).

2.2 The explicit-implicit divide: the relevance-theoretic approach

While human communication has been a subject of extensive and serious scientific investigation for at least half a century, certain fundamental issues have remained unresolved to the present day. One of them is the question about the explicit and implicit levels of communication. As hinted at above, it is almost unanimously agreed among researchers studying verbal communication phenomena that speaker meanings come in two distinct sorts, that is, as explicit and implicit meanings (cf. Chaves 2010). However, there is little consensus on how the division between the two should be made, and what criteria should be used to distinguish these two species of communicated content. Interestingly, while it may appear that exploring what is explicitly conveyed, as more direct and concrete, would be less problematic and more straightforward than dealing with implicit import, surveying the scene of pragmatic debates proves it is the other way round: there is a lot of controversy and dispute over what is principally explicitly delivered and where the borderline between the explicit and the implicit in communication should be drawn, and there seems to be much less violent disagreement over implicatures (see Ch.3.4), which does not mean that everything that concerns the implicit layer of communication has been described and explained.

The roots of the perennial dispute over explicitness are traceable back to Grice (1967/89),[3] who has introduced a distinction between what is said and what is implicated as instrumental for his working out schema for implicatures. Grice's major concern is to provide a principled explanation for how implicatures arise, so his preoccupation with the explicit level of communication is largely peripheral and, as a result, rather unsatisfactory.[4] Here is an extensive quote in which he introduces the technical meaning of *say* and provides the justification for it:

> In the sense in which I am using the word *say*, I intend what someone has said to be closely related to the conventional meaning of the words (and sentence) he has uttered. Suppose someone to have uttered the sentence *He is in the grip of vice*. Given a knowledge of the English language, but no knowledge of the circumstances of the utterance, one would know something about what the speaker has said, on the assumption that he was using standard English, and speaking literally. One would know that he has said, about some male person or animal x, that at the time of the utterance (whatever that was), either (1) x was unable to rid himself of a certain kind of bad character trait or (2) some part of x's person was caught in a certain kind of tool or instrument (approximate account of course). But for a full identification of what the speaker has said, one would need to know (a) the identity of x, (b) the time of utterance, and (c) the meaning, on the particular occasion of utterance, of the phrase *is in the grip of vice* [a decision between (1) and (2)]. This brief indication of my use of *say* leaves it open whether a man who says today *Harold Wilson is a great man* and another who says (also today) *The British Prime Minister is a great man* would, if each knew the two singular terms had the same reference, have said the same thing. But whatever decision is made about this question, the apparatus that I am about to provide will be capable of accounting for any implicatures that might depend on the

3   I will not report here on the notions of what is said as developed within a more philosophical perspective on language which focuses mainly (if not exclusively) on semantic rather than communicative aspects of sentences (cf. Stanley 2002a).

4   As argued by Wharton (2002: 209), one of the problems with Grice's concept of *saying*, quite ironically, originates in the difficulty of "working out what he meant by what he said (and wrote) about it." In an attempt to untangle the purported confusion between what Grice might have been aiming at and how his writing was interpreted, based on an in-depth analysis of the typescripts of *William James Lectures* and the content of *Studies in the Way of Words*, Wharton suggests that *what is said* might have been intended to have a much wider truth-conditional content than is generally attributed to Grice's programme. While certainly interesting, Wharton's ideas do not (and, in fact, cannot) go beyond mere speculation and offer a very subjective interpretation of different passages from Grice. In fact, there are quite a few other problems with Grice's term *what is said*, but since they are only tangential to the issues under investigation, they will not be explored here (for further discussion, see Bach 1999; Baptista 2011; Burton-Roberts 2010; Korta 2013; Levinson 2000; Saul 2002; Wilson and Sperber 1981).

presence of one rather than the other of these singular terms of the sentence uttered. (Grice 1975/89: 25).

As the above passage clearly reveals, and as many commentators on Grice underline (e.g., Ariel 2002; Bach 1994, 2001; Bezuidenhout and Cutting 2002; Carston 2002b, 2004a, 2007; Carston and Hall 2012; Clark H. 1996; Hamblin and Gibbs 2003; Ifantidou 2001; Iten 2005; Levinson 2000; Petrus 2010; Sperber and Wilson 1986/95, 2005), his notion of what is said is only minimally contextual and does not go beyond disambiguation and reference assignment. This kind of construal of explicitly conveyed content which is not inferentially arrived at makes it possible for Grice to draw a clear-cut dividing line between the two levels of communicated meaning, with any meanings recovered thanks to the workings of the conversational maxims of informativeness, truthfulness, relevance and manner, automatically counting as what is implicitly conveyed, however, it causes complications elsewhere in his theory.[5] Granting that, as Grice insists, what is said necessarily falls within what the speaker actually means (or to use the original terminology "M-intends", where "M" stands for meaning, Grice 1968/89: 123), defining *saying* in this manner creates problems in innumerable cases in which what is explicitly communicated departs considerably from what is said in the Gricean sense (Bach 1994; Carston 2002b, 2009; Carston and Hall 2012; Wilson and Sperber 1981). As Grice himself realizes, this kind of approach is difficult to reconcile with non-literal uses of language, in which speakers commonly do not mean what they actually say, hence his solution is to assume that in the case of irony, metaphor, hyperbole and other figurative uses of language "nothing may be said, though there is something which the speaker makes as if to say" (1978/89: 41),[6] and it is the reliance on the Cooperative Principle and the conversational maxims, which can be suitably exploited by the speaker, that leads the addressee to grasp the intended content (cf. Wilson and Sperber's 2002 criticism of this stance).

The theoretically dubious and psychologically unappealing Gricean notion of what is said is abandoned in the relevance-theoretic model and replaced with a

---

5   As pointed out by Katz (1972, in Carston 2004a: 829), reference assignment can depend on the maxims, so it is questionable whether the original neat distinction between what is explicit and what is implicit in verbal communication is tenable even within the original Grice's model.

6   While the idea that when uttering something on certain occasions speakers do not say anything but only "make as if to say" appears a bit preposterous (not to say slightly absurd), it needs to be borne in mind that the Gricean perspective is that of a philosopher of language, for whom epistemic concerns count, and psychological reality and plausibility are only of secondary significance (cf. Bezuidenhout and Cutting 2002; Wilson 2014). As Arundale (2008: 235) explicitly puts it, "Grice focused on developing a philosophical account of the nature of meaning, not a philosophical account of communication."

much richer notion of explicature. This broader conception of what is explicitly communicated that Sperber and Wilson (1986/95) have introduced reflects a fundamental and deeply held conviction of relevance theorists that, in general, pragmatic processes contribute to various aspects of the interpretation of utterances in an important way, and in particular, they are responsible for arriving at the speaker's meaning, both explicitly and implicitly conveyed. Strictly speaking, the rejection of the notion of what is said in the relevance-theoretic framework is programmatic, in that what is said in the Gricean sense is not recognized as a viable element in the comprehension process (Carston 2004a: 830) as it does not reflect a cognitively feasible level in the hearers' interpretation and is therefore not phenomenologically conspicuous (cf. Carston 2002a: 73).

The underlying claim about utterance processing on the relevance approach is that the decoded verbal signal comes underspecified in many respects: being the output of the language module (or parser), it surfaces as a mere logical form, that is, a semantic template or sub-propositional, "context-independent linguistically encoded meaning" (Carston 2008: 322), which necessarily needs to be inferentially completed, adjusted and enriched to yield the explicitly conveyed speaker-intended meaning (see, among others, Carston 2002a, 2010c; Carston and Hall 2012; Fretheim 2006; Ifantidou 2001; Jodłowiec 1991b; Pilkington 2000; Sperber and Wilson 1986/95, 2008; Wharton 2009; Wilson and Sperber 2002). The decoding process then, as carried out by the computational system, yields only a purely semantic representation of the utterance being processed, which, as a mere semantic blueprint, underlies a potentially infinite range of context-specific meanings. It is argued by relevance theorists (e.g., Carston 2002a, 2008; Carston and Hall 2012; Sperber and Wilson 1986/95, 2008; Wilson and Sperber 2002, 2004) that these kinds of output of the algorithmic, automatic and encapsulated language module constitute the proper territory of semantics, to be concerned with context-invariant meanings, while the study of inferentially-recovered, context-sensitive, propositional, and truth-evaluable content of utterances belongs to the realm of pragmatic investigation (for an in-depth discussion of how relevance views the division of labour between semantics and pragmatics, see, e.g, Carston 2008, 2009; Carston and Hall 2012)

Given this brief characterization of how explicit content is approached along relevance-theoretic lines and granting that implicatures, by definition, rely on inferencing, it should have become apparent by now that, unlike in Grice's framework, in RT the distinction between the explicit and the implicit does not coincide with the division between non-inferential and inferential. It is, on the one hand, the kinds of input on which a certain pragmatic process operates, and, on the other, its scope that help to establish if a given inferential procedure contributes to the explicit or the implicit level. Processes that apply to subcomponents of semantic representations recovered by the language module, whose function is therefore limited to just a local scope, are identified as explicature-developing procedures. By contrast, comprehension processes that deliver implicatures are assumed to take as input whole assumptions, so their range of operation is global: they necessarily affect and effect full assumptions rather than their parts (Carston 2002b, 2004b, 2009, 2010c; Carston and Hall 2012; Romero and Soria 2010). What provides a rationale for this kind of classification and what all this means in practical terms will become more obvious when the nature of explicatures and implicatures as conceived of by relevance theorists is discussed. Explicature as a pivotal notion in RT will be described in greater detail in the section that follows (2.3), whereas implicatures will be dealt with in the next chapter (see in particular Ch.3.2 and Ch.3.3).

2.3 The nature of explicatures

As noted above, the basic claim about utterance processing in RT is that the logical form, as generated by the language module or parser, becomes input to the pragmatic processor, and gets inferentially completed and enriched to yield the full content conveyed by the utterance that is being interpreted. This content includes both explicitly and implicitly communicated meaning. Let us consider how the meaning explicitly communicated by the speaker on a given occasion is taken to be recovered on this approach.

Virtually all researchers analysing the phenomena underlying human verbal communication agree that the semantic content of a given utterance severely underdetermines the intended meaning that the speaker is communicating through this utterance in context (e.g., Bach 1994, 2007; Jucker et al. 2003; Nerlich and Clarke 2001; Recanati 2002a, 2002b, 2004; Searle 1983; Seuren 2009; Sperber and Wilson 1986/95, 2002, 2008; Wilson and Sperber 2004; Žegarac 2006). As emphasized by Seuren (2009: 34), it is one of the central claims in pragmatics that "there is a trade-off between type-level, linguistically defined meaning, and token-level information." On the relevance-theoretic model this is known as the linguistic underdeterminacy thesis (Sperber and Wilson 2002).[7] Even a cursory look at

---

7   The thesis has been extensively developed and convincingly argued for by Carston (2002a: Ch.1), who contends that "the linguistic semantics of the utterance, that is, the meaning encoded in the linguistic expressions used, the relatively stable meanings in a linguistic system, meanings which are widely shared across a community of users of the system, underdetermines the proposition expressed (what is said). The hearer has to undertake processes of pragmatic inference in order to work out not only what the speaker is implicating but also what proposition she is directly expressing" (2002a: 19-

examples (1)-(10) below reveals that in order to understand the intended meaning, the interpreter must resolve a number of underdeterminacies of different kind.

(1)   She is lovely.[8] (33)
(2)   I will be retiring early. (563)
(3)   Even the sane ones are nuts. (385)
(4)   My service doesn't cover transatlantic. (383)
(5)   It's too heavy. (426)
(6)   Do you approve? (39)
(7)   Any of them real? (45)
(8)   Would you like to hear more? (24)
(9)   If I find which one of you provided that article, I'll have the consulate deport you. (24)
(10)   (a) 'How well did you know Jacques Sauniere?' the captain asked.
        (b) 'Actually, not at all.'(40)

So in order to recover the speaker-intended meaning of the utterances in (1)-(10), the interpreter needs to assign values to context-sensitive expressions (e.g., *I, she, it, you, them, his, my, ones*), deal with disambiguation (e.g., in (2) *retire* is ambiguous between "retire to bed" and "retire from the job or position"), identify the specific meaning of certain lexical items and phrases (e.g., words like *perfect, real, cover, approve, my service,* etc.), recover the ellipted material (e.g., in (6), (7) and (10b)), resolve illocutionary indeterminacies (e.g. (8) may function as a genuine or a rhetorical question; (9) may be taken as a humorous remark or a threat) and resolve an apparent contradiction in (3) – to list just the most obvious pragmatic tasks that must be performed to arrive at what is explicitly communicated in the context (of course, the actual communicated message may well go beyond the explicit meaning, but for the time being this is left aside and will be attended to only in chapter 3 below).[9]

20; see also Assimakopoulos 2008). This position is sometimes referred to as the strong underdeterminacy thesis (Carston and Noh 1996).

8   Examples (1)-(10) come from *The Da Vinci code* by Dan Brown, Corgi Books, 2004; the relevant page numbers are provided in brackets.

9   Accepting underdeterminacy as a phenomenon typical of how natural language functions in communicative exchanges is directly related to rejecting the principle of semantic compositionality. As Vicente and Martínez-Manrique (2005: 538) briefly explain, "the principle breaks down because there are terms in natural languages that suffer intrinsically from semantic underdetermination, such as comparatives, definite descriptions, demonstratives or universal quantifiers. We cannot ascribe a semantic value to terms of these types without pragmatic clues. We cannot construe the meaning of all sentences by semantic means alone." (For a more comprehensive discussion of why the principle fails, see also Carston 2002a: Ch.1; for a thought-provoking discussion on why the language of thought, by contrast with natural language, is compositional see Fodor 2003).

How does it happen that interpreters bridge all these gaps in the decoded output in order to understand adequately the actual meaning of utterances? RT provides a model of utterance comprehension which explains in very precise terms how the addressee arrives at the speaker-intended meaning. The Communicative Principle of Relevance and the presumption of optimal relevance (see Ch.1.5) map out the comprehension route for the interpreter, which is formalized on this approach as the relevance-guided comprehension heuristic:

(a) Follow a path of least effort in constructing an interpretation of the utterance (and in particular in resolving ambiguities and referential indeterminacies, in going beyond linguistic meaning, in supplying contextual assumptions, computing implicatures, etc.).

(b) Stop when your expectations of relevance are satisfied. (Sperber and Wilson 2005: 360)

The comprehension procedure introduced above predicts that all the pragmatic subtasks that need to be performed in order to arrive at the speaker-intended meaning, such as accessing appropriate contextual assumptions, making hypotheses about what is explicitly communicated (which embraces completing and strengthening the decoded semantic template in various ways) as well as constructing hypotheses about the intended implicatures, result from the addressee following the shortest route to achieving a satisfying level of cognitive effects (Wilson and Sperber 2004). All these interlocking processes are inferential and are assumed to run in parallel: an optimally relevant interpretation emerges in the course of mutual adjustments among hypotheses about the explicitly and implicitly communicated meanings, which are adequately adjusted and fleshed out in the course of interpretation (Carston 2002a; Noveck and Sperber 2007; Sperber and Wilson 1998, 2005, 2008; Wilson and Sperber 2002, 2004; Wilson and Carston 2007). This suggests that "a hypothesis about an implicature can both precede and shape a hypothesis about an explicature" (Carston and Hall 2012: 69).

To be more exact, on this approach rapid and relevance-constrained inferencing is deemed responsible for setting all aspects of communicated pragmatic meaning, so not just for generating implicatures on the basis of the recovered explicit meaning, but also for adjusting different components of the recovered explicature, which frequently comes about through the process of backward inferencing. Since the model predicts that in a certain communicative context, the interpreter may have quite precise expectations as to the contextual effects that utterance processing should return, a hypothesis about a particular implicated conclusion can be made first, and essential adjustments introduced in the explicature and the accessed background assumptions will follow so that this conclusion would be warranted (Sperber and Wilson 1998; Carston 2002b; Wilson and Carston 2007).

Acknowledging that inferential processes are a pivotal aspect of recovering not only the implicit, but also the explicitly communicated meanings, precludes the possibility of identifying the explicit layer of what is being communicated as derived non-inferentially, the way that Grice wanted to have it. Sperber and Wilson (1986/95: 182) define explicitness in the following way: "An assumption communicated by an utterance U is *explicit* if and only if it is a development of a logical form encoded by U." An explicature then is the outcome of developing and completing the decoded logical form, so it is necessarily a "semantic-pragmatic hybrid" (Carston 2004a: 819), with inferential processes mediating the transition from what is linguistically expressed to what is taken to be explicitly communicated (Carston 2002b: 133, 2007: 18).[10]

As a practical illustration of how utterance comprehension is assumed to proceed, consider the following mini-dialogue in (11) below. Let us assume that on coming home from work, Peter finds their flat in immaculate order, with Mary, his wife, putting the final touches to it by vacuuming the living-room, which she hardly ever does on weekdays, so puzzled he asks (11a):

(11)   (a) *Peter*: What's all this fuss about?[11]
      (b) *Mary*: Matilda is threatening to visit us.

The relevance-guided interpretation process for Mary's response in (11b), which is claimed to be automatically triggered in Peter's mind, can be schematically presented as follows:

Mary has said, "Matilda$_x$ is threatening to visit us$_y$."	*The encoded (incomplete) logical form of Mary's utterance, in which "Matilda" has an unresolved reference and the pronoun "us" remains uninterpreted, gets automatically embedded into a description of Mary's overt intentional behaviour.*

---

10   Two major classes of explicature are distinguished within RT. Apart from base-level explicatures (defined above), there are higher-level explicatures, which result from embedding the basic explicature under "a higher level description such as a speech-act description, a propositional attitude description, or some other comment on the embedded proposition" (Carston 2002a: 377). Generally, I will not be concerned in the present discussion with higher-level explicatures, so the term "explicature" will be used in this chapter exclusively to refer to base-level explicatures. (For a brief discussion of how higher-level explicatures, in particular those involving a propositional attitude description, may play a role in implicature derivation, see Carston 2010c.)

11   This is a slightly modified version of a dialogue from Stieg Larsson's novel *The girl who played with fire*, MacLehose Press, 2009, p. 17.

Mary's utterance is optimally relevant.	*The presumption of relevance conveyed by any stimulus produced in overt intentional communication (here: Mary's verbal behaviour) results in creating this expectation.*
(c) Mary's utterance will achieve relevance as an answer to Peter's question about the reason for THE FUSS* (THAT PETER SEES) AROUND.	*Expectation raised by (b) and the fact that such an utterance would be most relevant to Peter in the present communicative situation.*
(d) If Peter's sister, Matilda, a complete cleanliness freak, is threatening to visit Peter and Mary in the nearest future, there would be good reason for all the fuss.	*First assumption to be accessible to Peter, which, together with other adequate premises, might satisfy expectation (c); treated as an implicit premise of Mary's utterance.*
(e) PETER'S SISTER MATILDA IS THREATENING* TO VISIT* PETER AND MARY WITHIN HOURS.[12]	*First pragmatic enrichment of the logical form of (11b) to be made by Peter, which together with premise (d) will lead to the satisfaction of (c); treated as an explicature of Mary's utterance.*
(f) The reason for all the fuss that Peter sees around is Peter's sister's, Matilda's, forthcoming visit.	*An implicature based on premises (d) and (e) which satisfies the expectation of relevance in (c).*
(g) Matilda's obsession with cleanliness is going make Peter's and Mary's life very difficult for the period of Matilda's visit.	*Implicit inference from (e) and background knowledge, which is warranted by premise (e).*

Table 1. A relevance-theoretic schematic utterance interpretation model (Wilson and Sperber 2004: 616, cf. also Wilson and Sperber 2002) applied to (11b) as uttered by Mary in the Peter and Mary's home scenario.[13]

---

12 Capitalized words followed by an asterisk, in accordance with the convention adopted in relevance-theoretic analyses, represent ad hoc concepts, that is, occasion-specific senses of lexical items. The comprehension scheme presented here drastically simplifies the pragmatic lexical modulation processes underlying the explicature of the utterance under scrutiny. For an in-depth discussion on how RT approaches this aspect of verbal comprehension and ad hoc concept construction, see Sperber and Wilson (1998, 2008), Carston (2002a, 2010a, 2010b), Wilson and Carston (2007) and Wilson and Sperber (2004).

13 Inevitably, this kind of analysis suffers from some obvious but inescapable inadequacy. On the one hand, there is arbitrariness, which as the authors of RT point out (Wilson and Sperber 2002: 609), is due to the fact that the reasoning process is spelt out here in English sentences, whereas interpretive hypotheses will most probably be represented (if they reach a level of mental symbolization) in the language of thought. On the other hand, all these enrichments and adjustments happen simultaneously and not sequentially, unlike what Table 1 (and Table 2 below) presents (see also comments on schematic representations of the inferential steps that utterance interpretation is postulated to embrace in Sperber and Wilson 1998 and 2008).

The explicature represented in (e), as recovered by Peter interpreting Mary's utterance (11b), is assumed to be a fully-fledged proposition, with unique reference assigned to *Matilda*, the value of the pronoun *us* settled (probably partly on the basis of the highly salient contextual assumption (d)), the fixed temporal reference and the meanings of decoded words adequately adjusted to convey concepts denoting a very special kind of *threat* (signposted as THREATENING*) and an extraordinary kind of *visit* (VISIT*) associated with Peter's sister coming to stay, which is a bleak prospect. The implicit import as recovered by Peter in this context may go well beyond the implications spelt out in (f) and (g) above, but this issue will be taken on board in the discussion on implicatures (see in particular Ch.3.2-3.3).

As is widely acknowledged in the literature on verbal communication, the very same utterance can give rise to a number of quite different interpretations, which is not straightforwardly accountable for in terms of ambiguity or polysemy, but is an important property of how natural language functions (e.g., Bach 1994; Barwise and Perry 2004; Cappelen and Lepore 2005; Chapman 2001; Cresswell 1978/2004; Gleitman and Papafragou 2005, 2013; Grundy 2007; Neale 1993, 2004; Orrigi and Sperber 2000; Soames 2002; Vega Moreno 2007), and the apparatus of RT fully accommodates this potential of public languages (Sperber and Wilson 1986/95, 1998; Carston 2002a, 2010c). Thus the relevance-theoretic utterance comprehension procedure predicts that in a different immediate context, with a different set of highly accessible assumptions available to the addressee, the interpretation process will yield a completely different explicature from the one described above (cf. Mioduszewska forthcoming(a)).

So let us suppose for a change that the communicative situation of the dialogue in (11) is a hotel lobby scenario in Grenada in the Caribbean. There is a small group of guests gathered at the front desk, listening to the receptionist, who – as Peter can see – is reassuring everyone present that there is no reason to worry and all they need to do is just to follow instructions. Mary, who was one of the attentive listeners, currently joins Peter reading a paper in the lobby. To his enquiry concerning the fuss in (11a), Mary responds with (11b). In this context, the interpretation will result in a different explicature, as the analysis provided in Table 2 indicates.

(a) Mary has said, "Matilda_x is threatening to visit us_y"	*The encoded (incomplete) logical form of Mary's utterance, in which "Matilda" has an unresolved reference and the pronoun "us" remains uninterpreted, gets automatically embedded into a description of Mary's overt intentional behaviour.*

Mary's utterance is optimally relevant.	*The presumption of relevance conveyed by any stimulus produced in overt intentional communication (here: Mary's verbal behaviour) results in creating this expectation.*
(c) Mary's utterance will achieve relevance as an answer to Peter's question about the reason for THE FUSS* (_{THAT PETER SEES}) AROUND.	*Expectation raised by (b) and the fact that such an utterance would be most relevant to Peter in the present communicative situation.*
(d) If hurricane Matilda, mentioned in a recent weather forecast, is threatening to visit Peter, Mary and other people in Grenada in the nearest future, then there is good reason for all the fuss.	*First assumption to be accessible to Peter, which, together with other adequate premises, might satisfy expectation (c); treated as an implicit premise of Mary's utterance.*
(e) HURRICANE MATILDA IS THREATENING* TO VISIT** PETER, MARY AND OTHER PEOPLE IN GRENADA WITHIN HOURS.	*First pragmatic enrichment of the logical form of (11b) to have been made by Peter, which together with premise (d) will lead to the satisfaction of (c); treated as explicature of Mary's utterance.*
(f) The reason for all the fuss that Peter sees around is hurricane Matilda's forthcoming visit.	*An implicature based on premises (d) and (e) which satisfies the expectation of relevance in (c).*
(g) It is necessary to take precautions before hurricane Matilda strikes.	*Implicit inference from (d) and background knowledge, which is warranted by premise (e).*

Table 2. A relevance-theoretic schematic utterance interpretation model applied to (11b) as uttered in the Caribbean hotel scenario.

Even if it is the case that a moment before Mary approaches him, Peter was actually thinking about his sibling, Matilda, and her obsession with cleanliness which, in his opinion, she should discuss with a psychotherapist, the explicature of Mary's utterance that the relevance-guided comprehension procedure will lead him to access, will not concern his sister. The interpretation that Mary might have manifestly intended in the hotel lobby context, which Peter recovers as coming with a presumption of optimal relevance, is about hurricane Matilda and this is the way Peter understands his wife's utterance. The point is that the path of least effort that the interpreter invariably takes in choosing the right context and making hypotheses about the explicitly and implicitly communicated assumptions is necessarily constrained by considerations of the speaker's manifest intentions (see Ch.1.6-1.7).

Even though the analyses of (11b) proposed for the two different communicative scenarios presented above are simplified and cannot be treated as accurately demonstrating the interlocking mental operations going on in the interpreter's mind (see footnote 13 above), they clearly indicate that in recovering the explicitly communicated meaning intended by the speaker, the hearer does a lot of pragmatic inferencing, which results in fleshing out different subcomponents of the decoded semantic representation. These enhancements of the logical form (or logical forms which will be retrieved in the case of ambiguous utterances) are fully pragmatic, and apart from the resolution of ambiguities, saturation of contextual variables, and reconstruction of the ellipted elements, they "may require 'free' enrichment: that is, the incorporation of conceptual material that is wholly pragmatically inferred, on the basis of considerations of rational communicative behavior" (Carston 2004a: 819).

Free enrichment is taken to embrace two kinds of processes: the relevance-guided adjustment of meanings of lexical expressions as used in a specific communicative context, which is known as ad hoc concept construction (illustrated by capitalized words with asterisks in the analyses of (11b) in Tables 1 and 2 above), and the recovery of what some researchers refer to as unarticulated constituents (Carston 2010c; Perry 1986/93; Recanati 2002b)(e.g., WITHIN HOURS supplied in Tables 1 and 2 as part of the interpretation of (11b) is a typical example of this kind of free enrichment).[14]

2.4 Problems with free enrichment

While disambiguation, indexical fixing and ellipsis resolution seem fairly uncontroversial facets of utterance interpretation, the idea that explicitly

---

14 In fact, classifying both of these pragmatic processes as free enrichment is a relatively recent development in RT, not fully accepted by all researchers working in this paradigm (cf., e.g., Nishiyama and Mineshima 2010). In earlier relevance-theoretic analyses, free enrichment is associated with non-linguistically triggered completions of explicitly communicated meaning, while lexical modulation is treated as a separate process of ad hoc concept construction (Carston 2002a, 2002b, 2004b). In her paper "Explicature and semantics" Carston (2004a) briefly considers a hypothesis of elucidating all of the different kinds of pragmatic enrichment at the level of explicit content in terms of ad hoc concept construction mechanisms, but expresses doubt if this method can be capitalized on to account for all constituent enrichment cases. As notable later advances in this area of research reveal (Carston 2007, 2009, 2010c, 2012; Carston and Hall 2012), this kind of approach, apparently, has not been fruitfully exploited. For Recanati (2004), free enrichment is a different process from loosening meaning (that is, from ad hoc concept construction in RT terms), and semantic transfer (typical of metonymic uses of language), and it boils down to recovering unarticulated constituents. For a postulate concerning different types of free enrichment and critique of the notion *per se*, see Mioduszewska (2002, 2004).

communicated content involves free enrichment has received a lot of criticism from a number of researchers in the field and resulted in suggestions that the explicature as defined by Sperber and Wilson allows for some unjustifiable and unmotivated expansion in what is identified as explicitly communicated. To put it simply, structural and lexical disambiguation, resolution of indexicals (understood broadly to cover not only personal pronouns, but also demonstratives, context-dependent time adverbials, etc.) and ellipsis reconstruction are rather unproblematic, because there is a (usually easily) detectable linguistic basis (or an obvious linguistic gap to be filled in) for the identification of the relevant content in a given context. In other words, these completions of logical form are mandated by the underlying linguistic forms used, and even though the nature of the mechanisms employed leaves some room for debate,[15] there is no major disagreement as to what gives rise to them and what they result in, with the in-between path remaining somewhat controversial. So, for instance, it is standardly assumed that fixing reference for the pronoun *she* in (12a) is absolutely necessary to grasp the meaning conveyed, and the speaker's intention, in the context in which it appears, as spelt out in (12b), determines this reference unequivocally. In accordance with the relevance-guided comprehension procedure, the shortest interpretation route that will foreseeably yield enough contextual effects makes the interpreter identify the Eiffel Tower as the intended referent for *she* in this context.

(12) (a) She is lovely, no?
      (b) "She is lovely, no?" The agent motioned through the windshield toward the
          Eiffel Tower. (*The Da Vinci code,* 2004: 33)

As hinted at above, the major controversy in relation to explicatures has to do with free enrichment. This term was introduced by Recanati (1993, 2004) to

---

15 Answers to the question of how underdeterminacies of this kind are resolved in the course of interpretation differ across various frameworks. For instance, Bach (1994, 2001) assumes that recovering what the speaker expresses by saying what she does, and, in particular, fixing indexical expressions or choosing the intended meaning of ambiguous items, is due to completion and/or expansion of what is said into an impliciture, a term that emphasizes that the recovered meaning is communicated implicitly rather than explicitly expressed (on the similarities and differences between the relevance-theoretic explicature and impliciture, see Bach 2010). Setting all components of the impliciture, all expansions and completions are assumed to be necessarily constrained by the speaker's intentions and communicative context. On the other hand, Recanati (2004) assumes that assigning values to indexicals, as well as other linguistically controlled, bottom-up primary pragmatic processes are fully mechanical and non-reflexive, and are all due to "the dynamics of accessibility" (2004: 32), which remains totally non-inferential in nature (for the details of this approach to utterance interpretation, see Recanati 2004, and for some problems it faces, see Carston 2007 and Mazzarella 2011; for differences between inferential and associative accounts of comprehension, see Mazzarella 2013).

refer to mechanisms responsible for the fact that in certain cases recovering the proposition that is actually communicated in context requires an optional pragmatic enrichment. Free enrichment is viewed as truly pragmatic, since there is nothing in the underlying linguistic form that would license it, and it is claimed to be optional since without it, the utterance appears to express a complete (minimal) proposition, except that this proposition is either trivially true or obviously false, and therefore cannot constitute the meaning that is intentionally being communicated. To illustrate, let us consider some examples from Recanati (2004: 8). In (13) below, in order to grasp the meaning that the utterance conveys, as argued by Recanati (2004: 10), it is essential to expand the phrase *the table* by adding the bracketed material, because otherwise the absurd proposition that there is only one table in the universe which is covered with books would have to be recognized as the proposition actually communicated. In a similar vein, (14) can be fully made sense of only if the proposition is enriched by adding *from such and such group*; in fact, the blatantly false proposition that the unenriched utterance expresses is not even considered as its possible interpretation. The proposition literally expressed by (15) is inevitably true as it is highly improbable that anyone could have led a breakfastless life up to a certain point, so it is only the addition provided in brackets that yields its relevant meaning (Recanati 2004: 8-10).

(13) The table [in the living room] is covered with books.
(14) Everybody [from the UCLU Jazz Society] went to Paris.
(15) I've had breakfast [this morning].

As these examples show, free enrichment leads to the recovery of an interpretation that is much more fine-grained than what is literally said, through the "provision of (...) unarticulated constituents" (Recanati 2004: 24). Furthermore, it is assumed to be an unreflective, non-inferential, accessibility-based procedure, constrained by an associative network and background knowledge schemata, which is classified by Recanati (2004) as a primary pragmatic process: its output ("what is said" in Recanati's terminology) provides an important premise for inferring what is implicitly communicated (over and above what is said).[16]

While voicing some reservations and criticism concerning the utterance comprehension model that Recanati (2002a, 2002b, 2004) puts forth (Carston 2007), as indicated earlier, RT has adopted the term "free enrichment" to cover processes involved in augmenting explicatures beyond what is strictly linguistically mandated (Carston 2002b, 2004a, 2010c; Carston and Hall 2012; Hall 2008a, 2008b). To put it non-technically, free enrichment as included in the relevance-

---

16 Inferential processing, which takes into account the speaker's intentions, can influence interpretation at the primary level only when "the unreflective, normal process of interpretation yields weird results" (Recanati 2004: 38).

theoretic toolkit has to do with expanding the meaning of certain expressions at the level of explicature in order to arrive at their occasion-specific sense. As in Recanati's (2004: 10, 101) framework, these processes are claimed to be optional: that is, without them a full proposition is actually expressed, but this proposition can hardly be recognized as the one the speaker intends to convey, because it will not, generally, yield an expected range of relevant contextual effects (Carston 2002b), as is the case with (13)-(15) above. For this reason, "the relevance-theoretic position (…) is that, in the vast majority of contexts, it is the enriched propositions that are communicated as explicatures, with the uninformative, irrelevant, and, sometimes, truistic or patently false, minimal propositions playing no role in the process of utterance understanding" (Carston 2002b: 135-136). Also there may be utterances and contexts in which free enrichment will simply not apply (Carston 2009: 50).

A number of semanticists find this proposal difficult to accept (e.g., Corazza and Dokic 2007, 2012; Martí 2006; Stanley 2000; Stanley and Szabó 2000; Taylor 2001). In particular, they reject the idea of constituents not represented in the linguistic structure that should be added to arrive at the full explicature, contesting it as not well motivated, and suggesting that it causes an overgeneration problem (briefly discussed below in this section). Some of these critics (e.g., King and Stanley 2005; Stanley 2000, 2002b; Stanley and Szabó 2000) propose a solution in which all context-sensitive meaning adjustments would be linguistically mandated, positing the presence of hidden indexicals in the underlying logical form of the utterance (or, optionally hidden indexicals in Martí's 2006 analyses). Such covert variables are assumed to surface as an adequately constrained occasion-specific sense at the level of the utterance meaning, so in consequence, all enrichment is reduced to saturation.

The core of the debate revolves around Stanley's (2002b) examples in (16)-(17) and (18)-(20). Stanley's objection is that in a party context in which everybody invited is known to like and appreciate their mothers, in answer to a query whether another potential, though controversial guest, Sally, should also be invited, somebody uttering (16) cannot be communicating (17), even though the existence of a tacit pragmatic strategy responsible for enriching what has been expressed by the speaker allows for this kind of enrichment.

(16) Everyone likes Sally.
(17) Everyone likes Sally and his mother.

Another kind of overgeneration example that Stanley (2005) brings in is a sequence quoted in (18)-(20). It is a mystery, Stanley (2005) contends, why (18) can be enriched to express (19), but not to express (20), the latter obviously not conveyed in typical communicative contexts. So his question is, what blocks the generation of the superfluous (20) in a model that incorporates free pragmatic enrichment, which derives (19) from (18) on purely pragmatic grounds?

(18) Every Frenchman is seated.
(19) Every Frenchman in the classroom is seated.
(20) Every Frenchman or Dutchman is seated.

It is demonstrated by the defenders of free enrichment (e.g., Carston 2004a, 2009, 2010c; Hall 2008a, 2008b) that the purported overgeneration issue results from a misapplication of the pragmatic strategy, as RT presents it. On the one hand, only enrichments that produce intended and contextually relevant cognitive effects can be generated in the course of a relevance-driven comprehension process, which – in normal circumstances – rules out the enrichment of (18) into (20). On the other hand, all permissible enrichments must be truly local, that is, only those that operate on constituents of propositions (rather than on whole propositions) are legitimate, and only those that are minimal, that is, necessarily warrant the implicature which is evidently intended by the speaker, will go through.[17] So, for example, as Hall (2008a: 446-447) demonstrates, the enrichment of (21B) into (22) below is not sanctioned: the model predicts that (22) can only be recovered as the implicature (24) communicated by (21B). The point is that to be relevant, (21B) must provide a "yes" or "no" answer to the question in (21A). This kind of answer is recovered on the basis of (23c), which is the only required (and therefore, the only licensed) enrichment of (21B). Explicature (23c) processed together with highly accessible background assumptions like (23a)-(23b) yields (24). To recapitulate, the "no" answer is recovered as implicature (24) from processing (23c) in the context of assumptions (23a)-(23b), and the potential provision of (22) is blocked before (24) is recovered. Once (24) surfaces as the intended meaning conveyed by (21B),

---

17 As Deirdre Wilson has pointed out to me, this requirement is not satisfied by higher-level explicatures, which are necessarily derived from whole propositions. This is, for example, the case with "Today is your birthday" used to communicate that the speaker remembers it is the hearer's birthday on that particular day (this example is due to Deirdre Wilson, personal communication). I believe a possible solution might be to treat explicatures as resulting from one of two types of developments of the logical form generated by the language module, namely:
(a) developments involving local processes of meaning adjustment which apply to constituents of propositions and yield basic-level explicatures as their output;
(b) developments involving a global process of integration of a propositional form into a meta-communicative assumption schema (that is, one explicating the manifest communicative function of the utterance as intentionally used in the context; cf. Sperber and Wilson 1986/95: 82, 181, 224-225), which return higher-level explicatures as output; they are different from meaning adjustment processes typical of (a) in that they always consist in embedding the basic-level explicature under a speech act description, a propositional attitude description or another description of this kind (see footnote 10 above), with the exclusion of descriptions reserved for implicitly communicated assumptions (like, e.g., Mary has implicated that...).

comprehension stops, since the hearer's expectations of relevance have been satisfied.

(21) A: Do you want coffee?
      B: Coffee would keep me awake.
(22) B DOESN'T WANT COFFEE BECAUSE COFFEE WOULD KEEP HER AWAKE.
(23) (a) B DOESN'T WANT TO STAY AWAKE.
      (b) IF B DOESN'T WANT TO STAY AWAKE, THEN SHE DOESN'T WANT TO EAT/DRINK ANYTHING THAT COULD KEEP HER AWAKE.
      (c) COFFEE WOULD KEEP B AWAKE.
(24) B DOESN'T WANT COFFEE BECAUSE IT WOULD KEEP HER AWAKE.

The general rule that Hall (2008a: 447) formulates for free enrichment is as follows:

> if an assumption (developed from the logical form) is needed as a premise in the derivation of further intended aspects of meaning, as is frequently the case, then it cannot be developed any further at the level of proposition expressed. Further enrichment would block the inference, and thus prevent any inferential warrant for obviously intended conclusions. Any incorporation of additional material as a result of global inference, as opposed to local development, must therefore take place at a later stage, i.e. implicature derivation. Taking account of processing effort excludes the incorporation of more material into the proposition expressed if it serves no additional purpose, or if it will then have to be detached again to run the inferences needed to recover other communicated propositions.

This constraint eliminates not only illegitimate global enrichments, such as (17) alleged to be a possible development of (16) above, but also some other more complex cases of this type (for an exhaustive discussion, see Hall 2008a and 2008b: Ch.3).[18]

In fact, there is a series of publications by Carston (2002c, 2004a, 2009, 2010c), Hall (2008a, 2008b, 2009) and Carston and Hall (2012), in which they rebut the charges mounted against free enrichment filed by semanticists from the indexicalist camp, and compellingly argue against the covert indexical stance. They explain in detail how the locality of enrichment, which is part and parcel of the relevance-guided search for the speaker meaning, is just a minimal required

---

18 Nishiyama and Mineshima (2010) formulate a different type of constraint on free enrichment. Since free enrichment is claimed by the authors to operate only on referential expressions and the constraint is assumed to apply in the course of a sequential (rather than mutual) adjustment process of recovering the proposition expressed, it seems to have limited psychological plausibility. Nishiyama and Mineshima's semantic perspective does not take into consideration how their solution might fit into natural on-line utterance processing by hearers, whose minds may not readily distinguish between the referential and predicational use of nominal expressions.

development of certain subparts in the utterance's logical form and never operates over whole propositions, which rules out any possible overgeneration. They also expose some inadequacies in the hidden indexical programme, which may be shown to be burdened with overgenerating some nominal interpretations and urgently needs a set of adequate pragmatic principles to make the proposed saturation perform the vital contextual work (Hall 2008a). With reference to the latter point, a clearer division of labour between the bottom-up automatic processing (typical of saturation) and the top-down reflective processing (with access to speaker's intentions) needs to be implemented at the level of theoretical assumptions and postulates made by a researcher who opts for linguistic license for any enhancement of explicitly communicated content.

Some other opponents of free enrichment, Corazza and Dokic (2007, 2012), dispense with the concept altogether, advancing a model of situated minimalism or situationalism as they call it. Instead of contextually enriched propositions, Corazza and Dokic (2007, 2012) postulate situational anchoring for propositions expressed by utterances, which accounts for their context-sensitive meanings. On this approach, the specific truth-value (and, as a result, the meaning) of, for instance, (25) is simply (26). Depending on the implicit situation relative to which (25) is evaluated, the proposition expressed can either be that there is beer suitable for drinking in the fridge (for instance, if the speaker is making a suggestion about how the hearer could quench his thirst), or in a different situation (for example, in a fridge cleaning scenario), that there are still some beer stains in the fridge that need to be taken care of (Corazza and Dokic 2012: 186).[19]

(25) There is some beer in the fridge.
(26) An utterance of *u* of "There is some beer in the fridge" is true iff there is some beer in the fridge in the situation of *u*. (Corazza and Dokic 2012: 187)

As Corazza and Dokic (2012) point out, unlike free enrichment, in which the relevant aspect of the situation is singled out and becomes articulated as part of what is identified to be the proposition expressed by the utterance, situationalism posits only that truth-values of utterances are sensitive to implicit situations, relative to which they are evaluated. These situations need not be conceptually identified by subjects, who are simply *in them* (Corazza and Dokic 2007: 180, my emphasis). As the authors (2012: 190) maintain, "there is nothing incoherent in the idea of knowing or believing that an utterance is true relative to its situation without knowing *which* situation it is." Actually, the relevant standards for interpretation

---

19 As Corazza and Dokic (2007: 187) emphasize, the T-sentence in (26) "captures *all there is to capture* in order to understand the sentence 'There is some beer in the fridge' and to grasp the proposition that there is some beer in the fridge" in either of the scenarios presented above.

are assumed to be anchored to situations in which interactants happen to be rather than to reside in the discussants' minds (Corazza and Dokic 2007: 175).

On this approach, communicative exchanges do not need to rely on representing the mental states of the interlocutor, which is involved in identifying intentions or mind-reading (Corazza and Dokic 2012:192-193). While the situationalist T-sentences explicitly relativize utterance meanings to situations, it is by no means clear how and which contextual factors contribute to their truth-values. Even if it is evident that they materialize in two fundamentally different situations, it seems a bit of a miracle how the interpreter will get the two readings of (25). As Corazza and Dokic (2007: 189) admit, "a more detailed story on how the relevant contextual factors are determined" is needed.

Undeniably, the major attraction of situationalism is that it views communication as a less cognitively demanding enterprise than do models postulating free enrichment, in which some extra conceptual material gets incorporated into the interpretation of the speaker meaning. At this juncture it seems legitimate to pose a question about the necessity of holding on to free enrichment as an essential ingredient of explicature generation. If this cognitive burden, as Corazza and Dokic (2007: 176) refer to it, is found to be a disposable element in utterance comprehension, some controversy might be quelled. Let us have a closer look at the process of explicature generation in which free enrichment appears particularly problematic.

2.5 The enrichment fallacy?

One of the problems with free enrichment, which may have (inadvertently) contributed to some negative reactions that have emerged, may be related to the term itself. In the first place, as the discussion in the previous section makes clear, the process in question is by no means completely "free." On the contrary, the relevance-oriented comprehension procedure allows *only* enrichments necessary to achieve the expected and satisfying cognitive effects, so its range is restricted by the search for optimal relevance, which rules out any unjustified or gratuitous elaboration of explicatures. Besides, the developments that the logical form undergoes are additionally constrained by the local scope of the operation of pragmatic enrichment: only constituents or subparts of propositions can be "freely enriched."

Secondly, it is debatable whether "enrichment" is a felicitous term for the result of the process that is actually involved. What goes on has to do with making the meaning of underdetermining expressions specific enough, so the steps taken in the course of interpretation are geared towards pinning down the exact meaning (at least to the extent to which this is achievable or necessary, cf. the discussion below) or, more accurately, towards bringing this meaning into sharper focus (Recanati 2004: 24; Rubio-Fernández 2013: 725).[20] Strictly speaking then, what emerges is a context-specific sense, which should not be by definition either expanded or enhanced.

Furthermore, it appears that the mechanism of free enrichment is not fully compatible with some important assumptions that are generally accepted by RT researchers. As hinted at earlier, RT fully endorses linguistic underdeterminacy (e.g., Sperber and Wilson 1986/95, 2008) and Carston (2002a: Ch. 1) persuasively argues for the radical underdeterminacy thesis, in accordance with which it is a crucial feature of natural language sentences that they underdetermine the meanings that they are used to convey in communication. At the same time she indicates that no enhancement at the level of verbal expression can transform an utterance as used in context into a truly eternal sentence, that is, a sentence that will in a completely non-context-sensitive fashion (so eternally), carry the intended meaning. Even more importantly, she demonstrates that all additional linguistic material used either to turn a non-uniquely denoting expression into one that would make the entity uniquely identifiable, or to specify properties, relations, actions, etc., predicated in a sentence, tend to yield completions which are non-synonymous and which, therefore, surface as different propositions (Carston 2002a: 32-42). All this was very helpfully elucidated by Wettstein long ago (1979: 94):

> Given some utterance of 'It is covered in books', made in reference to some table, if we wish to obtain an eternal sentence, we can replace the indexical 'it' with any of several non-synonymous descriptions, each of which denotes the table in question, for example, 'the table Jones is sitting at at t_1', 'the table in room 209 at Camden Hall at t_1', and so on. Since these descriptions are not synonymous, it would seem that each of the resulting eternal sentences formulates a *different* proposition. The genuine eternal sentence counterpart will be the one that actually formulates the proposition the speaker asserted. But is there clearly one of these eternal sentences that, as opposed to the others, actually formulates what was asserted?
>
> It might be supposed that we can decide which of these eternal sentences captures what was asserted, by reference to the intention of the speaker. Surely the speaker, it might be supposed, knows which of these propositions he intended to express. This,

---

20 In principle the mechanisms under scrutiny resemble very much those typically associated with identifying context-sensitive lexical meaning. Specifization, which characterizes ad hoc concept construction (Recanati 2004: 25; cf. also Recanati 1995), and precisification, which is called for in the case of vagueness resolution (Cappelen and Lepore 2005; cf. also Korta and Perry 2007), involve exactly the same kind of mechanism as that involved in enriching the logical form of an utterance in order to arrive at the communicated explicature (see also 2.9 below).

> however, will not do. In many cases, the speaker will have no such determinate intention. The speaker will often be aware of several descriptions, each of which uniquely picks out his referent, and will not be able to select one of these descriptions as *the correct one*, the one that captures what he meant by his utterance of 'it'. Accordingly, if asked which eternal sentence formulates the proposition he meant to assert, he will not be able to answer. (original emphasis)

It is then an incontrovertible fact about how natural language functions as a means of communication that only a relatively small number of natural language sentences used by speakers could possibly (though not uncontentiously, as Vicente and Martínez-Manrique 2005 maintain) be analysed as determining the meaning conveyed without recourse to any pragmatic clues. However, using the required pragmatic clues to add linguistic material in order to arrive at the "full" (or "informationally exact", as Vicente and Martínez-Manrique 2005: 551 refer to it) meaning engenders taking a misguided course of action, since, to use Carston's (2002a: 30) own words, "[f]ormulating natural-language sentences of a progressively more determining sort may approach ever closer to a full encoding of propositions expressed, but the progression is asymptotic."

Looking at explicatures that are purported to result from free enrichment processes in the light of the above brings into question the validity and reliability of the pragmatic procedures involved. The problem is not only that different enrichments may result in different propositions (which they will), but also that usually there is indeterminacy as to which of the "enriched versions" is the one actually intended. This appears to cast a shadow on free enrichment as a credible explanatory mechanism that contributes to generating explicatures.

The point I am trying to make should become clearer when an example is analysed. Let us have a closer look at a paradigm case in which free enrichment might be called for, namely that of quantifier domain restriction. Quantifier domain restriction has been the topic of an extensive dispute between proponents of hidden indexicals and pragmaticists favouring unarticulated constituents (so on one side of the barricade there are, among others, Carston 2002a, 2004a; Carston and Hall 2012; Hall 2007a, 2008a; Recanati 2004,[21] and on the other, among others, Stanley 2000, 2002b; Stanley and Szabó 2000). The analysis provided below has been inspired by a relatively recent publication by Buchanan (2010),

---

21 In fact, there is some ambivalence in Recanati's approach to the class of expressions under scrutiny, because as he remarks, "[i]t remains an open question whether quantifier domain restriction is best treated as an instance of enrichment or as an instance of saturation" (2004: 114, see also Recanati 2004: 127 and 2010: 113), so he believes that it may viewed as an optional pragmatic enrichment or as a linguistically mandated process just as well, though, as he makes it explicit (2004:114), the hidden-indexicalist type of saturation is ruled out as theoretically ill-founded (for details see Recanati 2004: Ch. 7).

whose major goal is not so much to support one or the other side of the argument, but rather to show that what he refers to as the standard model of communication fails to account for certain important discourse data.

The widely-accepted standard model of communication, as Buchanan (2010: 342) states, rests on two fundamental assumptions about the content and success of communicative exchanges. It is assumed that what is communicated in terms of content must be a proposition (to be roughly understood as a conceptual representation that is semantically complete, i.e., truth-evaluable), whereas communicative success amounts to entertaining the proposition or propositions that the speaker *meant* by the utterance.[22] Admittedly, various theoretical frameworks may differ in detail as to how specific procedures and constraints responsible for identifying the content and achieving success will apply, but the central Lemma that is the common denominator for all of them will be: "If a speaker means a proposition p by her utterance U then her audience must entertain p if she [sic!] is to understand U" (Buchanan 2010: 348).

There are evidently some problematic cases which do not satisfy this Lemma. The example Buchanan builds up his argument around is (27):

(27) Every beer is in the bucket. (Buchanan 2010: 347)

It is stipulated that (27) appears as an utterance in the following discourse situation: in preparation for their apartment-warming party, Chet and Tim – in addition to the regular local keg beer – buy several cases of imported beer to cater for the sophisticated tastes of some of their female guests. They plan to serve this beer from a giant iced-filled bucket with a pirate motif to be placed in the backyard. Utterance (27) comes as part of Chet's response to Tim's question about whether everything is ready for the party. Chet says, "We are totally ready. The strobe lights are up. Every beer is in the bucket. I just need to find an eye patch for this pirate hat I'm going to wear" (Buchanan 2010: 347). As Buchanan (2010) demonstrates, on the standard view characterized above, Chet's utterance will be treated as underdetermining the intended meaning: the decoded logical form in (28) (or the "propositional radical" as Buchanan 2010: 348 prefers to call it) will have to be elaborated upon to yield the context-sensitive meaning.

---

22 As a description of the model in Ch.1 indicates, RT rejects the standard model of this kind, and places much less severe constraints on successful communication: (a) the intended array of propositions is assumed to merely be made manifest (rather than explicitly represented and entertained); (b) there is no requirement that the speaker must intend to express a single proposition which the hearer must identify exactly in order for communication to be successful (the goal is similarity rather than identity of thoughts, where similarity is assessed in terms of shared implications); (c) the speaker's informative intention may be more or less strongly manifest; and (d) its content may be more or less determinate (see also the discussion of strong and weak communication in Ch.3.5 below).

(28) [The ý: Bucket(y) &_ y] ([Every x: Beer(x) &_ x] (x is in y)) (Buchanan 2010: 348)

The major problem is that there is no single proposition that Chet can be identified as conveying in this context. There are a number of non-equivalent candidates for what Chet communicates by uttering (27), as the list in (29)-(32) shows, and possible further combinations of these, as (33)-(34) illustrate (Buchanan 2010: 349):

(29) Every beer *we bought at the bodega* is in the bucket *in the backyard.*
(30) Every beer *we will serve at the party* is in the bucket *decorated in pirate motif.*
(31) Every beer *for our guests* is in the bucket *filled with ice.*
(32) Ever beer *at the apartment* is in the bucket *next to the hot tub.*
(33) Every beer *we bought at the bodega* is in the bucket *next to the hot tub.*
(34) Every beer *at the apartment* is in the bucket *in the backyard.*

In principle, the list may be added to *ad infinitum*. Since all (or most) of these plausible candidate propositions have different truth conditions, they are substantially non-equivalent propositions. This reveals that the communicative success assumption as defined above cannot be upheld: "none of the foregoing candidates (or any other plausible candidate) satisfy the standard theorist's *Lemma*" (Buchanan 2010: 349), since there is no single candidate to be identified as the intended meaning. Under the circumstances, the speaker cannot reasonably cherish the expectation that the hearer will recover one specific proposition that the speaker has in mind, as the communicative intention made manifest in the discourse context does not allow the hearer to identify precisely this one proposition. As Buchanan (2010: 350) contends, Chet's communicative intentions in (27) "exhibit a certain kind of *generality* and *indifference* that precludes us from identifying any one of the candidate propositions as *the one he meant*" (original emphasis).

Buchanan examines four solutions that a standard theorist might come up with in order to save the standard view: a conjunctive propositions solution, a disjunctive proposition solution, and two appeal to vagueness solutions, and he provides convincing arguments that none of them works. The first one must be rejected, as the speaker could not have meant the conjunctive proposition (e.g. [29+30+31+32]), because there is no reason whatsoever to justify the identification of the conjunctive proposition as the one intended over any single proposition (say, (29)). The conjunctive proposition appears to have a status of yet another candidate proposition in no way licensed by the speaker's communicative intention. The same problem arises if each of potential candidate propositions were to come in succession, so that it could be suggested that the speaker meant that (29), the speaker meant that (30), and so on and so forth. Clearly, this does not make much sense, as there is no set of propositions that the speaker might evidently be recognized to require the hearer to form: that is precisely the problem with the generality and indifference of Chet's communicative intention.

The disjunctive proposition suggestion is similarly totally unrealistic, because it would force the interpreter to retrieve each of the disjuncts. Additionally, the disjunctive proposition will constitute yet another (entirely unsupported by the manifest speaker's intentions) proposition candidate to add and the interpreter will have no reason to choose this one rather than any other from among the propositions that the original utterance might give rise to. There are then very obvious reasons to discard this solution as well.

The other two solutions refer to vagueness. In the first place, a standard theorist might hold on to the idea that either "it is *vague* or *indeterminate* what Chet meant", or alternatively, that "Chet meant something *vague*" (Buchanan 2010: 354) by his utterance in (27). If the former is implemented, the claim could be that although there is no single definitely conveyed proposition, there is a whole range of vaguely communicated ones, including those in (29)-(32). It will be assumed that it is vague whether Chet meant (29) or (30) or any of the others. On this conception, "the various candidates are borderline cases of meant propositions" (Buchanan 2010: 355), so for each of them it can be stated that "it is not *definitely* the case that, for example, the speaker meant, say P_2, and it is not *definitely* the case that she didn't mean that proposition" (Buchanan 2010: 355). This does not work, since the speaker definitely did not mean P_2 for reasons provided above: there are no manifest speaker's intentions that, say P_2, is intended. Thus the speaker "*definitely* did **not** mean this proposition, and as such it is not vague whether she meant that proposition (in the standard theorist's favored understanding of 'means')" (Buchanan 2010: 355; original emphasis).[23] The first appeal to vagueness solution evidently fails.

The final rescue for the standard approach might be to argue that by saying (27) the speaker is actually communicating just something vague. Taking into account the fact that many propositions can be considered vague in that they are

---

23 As Deirdre Wilson (personal communication) has suggested, an alternative treatment accounting for the postulated indeterminate speaker's intention might involve analysing the communicative exchange under scrutiny in terms of what RT refers to as weak communication (see Ch. 3.5 for a discussion of weak and strong communication). There may be some evidence that the speaker intends to inform the hearer of P1, P2…Pn, although there is no conclusive evidence that she intended to inform him of any particular member of this array. Then the speaker might be seen as weakly communicating any particular member of the array, and the hearer would have to take some responsibility for deciding to accept one rather than another member from among this range. While this kind of analysis might adequately explain the indeterminacy problem that Buchanan is preoccupied with, it seems to me that, pace Buchanan (2010), in this communicative situation the speaker has a very specific referring intention with respect to both kinds of items referred to in (27), and makes these intentions mutually manifest in the context in which this utterance is used (see 2.6 below).

composed of one or more vague constituents, it might be claimed that Chet meant a vague proposition. Except that, as Buchanan is quick to point out, the problem of which vague proposition Chet had in mind remains unresolved. Principally then, it makes little difference if the theory offers no means of deciding which of a potential range of non-vague propositions the speaker actually means (which is the basic problem that gives rise to the whole predicament) or if the theory cannot identify which of a potential range of vague propositions the speaker actually means (Buchanan 2010: 356): each of them is detrimental to the model's credibility.

All this leads Buchanan (2010) to submit a proposal in which the content and success assumptions are eased. Instead of a proposition or a set of propositions that the speaker can be granted to intend to convey in the context, according to Buchanan (2010), it should be postulated that the communicative intention of the speaker concerns a property of propositions and not a certain proposition or a set of them. As a result, what is conveyed is assumed to be a restricted proposition-type, which can be identified and narrowed to recover the intended meaning in any way that will satisfy the speaker's (to a certain degree general and indifferent) communicative intention. As Buchanan (2010: 358) clarifies, "[t]he object of Chet's communicative intentions is not a proposition, but rather a property of propositions. (…) Chet's utterance is, in some sense, 'associated' with many non-truth-conditionally equivalent propositions – namely, those propositions that are of the intended (restricted) type", so many non-truth conditionally equivalent propositions of the restricted type (i.e. adequately contextually constrained) are assumed to be communicated. In consequence, communicative success is redefined in terms of the hearer entertaining one or more of the candidates of the restricted proposition-type that the utterance in (27) gives rise to.

Buchanan (2010: 361) concludes that analysing what is being communicated in terms of properties of propositions is a way of dealing with the problem of content and success in the case of expressions involving quantifier domain restriction. At the same time he admits that "a story is needed to show how a speaker's linguistic dispositions (…) at a particular context of utterance determine the intended proposition-type." More generally, it seems that his postulates need to be supported by a suitable theory of context. There is no principled explanation of how the intended proposition-type is identified or what exactly the thought that the speaker has in mind is. Is it also just a proposition-type thought? Furthermore, on this approach the recognition of the speaker's intention, however general and indifferent it may be, is very much up in the air and seems to be left out (or maybe left to metaphysics?).

Leaving aside these possible inadequacies in Buchanan's solution, I would like to suggest that his puzzle about the interpretation of utterances involving quantifier domain restriction is based on "the fallacy of enrichment." The propositions in (29)-(34), which are supposed to be candidates for the proposition that is actually meant, are nothing else but "freely enriched" explicatures derived from (27) in the context in which the utterance is used. As pointed out above more than once, they happen to be truth-conditionally different, so, strictly speaking, each of them conveys a different meaning. In my judgment, this creates an unwelcome proliferation (cf. Mioduszewska's 2002 concerns about explicatures). Of course, an ardent supporter of free enrichment might argue that these explicatures, even though not equivalent, are similar enough in terms of content to ensure that recovering, for example, any of the candidates in (29)-(34) as the explicature of (27) will do. On the one hand, the claim that all these explicatures are similar enough begs the question about the conditions of sufficient similarity. Besides, the fact that the range of potential explicatures featuring different enrichments is virtually infinite in number is a bit worrying. It seems that if criticism about overgeneration can be levelled at the relevance-theoretic treatment of explicatures, this aspect of explicature construction appears to be the real culprit. On the other hand, there is the hurdle of "cognitive burden" mentioned earlier, which free enrichment can be blamed for.

Another controversial issue that should not be ignored here has to do with the very nature of enrichment as a procedure allegedly contributing to constructing explicatures. As hinted at in the opening paragraphs of the present section, the interpretation of underdetermining expressions has to do with pinning down the meaning that is being conveyed. Therefore, reasonably enough, it involves zooming in on the actual referent, precisifying a property, specifying the kind of action that is targeted, identifying the location that is talked about, etc., rather than enhancing the meaning of the underdetermining expressions. This means that the precision of what is being conveyed rather than its expansion seems to be the goal, that is why viewing the process in terms of augmentation instead of zeroing in on the target is a misrepresentation. So it appears a mistake to think that we can account for how underdeterminacies are resolved by filling in some descriptive information: this kind of move negatively affects cognitive economy and in effect creates more problems than it solves.

I would like to argue that these problems can be by-passed on what will be called a contextual cognitive fix construal of settling underdeterminacies to be presented below. The proposal I would like to make is that neither the speaker's thought that gives rise to utterances like (27) nor the interpretation recovered by the hearer in context need to be viewed as enriched in the way (29)-(34) suggest.

2.6 Contextual cognitive fix instead of free enrichment

The point is that the contentious expressions *every beer* and *in the bucket* as used in (27) above can be taken to start as individuated mental representations in the communicator's mind and as components of mental representations formed in the interpreter's mind. Tacitly assuming that the first optimally relevant interpretation accessed by the comprehender will lead him to identify the entities referred to, because they are immediately available in their mutual cognitive environment (see 1.6-1.8),[24] the speaker produces (27), and as a result of processing (27), the hearer – following the relevance-guided inferential path – accesses very similar representations to those originally present in the speaker's mind. So, roughly (and, to be sure, very inadequately), the speaker's thought that is a trigger for utterance (27) can be schematically represented as (35), in which $BEER_a$ and $BUCKET_b$ are supposed to stand for the tokens of mental content actually representing the relevant objects in the world, or – more adequately – in the cognitive environment that the speaker shares with the hearer. At the receiving end, (36) is hypothesized to surface in the hearer's mind in the process of interpreting (27).

(35) $EVERY\ BEER_a\ IS\ IN^*\ THE\ BUCKET_b.$[25]
(36) $EVERY\ BEER_{a'}\ IS\ IN^*\ THE\ BUCKET_{b'}.$

So what (35) attempts to depict is the underlying speaker's thought which leads to producing (27). By the same token, (36) aims to portray the hearer's thought which emerges due to his processing of (27). Both (35) and (36) are seen as formulas reflecting the language of thought representations. Alas virtually nothing (beyond speculation that it is sensible to postulate it) is known about the language

---

24   The notion of cognitive environment was introduced in Ch. 1, but a short reminder might be in place here. A set of facts and assumptions that are manifest to an individual (where *manifest* means that a given person is capable of perceiving something or inferring an assumption and accepting it as true) constitutes this person's cognitive environment. People are said to share their cognitive environments if the same facts and assumptions are manifest to them. If, in this shared cognitive environment, one of the facts manifest is the fact that certain people share it, then Sperber and Wilson (1986/95: 41-42) call it the mutual cognitive environment of these people.

25   It must be emphasized that despite their superficial similarity to formulas used by the proponents of hidden indexicals, the above representations have nothing to do with this kind of analysis. The only affinity is notational, and the assumptions, claims and elucidations related to these formulas are completely unlike anything that comes close to the hidden indexicalist approach. Hidden indexicals are supposed to belong to the logical form of utterances, the schematic representations used here are supposed to depict (even if inaccurately) the components of language users' thoughts. As indicated earlier, an asterisk in (35) and (36) following the lexical item *in* signifies that an occasion-specific meaning of this word is intended.

of thought and the kinds of representations it uses. I do not intend to claim that formulas like (35) and (36) are "genuine" language of thought representations that inhabit human minds; my only purpose in manufacturing (35) and (36) is to advance an argument about the derivation of explicatures. Namely, I would like to propose that explicature generation, instead of enrichment, which is quantitative in nature, involves a procedure which is qualitative in character, which – for want of a better term – I will refer to as contextual cognitive fix. In a nutshell, while enrichment inevitably adds components to the recovered representation, the postulated contextual cognitive fix mechanism adjusts the representation so that the underdetermined components get a fully determined denotation at the level of the interactant's thought. Let me explain what the posited contextual cognitive fix pertains to, taking as a point of departure the comprehension of (27).

As stated above, it is postulated that the speaker's thought which triggers the production of (27) contains as its components the concept of *every beer (that is contextually relevant)* and *the bucket (that is contextually relevant),* whose representations in the speaker's mind are directly caused by the relevant real world objects. Thus in (35), $BEER_a$ is intended to symbolize the cognitive fix on the contextually relevant beers, which features as part of the speaker's thought, indicating the intended range of beers (in the world) which this constituent of the speaker's thought picks out. Likewise, $BUCKET_b$ represents the actual component of the speaker's thought, cognitively fixed on the relevant bucket in the world, and conveyed by the phrase "the bucket" in (27). The subscripts $_a$, $_b$, $_{a'}$ and $_{b'}$, which index the two components in (35) and two components in (36) respectively, are designed to indicate that the tokenings of the thought which is being schematically represented by the formulas are part of the mutual cognitive environment of the interactants, as if parameterized by the circumstances of context to which their thoughts are anchored (cf. MacFarlane 2007). The circumstances of context should be understood as those salient entities (or properties, actions, locations, etc.) that the immediately accessible context (emerging as part of the mutual cognitive environment of the interactants) affords the hearer, which help him determine, via relevance-constrained inferencing, what the speaker actually means (cf. Recanati 2007: 6).

To be more exact, by featuring in what functions as an explicature recovered by the hearer of (27), $EVERY\ BEER_{a'}$ represents the denotation of the phrase *every beer* that is accessed and cognitively fixed on in the hearer's mind. It is hypothesized then that the concept of *every beer (that is contextually relevant)* is the component of the hearer's thought, similarly to what it was like in the case of the speaker. However, the index in (36) differs in one minute detail from the index for this component in formula (35). The difference lies in the little sign of prime (') following the subscript $_a$ which indicates that there may be no full duplication of thoughts between the speaker and the hearer. For the same reasons, the equivalent of BUCKET$_b$ is depicted in (36) as BUCKET$_{b'}$. The prediction behind this is that, as convincingly argued by Sperber and Wilson (1986/95), the aim of communication should not be thought of in terms of "an exact duplication of thoughts in communicator and audience" (1986/95: 193). As Carston (2002a: 47) accurately summarizes the RT stance, "[v]erbal communication, on this view, is not a means of thought duplication; the thought(s) that the speaker seeks to communicate are seldom, if ever, perfectly replicated in the mind of the audience; communication is deemed successful (that is, good enough) when the interpretation derived by the addressee sufficiently resembles the thoughts the speaker-intended to communicate."

It must be emphasized that the schematic representations employed here have nothing to do with formal models of context representation: the relevant components of the hearer's thought are arrived at inferentially, via the relevance-driven utterance comprehension procedure. The explicature is assumed to be recovered by the recipient following the path of least effort and precisifying the meaning by evaluating interpretive hypotheses (based on their accessibility and compatibility with manifest communicator's intentions) until his expectations of relevance are satisfied. The only innovation is that instead of adding conceptual material into the explicature, which free enrichment would do, the explicit meaning surfaces as an unequivocal conceptualization, which is – just like free enrichment – wholly pragmatically motivated (cf. Carston 2004a: 818). Thus explicature remains "an amalgam of linguistically decoded material and pragmatically inferred material" (Carston 2004a: 824).

The present proposal can be seen as a development of the idea originally put forth by Sperber and Wilson (1986/95) with reference to mental representations underlying definite descriptions. As the authors emphasize, speakers and hearers need not describe to themselves intended referents "in terms of any external-language definite description. It seems plausible that in our internal language we often fix time and space references not in terms of universal co-ordinates, but in terms of a private logbook and an ego-centred map; furthermore, most kinds of reference - to people or events for instance - can be fixed in terms of these private time and space co-ordinates. Thoughts which contain such private references could not be *encoded* in natural languages but could only be incompletely represented" (Sperber and Wilson 1986/95: 192). Alas, later relevance-theoretic analyses do not follow this line of thought much further,[26] and instead, the process of free

---

26 A notable exception is Wilson's (1992) paper "Reference and relevance", in which the author analyses utterances of the type "The door is open" as "Door *d* is open", but – to my best knowledge – there is no follow-up on this kind of approach in further relevance-theoretic research.

enrichment involving the addition of extra conceptual material into the recovered representation is introduced and reinforced. Yet, for a number of reasons provided above (see Ch.2.5), free enrichment of this kind appears not fully adequate for specifying the proposition expressed by utterances.

On the present construal, the resemblance between the mental representations in the speaker's and hearer's mind seems to be rather transparent. Since thought duplication is assumed by relevance theorists to be neither expedient nor fully achievable, it seems important not to erase the little sign (') from the formula representing the hearer's thought. Anyone concerned about possible dissimilarities between what is taken to be basically the same concept should take into account the fact that all tokening in general, and mental tokening in particular will never be the same for different individuals.[27]

How can communication failure be accounted for in the model incorporating cognitive contextual fix as part of the utterance comprehension procedure? As may have become apparent by now, erroneous resolution of underdeterminacy is predicted to arise from a context-index error which occurs when the speaker-intended context and the one retrieved by hearer do not coincide. The claim is then that potential errors that result from the interpreter's not accessing the right kind of context will give rise to the representation in the hearer's mind in which the contextual index for a given expression differs from the one in the speaker's thought, as shown in (37) and (38) vis-à-vis (36).

(37) EVERY BEER$_i$ IS IN* THE BUCKET$_{b'}$.
(38) EVERY BEER$_{a'}$ IS IN* THE BUCKET$_j$.

In more practical terms, the above means that either the beers that the hearer fixes on or the bucket conceptualized as the one intended are different objects in the world from those represented in the speaker's mind.[28][29]

But isn't it the case that the hearer may actually think of *every beer* from (27) as *every beer bought at the bodega* or *every beer for the guests*, and of *the bucket* as, for instance, *the bucket next to the hot tub*? Such mental representations are by no means barred from being generated by the contextual cognitive fix mechanism:

---

27 As Carston (2002a: 339) aptly puts it, "there is always leeway for individual differences where pragmatic inference is concerned."

28 In principle, of course, the addressee may wrongly resolve both underdeterminacies (as represented by: EVERY BEER$_i$ IS IN* THE BUCKET$_j$), but such a situation will be rather rare, revealing that there is a major incapacity related to the identification of the speaker's informative intention (cf. Ch 1.6).

29 The subscripts $_i$ and $_j$, which index the erroneously picked denotations, are not marked by the prime (') sign as they are a complete mismatch to the speaker's intended entities, so the speaker's and the recipient's thoughts diverge in this respect and it is not the case that they are just mental tokenings of the intended denotations, which the prime serves to indicate.

it is possible that the actual representation of the intended beer and bucket will take an enhanced form, for instance, similar to one of those in (39)-(40), however, this kind of "supplemented" representations should no means be taken as a standard, usual and natural procedure which the relevance-guided comprehension process recovers, but rather as an idiosyncratic variation in the representation of the speaker-intended meaning in the recipient's mind.

(39) EVERY BEER$_a$,(BOUGHT AT THE BODEGA$_c$) IS IN* THE BUCKET$_b$,.[30]
(40) EVERY BEER$_a$,(FOR THE EXPECTED GUESTS$_d$) IS IN* THE BUCKET$_b$,.
(41) EVERY BEER$_a$, IS IN* THE BUCKET$_b$,(NEXT TO THE HOT TUB$_c$).

As a matter of fact, it can only be expected that internal language representations that are formed in the course of utterance interpretation will be to a lesser or greater degree idiosyncratic (as indicated above, and as hinted at by Sperber and Wilson 1986/95: 192 in the quotation concerning definite descriptions cited earlier): depending on the mental effort that the hearer will be willing and/or able to invest in the interpretation process, depending on the thoughts present in his mind prior to utterance processing, depending on the range of specific contextual assumptions brought to bear on the comprehension process, depending on the content of the concepts featuring in these assumptions, etc., different individuals processing the same utterance in (principally) the same communicative context may end up with slightly different mental representations of the speaker's meaning. On the contextual cognitive fix construal, cognitive enhancements of the kind illustrated in (39)-(41) are viewed just as elaborations on the recovered explicit meaning: the basic explicature generated by the relevance-guided comprehension heuristic is assumed not to contain any extra cognitive material, with contextual cognitive fixes on the same entities, properties, actions, relations, locations, etc., as marked by co-indexed constituents in the internal language representations of the speaker and the hearer, being one of the requirements of communicative success.

This indicates that the manner of conceptualizing entities (or, for that matter, of properties, actions, relations, locations, etc.) may be to a certain extent specific to a given recipient at a particular moment, but as long as it is nested in the same type of shared cognitive environment, it will (usually) pick out the same intended entities. Thus it may happen that the thought that originates in the speaker's mind will be more schematic (as represented in (35) above) whereas what the hearer

---

30 There should be many more asterisks in these explicatures to account for different kinds of meaning modulations involved, but since the goal is to show how contextual cognitive fix works rather than to provide formally accurate language of thought formulas (which, as stated earlier, is not attempted here), they have been left out to avoid unnecessary proliferation of symbols.

recovers will be more conceptually encapsulated as (39)-(41) depict, or the other way round. Whichever way it proceeds, the overlap between the original and the retrieved meaning is transparent from the postulated formulas.[31]

It seems that some generalizations can be offered at this stage. On the construal proposed here, the actual concepts of the intended objects or mental tokenings of properties, actions, relations, locations, etc., are posited to feature in both the thought that originates in the speaker's head, being a (potential) prompt for her verbal output, as well as in the thought that occurs in the hearer's mind as a result of utterance processing. The underlying claim is that thought constituents, that is, concepts that originate in the speaker's mind which – as a result of utterance processing – will be also (hopefully) entertained by the hearer, are in a causal relationship to the entities, properties, actions, relations, locations, etc. in the world (in fact, real or possible, as the case may be) in that they may be directly caused by them or by processing ostensive verbal stimuli that make reference to them (cf. Carston 2002a: 1.7.1). Thus what Carston (2002a) claims to be true of indexical reference, is here generalized to all uses of language which underdetermine the communicated meaning. Each case of this kind is assumed "to be irrevocably context-bound; it is not reformulable in terms of a uniquely denoting description [or any other description for that matter], but depends on the addressee's capacity to identify the intended entity [or property, action, relation, location, etc.] by some means which is non-linguistic or, at least, not wholly linguistic" (Carston 2002a: 36-37).

This kind of modelling of explicatures avoids including the somewhat troublesome enrichment process as an element of explicature generation, at the same time allowing for relevantly (though not freely enriched) complete explicatures to surface. The resulting explicature can be more (or less) conceptually satiated, depending on where the shortest relevance-oriented route will take the hearer (see Ch.2.8).

This proposal fully acknowledges that linguistic underdeterminacy is not just an inherent, but, as Carston (2002a: Ch.1) argues, an essential feature of natural language in general and of verbal utterances in particular. More importantly, the contextual cognitive fix mechanism postulated to underlie speech production and reception appears to offer some natural motivation for underdeterminacy: thought components frequently have a form of concepts which cannot be uniquely expressed by linguistic means, as the above quotes from Sperber and Wilson (1986/95:

---

31 This brief discussion of how the contextual cognitive fix contributes to explicatures provides at least a partial answer to Mioduszewka's (2004: 165) query about possible intersubjectivity of explicatures (cf. also Mioduszewska forthcoming(a)).

192) and Carston (2002a: 36-37) aptly emphasize.[32] The slight amendment to the relevance-driven comprehension model proposed here has to do with replacing free enrichment with contextual cognitive fix, which is not specific for what the hearer recovers, but characterizes thoughts in general. No extra information needs to be fed into explicatures, so the "cognitive burden" (cf. Corazza and Dokic 2007: 176) associated with enrichment disappears: explicatures become "informationally exact" (to borrow again the convenient phrase from Vicente and Martínez-Manrique 2005: 551) as language of thought formulas.

The proposed construal not only follows the important tenets of RT, but also seems to fit well into the underlying assumptions of RT as a model of ostensive verbal communication. The relevance-theoretic model of verbal communication posits that a speaker in a certain mental state, let us label it MN_1, which involves entertaining a certain thought T_1, who wants to communicate verbally T_1 to an addressee, needs to use for that purpose an ostensive (most frequently) verbal stimulus, that is, an utterance, say U_1. U_1 is a representation of T_1, which is produced as evidence for the speaker's informative intention and is taken as such by the hearer. The hearer then uses U_1 as a piece of evidence for the thought T_1 that the speaker is communicating. Recovering the speaker-intended meaning results in the hearer entertaining a thought $T_{1'}$. If communication has been successful the hearer retrieves $T_{1'}$, which resembles T_1, and the two thoughts contribute their shared implications to the mutual cognitive environment of the interactants. If communication is not successful, then the recipient retrieves a different thought, for instance, T_2, which does not contribute to the mutual cognitive environment. Since a thought is a mental state, the mental state MN_1' of the hearer after interpreting U_1 should resemble the initial MN_1 of the speaker if communication succeeds, otherwise the two mental states are different, MN_1 and MN_2 respectively. The formulas used to illustrate how the contextual cognitive mechanism operates are in full harmony with these theoretical postulates of RT.

The description of how the contextual cognitive mechanism underpins utterance production and comprehension offered in this section needs to be substantiated by analyses of a number of examples, so let me proceed to demonstrate how the contextual cognitive fix can be applied to some interesting examples.

---

32   This brings to light a very basic fact: "We think in Mentalese and communicate in English" (Fodor 2003: 153), and these are two very different systems, the former being compositional and the latter non-compositional (Fodor 2003; for a well-reasoned argument why this is so, see Carston 2002a). Therefore, while the content of thought as a complex mental representation is determined by the content of its constituents, no similar principle functions for natural language complex expressions. (For an intellectually stimulating discussion on how natural language and thought are dissimilar, see Fodor 2003.)

2.7 How contextual cognitive fix works

In order to see how contextual cognitive fix can account for generating explicatures for different kinds of utterances, let us consider a couple of examples. It appears only logical that the focus should be on examples in which free enrichment as an essential explicature-generating tool is standardly employed. The focus in what follows will be mainly on some classic examples, which have been used and re-used in various kinds of discussions on how natural language works not only by pragmaticists, but also by semanticists and philosophers of language. The primary aim is to show in what way the proposed treatment can cope with the interpretation processes.

Non-sentential assertions (Buchanan 2010; Stainton 1994) are the class of utterances which, in a sort of natural way, yield themselves particularly well to the contextual cognitive fix processing. It is difficult, if not virtually impossible, to come up with a plausible explicature the speaker who utters (42) actually communicates.

(42) John's father. (Stainton's 1994: 271)

As argued by Stainton (1994), (42) can be used as an assertion which in a given context would communicate, for example, that the man standing near the door is John Adams's father. The question that arises has to do with the content of the (intended and recovered) explicature, because if it were to be an enriched version of (42), then there exists no single candidate for the hearer to identify as the intended meaning, as (43)-(45) indicate.[33]

(43)　THE MAN LEANING AGAINST THE DOOR IS JOHN ADAMS'S FATHER.
(44)　THE MAN IN THE WHITE HAT IS JOHN ADAMS'S FATHER.
(45)　THE MAN WITH A BIG MOUSTACHE IS JOHN ADAMS'S FATHER.

The problem can be overcome if the intended meaning is identified by the cognitive fix mechanism. Assuming that "That is" can be supplied as the ellipted material in (42), the explicature which the contextual cognitive fix helps to retrieve is (46).

(46)　THAT$_X$ IS* JOHN$_{a'}$'S FATHER$_b$.

The processing of (42) based on the contextual cognitive fix procedure predicts that the intended meaning will surface in the hearer's mind as a mental representation of the concept of the intended referent in the shared cognitive environment of the speaker and the hearer. The regular search for relevance and manifest speaker's intentions underpin the contextual cognitive fix, which yields this interpretation.

33　Carston (2002a: 35-37) comments on such cases arguing against eternal sentences and the third effability principle.

An analogous analysis can be provided for a number of definite and indefinite descriptions used in subsentential utterances of assertoric sort. As Buchanan (2010) points out, (47) below causes problems similar to utterances involving quantifier domain restriction, since there is no identifiable candidate for the actual explicit meaning that is conveyed in the context, in which, let us assume, a waiter taps the chef on the shoulder and utters (47): there is a whole range of plausible explicatures (e.g. (48)-(49)), but none of them can have the status of the unique one actually endorsed by the speaker.

(47) A health inspector. (Buchanan 2010: 350)
(48) THE MAN WE ARE LOOKING AT IS A HEALTH INSPECTOR.
(49) THE CUSTOMER WHO IS SNIFFING HIS PLATE IS A HEALTH INSPECTOR. (Buchanan 2010: 351)

As previously, the direct contextual cognitive fix (represented as: THAT IS A HEALTH INSPECTOR$_a$.) that the relevance-guided interpretation procedure is posited to involve, will result in the direct representation of the intended referent in the hearers' mind.

Let us now turn to an example that has provoked a lot of discussion ever since it was seriously examined for the first time about thirty years ago by Perry (1986/93). Perry's observation is that an utterance like (50) is always a statement about some place: *rain* is a predicate with a dyadic relation which necessarily specifies the time (expressed in (50) through the present continuous tense) and the place (unarticulated in (50)).

(50) It is raining.

As Perry (1986/95: 206) emphasizes, for a specific time at which it is raining, it must always be raining at some specific locale, as inevitably "it rains in some places while not raining in others." He contends that while the place argument will frequently remain unarticulated, it will necessarily (tacitly) be supplied in context.[34]

This line of argument is challenged by Recanati (2002a), who comes up with the following hypothetical situation. Because of a disastrous drought on earth, every event of raining is being monitored by special rain detectors, which have been placed all over the planet, and information about each occurrence of rain not only immediately appears on the rain-detection map at the rain-detection headquarters,

---

34 Taylor (2001), who draws on Perry's analysis, makes the case for unarticulated constituents by suggesting that utterances like (50) are semantically incomplete, because in the "subatomic structure" of the verb "to rain" (it is actually not clear what Taylor means by this subatomic structure) there is a place argument, which remains unarticulated at the level of the logical form. See Cappelen and Lepore (2007a) for some arguments against Taylor's suggestions.

but is signalled by an alarm bell that alerts the staff to each incidence of rain. After a really long rainless spell, a weatherman at the rain-detection centre hears the alarm bell go off. He is in a different room, so he is oblivious to where the rain has been recorded by the apparatus, but his utterance of (50) will be true (so it will be a full proposition) regardless of where the rain comes down and in spite of the speaker's total ignorance of the actual location of the rain. On this basis, Recanati (2002a) argues that semantically *rain* is a "zero-argument" predicate, which can be (if there is a pragmatic need) optionally enriched in a given communicative context by adding the actual site for the rain-action, "even though the sentence itself involves no (overt or covert) reference to a place" (Recanati 2010: 82).[35]

Cappelen and Lepore (2007a: 213, fn. 3) find Recanati's example not sufficiently strong to argue that rain predicates require no place value: they remark that "Recanati is arguing that the location-*general* proposition, not the location-*neutral* proposition, gets expressed" (original emphasis) in utterances like (50). Strictly speaking then, in the rain-detection scenario, (50) conveys the meaning that it is raining in some place or other, so the place is tacitly invoked even if it remains unspecified (at least before the weatherman looks at the map).[36]

In order to show that an unarticulated place constituent may be totally absent from utterances about rain, Cappelen and Lepore (2007a) present a different example. They invent The Rain-Ache Universe in which the following is true: there is no agriculture there, so rain is totally irrelevant to crop success, rain drops immediately evaporate as soon as they come into contact with anything, so one cannot get wet by being exposed to rain, but whenever it rains, no matter where the precipitation occurs, it is the cause of headaches of the inhabitants. Fortunately, in the Rain-Ache Universe it is enough to put a yellow hat on before the rain starts to prevent the headaches, therefore, constant rain monitoring is very important to everybody's well being. When rain-detectors fail to issue relevant warnings, one can hear grumbles like those in (51) and (52) expressed by the dwellers (Cappelen and Lepore 2007a: 209).

(51) Ugh, it's raining; those rain detectors never work.
(52) Oh, it's really raining today.

---

35 Marti (2006) argues that the rain-detection centre example has the parameter "in the territory" supplied as the implicit location, due to the fact that rain predicates have a "location slot" for contextually assigned values in the logical form of utterances in which they appear. It is not a very convincing alternative, and it is cogently refuted by Recanati (2010: 107-113) on the basis of a solid analysis of the underlying semantics for *rain*, vis-à-vis *arrive* and *dance*.

36 In his more recent publication, Recanati (2010: 87) does provide what appears to be a location-neutral example:
(a) Once, in Antiquity, it rained blood. Since then, no such thing ever happened again.

For obvious reasons, the place parameter remains outside the sphere of interest of the inhabitants of the Rain-Ache Universe, who as a result, produce place-insensitive rain utterances. "The only thing they (…) care about is not where it rains but whether it rains" Cappelen and Lepore (2007a: 209). The authors draw two useful conclusions from the way rain-utterances function in the Rain-Ache Universe, which are directly applicable to how earthlings process utterances about rain.[37] First, it is people's experiences with the rain and the direct effects it exerts on their lives that are responsible for location-completion that interpreters are likely to come up with for most rain-announcements that they hear.[38] Second, since place-insensitive rain-predicates are conceivable and the nonlocalized proposition does exist, hence the underlying semantics of the verb under examination is location-neutral. While rain as an activity always takes place somewhere, this fact need not always be part of the interpretation of rain-utterances, in the same way that dancing – which always takes place somewhere – does not require that all utterances with *dance* will specify it. So, although dancing necessarily is an action happening in a certain location, this does not lead anyone to postulate unarticulated constituent for an utterance like (53), as Taylor (2001) and Cappelen and Lepore (2007a) argue:

(53) Laura danced the tango all night last night. (Taylor 2001: 53).

Rain-utterances have also been studied by relevance theorists. On the relevance-theoretic treatment, it is proposed that the location element is added in the explicature via free enrichment as is contextually appropriate and required for the expected cognitive effects to be brought about. So, as it is reasonably claimed by Carston (2004a), if (50) is uttered in the context of a telephone exchange, and the speaker is in New Zealand and the hearer in London, the recipient gets a proposition like (54).

(54) It is raining in Christchurch, New Zealand, at t_x. (Carston 2004a: 818)

I would like to point out that there is a minor worry related to this kind of treatment. While vulnerable to the (by now well-familiar) charges that free enrichment

---

37 Cappelen and Lepore (2007a: 205-206) bring in more examples of what they refer to as location-neutral rain utterances, such as (a)-(d) below, but these are much less interesting than the Rain-Ache Universe case discussed in this section and it is debatable if they can be viewed as fully analogous to (50).
   (a) Rain is Nina's favorite weather condition.
   (b) Rain is the topic of our next book.
   (c) I don't care *where* it rains, I only care *whether* it rains.
   (d) Why does it rain?
38 Recanati (2010: 94) makes a similar point by remarking that we care about where precipitation occurs simply because it is likely to affect us directly.

provokes, this kind of example is particularly worrisome. To make what I am driving at clearer, let us first give some consideration to the following situation: Peter and Mary have been planning to do some long-overdue garden chores first thing that weekend. On Saturday morning, Mary is the first one to get up, she looks out of the window and utters (50). The obvious question to ask is: what kind of place does Mary have in mind, and, as a consequence, what location name can be identified as adequately completing (50) to get the full-fledged explicature? Will it be the italicized expression in (55) or maybe more adequately the one used in (56) or (57)?

(55) It is raining *in Peter and Mary's garden.*
(56) It is raining *where Peter and Mary live.*
(57) It is raining *in north London.*

At first blush, it looks as if the problem is exactly the same as with the enrichments of (27) ("Ever beer is in the bucket"), as discussed in section 2.5 above, but (55)-(57) appear a bit more controversial. In principle, all the enriched versions proposed in an earlier discussion of (27) are sensible candidates for the intended meaning. Unfortunately, (55)-(57) seem rather counterintuitive: it certainly is the case that Mary's announcement about precipitation is not about just anywhere in the world – it is about a location that is directly relevant for Peter and Mary's plans, but there seems to be *no* good candidate for how this place should be described. There is an imminent oxymoronic indeterminate-exactness about where it is raining: it is raining in the location that is most relevant for Peter and Mary on this very Saturday morning. The crux of the matter is that, as pointed out above, the intended location, whose existence is part of their mutual cognitive environment, is conceptualized in Mary's and Peter's thoughts, but it cannot be straightforwardly identified via a full conceptual description expressed as part of the explicature. The explanation seems to be that the location is conceptually grasped via the thought that Mary has on seeing what is going on outside, and the relevant location is identified adequately by Peter, who instantly interprets what his wife said, most probably without consciously attaching to Mary's words any location-phrase. The thoughts seen as underlying the production of (50) as used in this context and its interpretation can be schematically represented as (58) and (59) respectively.[39]

(58) IT IS RAINING$_f$.
(59) IT IS RAINING$_{f'}$.

---

39 Most probably, the "It is" structure will not be part of the Mentalese representation of the thoughts under scrutiny, but since no claims are made here about the syntax and/or the lexicon of the language of thought, the "dummy-it" is left where it is in the corresponding English sentence in the formulas.

The place at which it is raining remains *implicit* in the immediately available context conceptualized by the communicator and (hopefully) the interpreter, as part of the shared cognitive environment of the interactants. The shared cognitive environment, it needs to be emphasized, may not be physically shared by the interlocutors, as is the case with a long-distance phone call during which the utterance about raining is produced in Carston's example (54) above: the contextual cognitive fix will be on the speaker's location of course. In fact, in more general terms the cognitive fix will be on the location that is relevant to the circumstances of discourse, that is, on the location that the relevance-theoretic comprehension heuristic yields and the presumption of optimal relevance backs up. This provides a straightforward explanation to one of Perry's (1986/93: 175) examples in which the situation is as follows. Perry's son, currently in Palo Alto, has just finished a phone conversation with his older brother, at the moment staying in Murdock. To the father's query: "How are things there?" the younger son replies with "It is raining." This utterance will obviously be about the rain in Murdoch and not in Palo Alto, as Perry (1986/93: 175) points out, and as the relevance-theoretic analysis with the contextual cognitive fix predicts.

This is not to say that the specific location name will never "enter" a thought about raining which will emerge as a result of processing an utterance like (50). It may happen that due to the manifest contextual assumptions, speaker's intentions, and relevant cognitive effects expected to be derived from the utterance, the contextual cognitive fix will lead the hearer to recover the representation of the explicitly communicated meaning in which the intended place name will appear. In such a case, the mental representation of the relevant rain-thought will be similar, for instance, to (60) or (61).[40]

(60) IT IS RAINING$_g$ (IN LONDON).
(61) IT IS RAINING$_h$ (IN SOUTHERN ENGLAND).

Such thoughts are likely to be formed, for instance, when a recent weather forecast in which rain in London (or in southern England) has been predicted is vivid in the individual's mind, and this information is brought to bear on the thinking process (either in the speaker's and/or in the hearer's mind). As before, such conceptual additions should be viewed as (idiosyncratic) conceptualizations which result in fleshing out the basic explicature recovered by the relevance-guided comprehension heuristic. Thus the suggestion is that for the utterance in (50), the explicature will invariably be like the one in (62), with any potential – albeit optional – enhancements being due to particular, personal and private cognitive preferences and inclinations of a given individual, which are pretty much rooted

---

40 Cf. the discussion of (39)–(41) above.

in the here-and-now of the communicative situation in which the individual is functioning.[41]

> (62) IT IS RAINING$_{x\ at\ time\ t}$.

In contrast to the standard free enrichment analysis, such "supplementations" are assumed to go beyond the meaning that can be unequivocally attributed to the speaker,[42] even though as long as the hearer-represented place denotation and the speaker-intended one coincide (as marked by the relevant indices), they remain compatible with the basic explicature endorsed by the speaker's informative intention.

The claim about the implicitness of the location in many rain-utterances may suggest strong affinity with Corazza and Dokic's (2007, 2012) situationalism. Just like situationalism, the contextual cognitive fix construal, "dispenses with free enrichment at the level of both utterance and thought" (Corazza and Dokic's 2012: 185). Just as in Corazza and Dokic's (2012) model, there is indeterminacy involved: with reference to the interpretation of (50), indeterminacy is transparent in the implicitness of the location concept in the underlying thought. However, there is a profound and radical difference between the two approaches, which places them in two distinct and distant realms of linguistic investigation. The contextual cognitive fix construal is seen an instrument in the relevance-theoretic toolkit, while situated minimalism is a semantic framework, concerned more with the philosophical perspective on the nature of language than with the psycholinguistic mechanisms of utterance production and reception. As has been already emphasized, contextual cognitive fix is assumed to arise in the course of the relevance-guided comprehension process,[43] in which explicature generation, forming implicatures and context construction are all inferential through and

---

41 This line of reasoning fits in with suggestions that the human mind is likely to come up with different conceptualizations of the same perceived objects, properties, relations, etc., depending on the cognitive goals pursued, earlier cognitive tasks performed, etc. (cf. Vega Moreno 2007: Ch.1). Ariel (2002) advances the same main argument with reference to verbal communication, though on her approach, the meaning actually recovered by the addressee involves a great deal more subjectivity (cf. arguments challenging free enrichment and ad hoc concept construction in Mioduszewska forthcoming (a) and (b)).

42 As was the case with example (27) discussed in section 2.5 above, there are infinitely many possible enhancements of this kind for the interpretation of (50) uttered in a particular communicative situation. So while by producing (50) the speaker makes manifest the intended location, this location is, strictly speaking, not expressible through a conceptual description, even though it is manifest in the shared cognitive environment of the speaker and the hearer, and is identifiable by a suitably indexed thought.

43 To be sure, it seems that cognitive fixes of the type discussed here are needed for purely cognitive and not exclusively for communicative reasons. I would like to thank Deirdre Wilson for pointing it out to me.

through, and result from the workings of a single pragmatic system, at the heart of which there is the Communicative Principle of Relevance (see Ch.1.5). All this means that if the contextual cognitive fix construal can profess any explanatory power, this can only be within the machinery of RT. In other words, any explanatory power that the present construal could claim cannot be attributed to the procedure *per se* but is inherited from and deeply ingrained in the relevance-theoretic framework.

I would like to submit a contextual cognitive fix analysis for yet another interesting case. Let us assume that Peter and Mary are going out for dinner. As usual, Peter is waiting at the door for Mary to finish getting dressed and making herself up. When Mary finally comes down and utters (63), Peter is assumed to access (64) rather than the enriched versions (65) or (66) in the process of interpreting what Mary has said.

> (63) I'm ready.
> (64) MARY IS READY$_k$.
> (65) MARY IS READY TO LEAVE THE HOUSE.
> (66) MARY IS READY TO GO OUT TO DINNER WITH ME.

In the situation in which he happens to be when he hears (63), Peter does not need to enrich in any way what he has heard: a proper saturation of the speaker indexical (which will yield MARY) and interpreting *ready* in the way that contextual cognitive fix ensures return an informationally exact thought. READY$_k$ that surfaces in the hearer's mind is intended to stand for the particular state of being ready that Mary declares in the context, so this constituent of Peter's thought tokens the specific type of readiness in this concrete situation.[44] It is, in the circumstances, the state of readiness that has to do with going out, but to understand this meaning, Peter does not have to enrich what he has heard in any way: he merely processes the decoded signal, and the relevance-guided comprehension procedure results in the thought with an occasion-specific interpretation of *ready*. This means that the actual meaning as delivered by the relevance-guided comprehension mechanism is relativized to the specific context immediately available to the hearer and is realized as a certain conceptualization in Peter's mind. This meaning is part of the language of thought representation, so it cannot be adequately rendered as an

---

44 An adequate recognition of the common core meaning that is context-insensitive has provided the major motivation for the semantic minimalism programme, whose main proponents are Cappelen and Lepore (2005). Whereas this line of research has come under considerable criticism (Bach 2006a; Bezuidenhout 2006; Carston 2008; Corazza and Dokic 2007; King and Stanley 2005; Wedgwood 2007), the focus on shared content, which is claimed to be "a central feature of our self-conception as communicating creatures" Cappelen (2007: 18), appears worthwhile. For an interesting presentation of how similar Cappelen and Lepore's and RT positions are, despite the claims to the opposite from both sides, see Wedgwood (2007).

enriched phrase: it is the occasion-specific meaning of *ready* that the addressee recovers in the context.

For the sake of argument, let us assume that as soon as this interpretation reaches Peter's consciousness, he turns to unlock the door. But then he hears Mary say:

> (67) Wait a moment! I'm not ready to leave yet. I am ready with the dress and now you can do the necklace clasp for me. Have you forgotten?

Only on hearing (67) does Peter remember that Mary has mentioned earlier that she will need his help with the pearl necklace. So in his processing of (63), he failed to access the actual context that Mary intended: instead of (64), the intended meaning should have been identified differently. Assuming that the original thought that gave rise to Mary's utterance can be schematically represented as (68), Peter should have recovered (69): there is an obvious mismatch between (64) and (69) as the subscripts depict.

> (68) I AM READY$_i$.
> (69) MARY IS READY$_{i'}$.

Peter's recovery of (64) rather than (69) was responsible for the misunderstanding that occurred.

A careful reader will have noticed that this kind of analysis easily allows us to account for intuitions about the content that all occurrences of a certain sentence share across the diverse contexts that they are used in, which is referred to in the literature on the subject as shared content (for a thorough discussion of the shared content argument, see Cappelen and Lepore 2007b). The meaning of *ready*, as the formula in (64) indicates, is recovered as a stable meaning, which – by being anchored to the situation in which Peter and Mary are – gets its intended situation-specific interpretation as a result of contextual cognitive fix, which is a fully pragmatic operation. But the nucleus of the formula depicting the recovered explicature will be the same for many (if not all) instances of interpretation, with different parameters that the context sets constraining any given interpretation, as shown by the relevant indices.

Let us have a look at another example which has been often used to demonstrate the range of enrichment processes necessary for explicature generation. It was originally introduced as early as 1988 by Carston, who employed it to show how explicatures are different from implicatures. Carston (1988) was interested in developing relevant criteria to keep the two layers of communicated meaning apart that would replace the Gricean condition in accordance with which implicatures required the operation of inferential processes while explicatures did not, which provided a useful distinguishing principle between the two. As indicated above, this neat but unappealing distinction cannot be kept in RT, since the model assumes what some researchers (e.g., Bach 1999, 2001, 2004; Capone 2006, 2011; Horn 2004, 2010; Levinson 2000) refer to as "pragmatic intrusion" into the truth-conditional content, by allowing inferences to play an important role in generating explicatures. As a consequence, some new criteria need to be identified to account for keeping explicatures separate form implicatures in RT (see Ch.2.4 and 3.2). The starting point for Carston's (1988) analysis is the example I would like to refer to now. In fact, she uses it in some later writings (Carston 2004b, 2008) to illustrate how the decoded form of an utterance needs to be expanded in many ways to arrive at the meaning actually communicated by the speaker, and it is precisely these expansions that cause my concern and therefore will be focused on here. To put it openly, this example, provided in (70) below, appears to demonstrate that free enrichment does create problems and may indeed be charged with causing an unnecessary and taxing conceptual burden for the interpreter. According to Carston (1988, 2004b, 2008), what Y communicates in (70) amounts to the assumptions listed in (71), with (71a) being an explicature of Y's utterance and (71b) its implicature.

(70) X: How is Mary feeling after her first year at university? (Carston 2004b: 635)
      Y: She didn't get enough units and can't continue.

(71) (a) MARY$_X$ DID NOT PASS ENOUGH **UNIVERSITY COURSE** UNITS **TO QUALIFY FOR ADMISSION TO SECOND-YEAR STUDY** AND, **AS A RESULT,** MARY$_X$ CANNOT CONTINUE **WITH UNIVERSITY STUDY**.
      (b) Mary$_x$ is not feeling very happy.

While identifying (71b) – or for that matter, any assumption that characterizes Mary's psychological state after her failure at university which follows from the premise provided by Y's utterance and other assumptions highly accessible in the context and backed up by the speaker's intention[45] – as the meaning implicitly communicated by Y appears uncontroversial (cf. Romero and Soria 2010: 4), there seems to be a problem with (71a) as the assumption explicitly communicated. There is a considerable amount of conceptual material, highlighted in bold, fed into explicature (71a). It is not only the number of enhancements introduced that is worrying: as with other utterances enriched in this manner, there is a whole array of possible additions like, for instance, those in (72), each producing a proposition with different truth-conditions, for which there is no principled means of favouring one over the others.

(72) (a) MARY$_X$ DID NOT PASS ENOUGH **COURSE** UNITS **REQUIRED BY THE UNIVERSITY TO BE ABLE TO ENTER SECOND-YEAR**

---

45 Conceivably, Mary may have been forced to enter university by her parents, may have been very unhappy as a student and may be feeling relieved that she no longer has to study.

STUDY AND, **AS A RESULT,** MARY$_X$ CANNOT CONTINUE **WITH THE STUDIES THAT MARY$_X$ HAS UNDERTAKEN.**[46]
(b) MARY$_x$ DID NOT PASS ENOUGH **UNIVERSITY COURSE** UNITS **REQUIRED OF YEAR ONE STUDENTS** AND, **AS A RESULT,** MARY$_x$ CANNOT CONTINUE **WITH STUDYING CHEMISTRY.**
(c) MARY$_x$ DID NOT PASS ENOUGH **UNIVERSITY COURSE** UNITS **THAT WERE OBLIGATORY** AND, **AS A RESULT,** MARY$_x$ CANNOT CONTINUE **STUDYING.**
(d) MARY$_x$ DID NOT PASS ENOUGH **COMPULSORY COURSE** UNITS **AT YEAR ONE** AND, **AS A RESULT,** MARY$_x$ CANNOT CONTINUE **WITH MARY$_x$'S TERTIARY EDUCATION.**

Moreover, unlike in some other communicative contexts (see footnote 23 above), it would be difficult to postulate here that what the speaker conveys is weakly communicated. In a nutshell, instances of weak communication involve a whole range of similar propositions that the utterance makes manifest and no conclusive evidence that one is actually intended by the speaker, so the hearer can just decide on any from the gamut of manifest assumptions (e.g. (71a) or (72a)), at the same time accepting responsibility for this particular choice (for a more detailed description of strong vs. weak communication see Ch.3.5).

A contextual cognitive fix analysis for (71) would be something like (73), which is much simpler than any of the freely enriched explicatures.

(73) MARY$_x$ DID NOT PASS ENOUGH UNITS$_1$ AND* MARY$_x$ CANNOT CONTINUE$_m$.

The above schematic representation is supposed to depict that the hearer recovers a complete representation of the speaker's intended explicit content, in that occasion-specific meanings are contextually fixed (as the indices show) by the relevance-oriented comprehension process. The meanings of certain components, in particular *units* and *continue*, even though not fully conceptually developed, are read off as unequivocal in the context in which they are used. This kind of "conceptually frugal" construal, as argued above, not only avoids some problems that free enrichment gives rise to,[47] but also allows for a natural and fairly straightforward explanation of a comprehension phenomenon that is widely

---

46 Conjunction *and* (as well as many other conjunctions, discourse markers and function words in general) has been the subject of extensive discussions and analyses in neo-Gricean and post-Gricean literature, which will not be reported here as they go well beyond the scope of the present work. For this reason, I do not dispute the meaning of *and* in any way and stick to Carston's analysis in this respect.

47 In particular, the conceptual burden can be seen as taken off the interpreter's shoulders. Besides, a proliferation of possible enhancements of the explicature is curbed, while at the same time subjective and idiosyncratic conceptual additions are legitimized under certain circumstances (see the discussion of (39)-(41) and (60)-(61) above).

attested in empirical studies, namely that of shallow interpretations or good enough interpretations. I would like to pass on to this topic in the next section.

2.8 Shallower interpretations

As stated above, while free enrichment assumes conceptual elaborations of different sorts as a way of resolving linguistic underdeterminacies at the level of explicature, the contextual cognitive fix mechanism involves adequate meaning narrowing without adding conceptual material. As a result, explicatures tend to be more abstemious on the latter construal. Conceptual additions are allowed, but only as "supplementations" that result from specific cognitive preferences of the interpreter at a given moment, and are treated as a non-systematic practice, which should not be viewed as standard.

The idea that explicatures may be more or less developed remains in full agreement with RT, in which explicitness of utterances is seen as a matter of degree. As Sperber and Wilson (1986/95: 182) convincingly argue, "[a]n explicature is a combination of linguistically encoded and contextually inferred conceptual features. The smaller the relative contribution of the contextual features, the more explicit the explicature will be, and inversely. Explicitness, so understood, is both classificatory and comparative: a communicated assumption is either an explicature or an implicature, but an explicature is explicit to a greater or lesser degree."

Without doubt, the amount of linguistic encoding involved affects the amount of inferencing that the hearer needs to go through to recover what is explicitly expressed. If a passer-by asks what the time is, there is little that needs to be inferred by the hearer to get the explicit content as communicated by, for instance, the utterance in (74).

(74) It's 16.25.[48]

However, in a different situation, if – when asked a question about the time – Mary utters (75), Peter must not only infer the implicature that Mary does not know what time it is and suggests he may possibly find it out for himself by looking at her watch, but to understand her explicit meaning he must also infer which worktop she is referring to, as (76) indicates.

---

48   Once the explicature is recovered, it may combine with assumptions that the hearer has in mind, which will potentially lead to inferring some implications, for instance, that he needs to hurry up in order not to be late for the 17.00 train, but these will not be intended by the speaker, and therefore not communicated (cf. Sperber and Wilson 2008; cf. also Ch.3.3)

(75) My watch is on the worktop.
(76) MARY'S WATCH$_{n'}$ IS ON* THE WORKTOP$_o$.

However, the contextual cognitive fix construal suggests also that, to a certain degree and within certain limits, explicatures themselves may be retrieved as more or less explicit, depending on how deep the hearer goes in the interpretation process. On the one hand then, the degree of explicitness is inversely proportional to the amount of inferencing involved in generating explicatures, as Sperber and Wilson (1986/95) point out. On the other hand, the explicature derived by the relevance-guided comprehension procedure may determine the explicitly communicated content with a greater or lesser degree of elaboration for a particular hearer in a certain communicative context. This latter conception has support in the idea, which has been around for quite some time, that the depth of interpretation of utterances may vary.

There is a lot of experimental evidence which shows that when people process utterances they may not engage in their full syntactic or semantic analysis, and often end up with incomplete meaning representations. For instance, in a series of Moses illusion experiments it has been shown that a vast majority of respondents fail to see the factual mistakes in questions like: "How many animals of each kind did Moses take on the ark?" (cf., among others, Bredart and Modolo 1988; Park and Reder 2004; Reder and Kusbit 1991; Van Oostendorp and de Mul 1990). Semantic illusions of this type have been investigated on a wide scale (Barton and Sanford 1993; Natsopoulos 1985; Sanford 2002; Sanford and Graesser 2006) to reveal that "a more heuristic, on-the fly" (Holtgraves 2008: 628) processing is often performed. The hypothesis is that, because of severe time constraints and considerable cognitive demands typical of on-line conversations, a "good-enough" interpretation (Ferreira et al. 2002) is often preferred to an in-depth full representation.

The underlying idea is that the language comprehension system is very frequently satisfied with "representations that are suitable for the task that the listener wants to perform with the help of the linguistic input" (Ferreira and Patson 2007: 71) instead of pursuing full-fledged and precise representations of utterances. As Ferreira and Patson (2007: 75) report, ungrammatical sentences of the garden-path type, such as "Katie fixed the car hit a fire hydrant", are judged grammatical on about 30% of trials, which by far exceeds rates of judgments for regular ungrammatical sentences. There seems to be ample evidence that frequently local meanings, which prove wrong if a more global scale of interpretation is taken into account, tend to be retained by subjects despite the incoherence of the overall interpretation which cannot pass unnoticed. For instance, after reading the sentence: "While Anna dressed the baby played in the crib", almost 100% respondents answered correctly the question about whether the baby played in the crib, but at the same time many of them incorrectly answered the question about whether Anna dressed the baby (Ferreira et al. 2002). Furthermore, people are ready to modify implausible sentences (like, e.g. "A fox shot a poacher") to carry plausible meanings, which as the authors speculate, may be due to the strategy normally employed in interpreting discourse, where slips of the tongue and some other mistakes that lead to absurd meanings, are automatically corrected by comprehenders. As Ferreira and Patson (2007: 76) maintain, "there is growing evidence that the system computes a sensible meaning and then tries to reconcile it with the sentence's form. If the two conflict, then the parser appears to try to restructure the sentence, and then either goes with the altered structure or adjusts the meaning to conform to the structure and to allow expression of the unexpected idea." This suggests that very often pragmatic considerations override the meaning that syntactic or semantic rules return, as is the case with the frequently quoted example: "No head injury is too trivial to ignore." Found by Wason and Reich (1979, in Elugardo 2007) in one of London's hospitals, the sign with this sentence was evidently intended to alert people to the fact that no head injury however small should be disregarded, but the actual meaning of the sentence is quite opposite (in parallel with "No missile is too small to be banned", as Sanford 2002: 191 points out; cf. also Natsopoulos 1985: 386). The relevance-theoretic explanation of what is involved in this illusion is based on the highly accessible assumptions in the interpreter's mind. As convincingly argued in one of her talks by Wilson (1996, in Carston 1997), in the hospital setting in which the notice is displayed, the highly accessible contextual assumptions are similar to those in (77a-b), and they lead the interpreter to the interpretation in (77c).

> (77)   (a) All head injuries should be attended to.
>   (b) Head injuries are generally a serious matter and should not be ignored.
>   (c) No head injury is too trivial to ignore.

So it appears that if a result is found "relevant in the expected way, then processing is ended, in some cases prematurely" (Allott 2007: 273).

It is the orientation towards the optimally relevant interpretation that the speaker *manifestly intends* to covey (cf. Ch. 1.6), which, on the relevance-theoretic model, underpins ostensive communication in general and verbal comprehension in particular. For example, considerations of this kind provide a straightforward, plausible and natural elucidation for the repairs that hearers can (usually) easily make when confronted with slips of the tongue of the speaker, as is demonstrated by Wilson (2000). So when recovering the intended meaning of (78), Peter needs to ask himself "on what interpretation Mary *might have thought* her utterance would be relevant enough to him" (Wilson 2000: 422), which will at once lead him to replace *penguins* with *pigeons*.[49]

(78) I've been feeding penguins at Trafalgar Square. (Wilson 2000: 422)[50]

The main point I would like to pursue here does not centre on misinterpretation though, but on the depth of processing of utterances, as hinted at above. The fundamental assumptions of RT and especially the relevance-guided comprehension heuristic (see Ch.2.3) predict that the major driving force for the utterance interpretation process, which both shapes it and determines its goal, has to do with the level of relevance sought by the interpreter. The adequate level of relevance, on the one hand, is one which may have been anticipated by the communicator, and on the other, is one considered adequate for the current communicative purposes by the addressee (Sperber and Wilson 2008: 89-90). This means that in performing different tasks which utterance interpretation may involve, that is, in fixing on the intended referents and senses in order to recover what is explicitly communicated as well as in calculating the implicit content, the path of least effort takes the interpreter to the terminus of cognitive satisfaction in which the effort invested in processing the verbal input returns sufficient gratification in terms of cognitive effects. And he is entitled not to proceed any further.[51] Obviously, all this should be understood to take place at the subconscious (or subpersonal, see Ch.4.7) level, and it is the pragmatic system operating in the hearer's mind rather than the consciously acting interpreter that is responsible for all that is going on.

Since on-line communication, with which RT is primarily concerned, is very economical, extremely fast and amazingly successful, it should not be surprising that shortcuts are taken and in depth-representations are eschewed whenever possible. With reference to generating explicatures, as they are the major focus of the present chapter, if the locus of pragmatic meaning conveyed in a given communicative context lies beyond the explicit meaning *per se* and has to do with what is implicated, shallower interpretation will often be perfectly sufficient. What is pivotal in such cases is that the content of the explicature provides the inferential basis for implicatures that carry the core pragmatic meaning. To

---

49 The major focus of Wilson's (2000) paper is on metarepresentational abilities related to verbal communication, so her analysis of the example under scrutiny is strictly speaking metarepresentational. For multi-level metarepresentations that the search for an optimally relevant interpretation adjusted to the speaker's capabilities and intentions may require, see Sperber 1994a.

50 It is also worth pointing out that highly accessible assumptions about birds at Trafalgar Square and shallower processing of the utterance may result in a failure to notice this minor mistake, and the hearer will automatically recover *pigeons* instead of *penguins* (cf. Vega Moreno 2007: 26).

51 Ariel's (2002) argument is based on a similar assumption.

illustrate this point, let us look at another frequently quoted example in (79b), which in this form is a slightly modified version of the mini-dialogue that Wilson and Sperber (2002) discuss.[52]

> (79) (a) Alan Jones: Do you want to join us for super?
>   (b) Lisa: I've eaten, thanks.

Obviously, the main point of (79b) is to decline the invitation to supper. This is the interpretation that yields the expected and required cognitive effects (cf. Wilson and Sperber 1998: 13). That is why, the kind of contextual cognitive fix that secures this interpretation and returns a rather "bare" explicature in (80) would be entirely satisfying.

> (80) LISA_X HAS EATEN_p.

(80) indicates that Lisa's having eaten gets constrained in the context of the present exchange by the relevance-guided comprehension heuristic, so that in the mutual cognitive environment of Lisa and Alan the fact that she has eaten can constitute an operational premise from which her refusal to join Alan and his companions for supper directly follows. In other words, contextually relevant meaning of Lisa's having eaten is fixed on, as the subscript $_p$ indicates, and becomes part of the mutual cognitive environment of the speaker and the hearer, so that the explicit meaning conveyed by (79b) can provide an inferential basis for the straightforward conclusion that she refuses to join Alan and the others for supper. Naturally, were Alan to engage in a deeper interpretation, he might access a salient background assumption that the "fact that one has already eaten supper on a given evening is a good reason for refusing an invitation to supper that evening" (Sperber and Wilson 2002: 608). This might lead Alan to generate (through backward inference, see Carston 2007) an enriched explicature: LISA HAS EATEN_p SUPPER THAT EVENING, as Sperber and Wilson (2008:608) suggest (the subscript is my addition). This is a very plausible scenario, but in another situation it may just as well be that Alan accesses a different salient assumption, for instance, that Lisa only eats bread and butter at tea time on Fridays, and remembering that it is a Friday, he will take Lisa to have explicitly communicated that she has already eaten her Friday meal of bread and butter, which provides a perfect reason for declining the supper invite. In this context, the explicature will be similar to: LISA HAS EATEN_p BREAD AND BUTTER THIS FRIDAY. Many other scenarios are of course possible. The two alternative explicatures referred to here differ from (80) only in the amount of detail about Lisa's eating that the recipient

---

52 Wilson and Sperber's (2002: 607) original example involves an explicit refusal:
     (a) Alan Jones: Do you want to join us for super?
     (b) Lisa: No, thanks. I've eaten.

is willing and/or able to take into account. Whether such conceptually richer interpretations surface in the recipient's mind will, as pointed out more than once above, depend on the current conceptual state of the interpreter, his present state of cognitive agility and volatile cognitive preferences. The suggestion is that the schematic interpretation like (80) will frequently be sufficient. I assume then that such shallow interpretations at the level of explicature are standardly pursued in on-line communicative situations in which the focal meaning is conveyed by implicature (rather than explicature which functions under the circumstances "merely as a vehicle" for implicitly conveyed content, Romero and Soria 2010: 11) and for which this kind of schematic and conceptually frugal representation is quite sufficient.

To move to a different range of examples, it seems reasonable to postulate that genitive resolution will not always have to be executed in the course of explicature generation, as long as all the relevant contextual effects can be generated without a full contextual saturation of the genitive phrase as used in a given utterance. Let us consider briefly the following exchange in (81).

(81) (a) Peter: Shall we go to the cinema tonight?
      (b) Mary: I have Joanne's text to work on.

Evidently, (81b) provides the "no" answer to the cinema offer. It appears that this interpretation does not require the addressee to come up with a full contextual instantiation of the genitive. Regardless of whether *Joanne's text* stands for the text that Joanne has written and asked Mary to proofread, or refers to the text that Joanne has translated and asked her friend to revise, or denotes the text that Joanne has asked Mary to translate, Peter will without much problem understand Mary's refusal and does not need to fully identify the type of relationship that exists between Joanne and the text.[53]

To recapitulate, the explicitness of explicatures is a matter of degree, as Sperber and Wilson (1986/95) astutely observe. This is fully supported by analyses that are viewed as involving the contextual cognitive fix mechanism. The point is that conceptual saturation of explicatures generated on a given occasion may differ due to different depths that the processing will reach. Instantaneous and cursory comprehension[54] may very often return a very unrefined explicature, which

---

53   By the same token, Peter may not bother to pin down the occasion-specific meaning of the decoded phrase "work on." While adequately contextually constrained, it may surface as mere ad hoc concept WORK ON* without any deeper penetration of the actual meaning conveyed. This means that the meaning of this constituent may remain partly vague on a shallow interpretation.

54   A related point concerns partially successful communication, which in many communicative contexts may prove completely sufficient (Maitra 2007). So even though the hearer may miss some semantic information (e.g., due to lacks in competence or inadequate

will nevertheless be sufficient to initiate a more elaborate process of recovering the implicitly conveyed import. Fairly recently, when the Ukraine crisis was dangerously unfolding just after the Crimean Peninsula was taken over by the supporters of the pro-Russian movement, one of the Polish radio stations organized a debate whose title (*Puszkin–tak, Putin–nie*) translates into English as "Pushkin–yes, Putin–no." It appears that in this context little more is communicated explicitly than the bare (82), but there is a load of implicitly communicated meaning behind this.

(82) $[PUSHKIN]_x$ YES*; $[PUTIN]_y$ NO*.

I think it is uncontroversial that the explicit meaning here is grasped immediately, and the huge meaning potential has to do with recovering a number of background assumptions evoked by the presence of the words used and the implicit import that the recipient can retrieve. But this takes us directly to the subject matter of the chapter that follows, the focus of which is the relevance-theoretic treatment of the implicit layer of utterances. Before leaving explicatures, though, it seems important to tackle one more issue that has to do with the relationship between the contextual cognitive fix mechanism and ad hoc concepts.

2.9 Contextual cognitive fix and ad hoc concepts

As Wilson (2004) convincingly argues, RT offers a unitary approach to a number of lexical pragmatic adjustment processes, which apply "spontaneously, automatically and unconsciously to fine-tune the interpretation of virtually every word" (2004: 343). The relevance-driven comprehension procedure results in adjusting the meaning of decoded lexical items to yield a relevant occasion-specific identification of the intended concept which secures a satisfying range of cognitive effects in a given context (Sperber and Wilson 2008). Since these concepts are occasion-specific, they are referred to as ad hoc concepts – a term

---

processing), he may arrive at an interpretation that is "good enough for partially successful communication." In relevance-theoretic terms, this kind of partial interpretation will return satisfying cognitive effects despite the fact that complete explicature cannot be generated. As Maitra (2007) shows, depending on the type of semantic information missed and the current communicative goals of the recipient, partially successful communication can be judged to be so to varying degrees. What is most important in the context of my discussion is that "for many (though not all) practical purposes, this approximate knowledge on the part of the hearer, and the resulting partially successful communication, will be sufficient" (Maitra 2007: 130).

which goes back to Barsalou's (1982, 1983) research[55] and is used also outside the circle of relevance theorists (e.g., by Ariel 2002 and Recanati 2004).

The key underlying assumption which follows from Barsalou's experiments is that human beings are perfectly capable of reorganizing bits of encyclopaedic information and creating novel categorizations if their present cognitive task or goal pursued requires it. This does not happen in a haphazard fashion, but is based on well-established cognitive routines, and may lead to different results depending on the trigger (e.g., in the form of contextual information that is accessible). Thus Barsalou (1982: 82) claims that concepts contain both context-independent properties, that is, those "activated by the word for a concept on all occasions", and context-dependent properties, which "are activated only by relevant contexts in which the word appears", contributing to "cross-classification, problem solving, metaphor and sentence comprehension" that the human mind regularly performs. As Barsalou (1982: 89) concludes, "[g]iven the existence of CD [context-dependent] properties, the meaning of a word is not a fixed set of properties that is activated as a whole every time the respective word is encoded. Rather, the meaning of a word also contains weakly associated and inferable properties that are inactive in irrelevant contexts and active in relevant contexts. Given the existence of CI [context-independent] properties, the meaning of a word is not completely determined by context. Rather, certain properties appear to be automatically activated by a word independently of context."

In full agreement with these ideas, utterance comprehension on the relevance-theoretic view is assumed to involve, more often than not, ad hoc concepts construction. This means that RT predicts that the process of mutual parallel adjustment embracing explicature derivation, accessing immediately available contextual assumptions and formulating implicatures communicated by a given utterance may lead the interpreter to construct[56] a new concept, based on the linguistically encoded one, whose denotation differs from that of the encoded concept.[57]

---

55 Barsalou's (1983) focus was on ad hoc categories, like "things that conquerors take as plunder" or "ways to escape being killed by the Mafia." His findings show that people not only have no problems with listing exemplars for them, but also that ad hoc categories show inner structuring (just like common taxonomic categories) and may potentially change from one-off categories to a more enduring class when subjects find them cognitively useful: e.g., "things to take on a camping trip" may change the status from an ad hoc to a well established category (Barsalou 1983: 224; cf. also Vega Moreno's 2007: Ch.1 comments on ad hoc categories).

56 As Orrigi and Sperber (2000: 152) contend, "[m]eanings are not just disambiguated, they are in part disambiguated, in part constructed in context."

57 Mioduszewska (forthcoming(a)) views this as a potential threat to intersubjectivity (cf. also footnote 31 above). Mioduszewska (forthcoming(b)) voices concern about the nature

Depending on how the denotation of the encoded and the occasion-specific concept constructed in an ad hoc manner differ, lexical narrowing or lexical broadening may be seen at work. If the denotation of the concept recovered by the addressee searching for an optimally relevant interpretation, as intended by the speaker, is narrower than the decoded meaning, so that it includes only a certain subset of the denotation of a given lexical item, then lexical narrowing is at play. By contrast, if the intended meaning ranges beyond the denotation of the decoded word, picking out items which, strictly speaking, "fall outside its linguistically specified denotation" (Sperber and Wilson 2008: 91), then lexical broadening is in operation. Examples (83) and (84), quoted from Sperber and Wilson (2008: 91), illustrate concept narrowing and broadening respectively.

> (83) I have a temperature.
> (84) Holland is flat.

As Sperber and Wilson (2008) point out, by uttering (83), the speaker is communicating something much more specific than what the literal meaning of the word *temperature* denotes. The property of having a temperature of a certain value is inherently characteristic of any physical object, therefore for (83) to be relevant, that is, to yield an expected range of cognitive effects, the temperature referred to must relevantly diverge from the norm. Concept narrowing is involved, because the relevant meaning denoting a higher than normal human body temperature in the context picks out a restricted range of the temperature scale, with the contextual construal in this case to be represented in the explicature as TEMPERATURE*.

Lexical broadening, as illustrated by (84), involves relaxing the decoded meaning of *flat* to include features typical of landscapes with relatively few hills and virtually no mountains, "where the ad hoc concept FLAT* represents an approximation to flatness which is close enough to yield the implications that make the whole utterance contextually relevant" (Sperber and Wilson 2008: 92).

As convincingly argued by Carston (2002a) and Sperber and Wilson (2008), these two types of concept adjustment are the outcome of a single relevance-driven process of on-line meaning construction, and it may happen that the fine-tuning required to get the precise sense as intended in the context will embrace both narrowing and broadening. This is the case, for instance, with understanding the meaning of *French* in (85b):

---

of ad hoc concepts, the stability of concept content and, as a result, shareability of explicit content in general. The above analyses showing how contextual cognitive fix works and the comments on how communicative success is approached along relevance-theoretic lines which have been made earlier provide a rejoinder to the line of criticism directed at explicatures (cf. also Carston 2010b, 2010c; Sperber and Wilson 2008; Vega Moreno 2007; Wilson 2004; Wilson and Carston 2007).

(85) (a) Does Gérard like eating? (Sperber and Wilson 2008: 91)
      (b) He is French!

Utterance (85b) evidently implicates that Gérard likes eating. Let us suppose, as Sperber and Wilson suggest, that the speaker knows that Gérard is a citizen of Monaco. Under the circumstances, she is using the word *French* to denote "a concept FRENCH** which is narrower in some respects and broader in others, denoting people who fit some prototype of a French person without French nationality being either a sufficient condition or an absolutely necessary one for inclusion in its extension" (Sperber and Wilson 2008: 92-93). Most metaphorical meanings, as Sperber and Wilson (2008) contend, involve both narrowing and broadening. In more general terms, RT posits that while the human lexicon consists of a stable inventory of concepts, these undergo various modulation processes in concrete communicative situations, affecting the explicatures recovered.[58]

This short description[59] clearly indicates close affinity between ad hoc concept construction and the contextual cognitive fix mechanism introduced earlier in this chapter. Each is triggered by and has its rationale in the relevance-theoretic verbal comprehension model. Both are processes of pragmatic meaning construction, and both are inferential in nature.

But it seems that there exist some important differences between the two. First, the contextual cognitive fix mechanism, as emphasized earlier (see, in particular, Ch.2.7 and Ch.2.8), may result in rough-tuning of the recovered explicature, whereas ad hoc concepts are, by definition, fine-tuned. Second, in the case of contextual cognitive fix, a given entity, property, action, relation, location, etc., becomes anchored to the dynamic context that is brought to bear in the utterance comprehension process, which is depicted as an index on this component in the language of thought formulas. Ad hoc concepts arise from utterance comprehension as occasion-specific senses which provide first and foremost access to contextual implications directly evoked by encyclopaedic information that the newly emergent concept evokes. This means that the former mechanism consists mainly in singling out the intended item (whether it is an entity, property, action, relation or whatever), with the interpreter's thought fixing on it, as the very term suggests, whereas in the case of ad hoc concepts, it is immediate access to contextual implications evoked by the emergent sense that

---

58 For a detailed and comprehensive account of ad hoc concept construction, see Carston (2002a: Ch. 5).

59 Since recovering implicitly communicated import depends crucially on the information stored in encyclopaedic entries and, in particular, on (intended and potential) implications that may arise because of the background assumptions made accessible by concepts that words evoke, this idea will be developed further in the next chapter (see specifically Ch.3.6).

is afforded in the context. This is directly related to the third important point to be made here. In principle, the contextual cognitive fix procedure is designed for cases in which so-called unarticulated constituents are postulated as underlying explicature generation, whereas ad hoc concept construction is just a lexical pragmatic process of meaning modulation.

So even though, undeniably, the two processes are very similar in nature and are rooted in the relevance-theoretic comprehension heuristic, they have different motivations and they lead to different outcomes. It would really be difficult (though not impossible) to account for a full range of cases simply in terms of either ad hoc concepts (e.g., for quantifier domain restriction expressions or weather report utterances) or in terms of the contextual cognitive fix: there is a division of labour between the two processes, which seems both desirable and useful.

Hopefully, the present proposal will open some interesting and critical exploration of what it is that shapes explicatures, which may lead to an even more uniform and cognitively more economical model of relevance-guided comprehension process.

2.10 Concluding remarks

In an attempt to create a comprehensive and coherent framework for human intentional communication and to account for the intricate processes underlying verbal communication in a psycholinguistically plausible way, Sperber and Wilson (1986/95; Wilson and Sperber 2004) have created a model which is inferential through and through. On this approach, it is proposed that inferencing is crucial not only for recovering implicatures, but also for understanding the intended meaning that is explicitly conveyed. As a result, the neat distinction between the explicitly and implicitly communicated content based on the contrast between non-inferential (and not based on pragmatic maxims) and inferential (based on pragmatic maxims) interpretation processes cannot be maintained.

The explicature/implicature differentiation postulated within RT is probably subtler, but at the same time more intuitively appealing. It is based on a definition of explicitness which admits only local developments of the logical form encoded by the utterance to be identified as its basic explicature.[60] It is assumed that the developments of the logical form underlying explicature generation may be linguistically mandated, as is the case with filling in ellipted elements or

---

60   See footnote 17 above about the distinction between local processes that are assumed to contribute to generating basic-level explicatures and global processes that return higher-level explicatures as output.

semantically incomplete elements or with saturation of indexicals, or they can be motivated on purely pragmatic grounds, as is the case with free enrichment and ad hoc concept construction. The latter processes prove particularly controversial, since they lack objective criteria for application. Free enrichment incorporated into the relevance-theoretic toolkit appears highly contentious, since, on the one hand, it relies on adding extra conceptual material to what is decoded, which appears cognitively strenuous, and on the other hand, there is usually a range of possible conceptual enhancements to be applied in a given context, each returning a different proposition.

I have tried to argue above that free enrichment can be changed into a different pragmatic procedure, namely a contextual cognitive fix mechanism, which is fully compatible with the relevance-theoretic assumptions and claims, and which can deal with precisifying the explicit meaning of utterances as required. It seems cognitively more economical, avoids some of the disadvantages of free enrichment, can be appealed to to account for different depths of processing that utterance comprehension may involve and can throw some light on shared content as communicated by a certain utterance across different contexts of use.

It would be naïve to see the postulated contextual cognitive fix as a panacea that solves all problems at the level of explicitly communicated content that free enrichment runs into. Since it is based on some hypotheses about the underlying thought representations about which very little is known, it suffers from all the inadequacies of an account that rests on intuition and speculation. The formulas used to represent the meanings recovered via contextual cognitive fix are rather tentative. It should be remembered though that their role is not to depict the exact language of thought format, but rather to elucidate the underlying processes thanks to which speakers and hearers can converge on getting the explicitly communicated utterance content (cf. Sperber and Wilson 2008). The issue of the propositional status of explicatures which are schematically represented as indexed cognitive representations needs an in-depth exploration too.

Since the ideas presented here are quite new, they will hopefully provoke reflection, comments, and criticism, which may contribute to pushing the wheel of pragmatic investigations forward.

Chapter 3
Within and beyond implicature

3.1 Introduction

As remarked earlier, while there seems to be a broad consensus among pragmaticists and other researchers investigating language use phenomena that there are two planes on which meaning is communicated: the explicit level and the implicit level, the robust debate as to how they should be discriminated is far from settled. In the relevance-theoretic framework, a clear-cut and straightforward distinction between the explicit and implicit import, in accordance with which all aspects of communicated meaning arrived at inferentially would necessarily belong to the implicit layer of communication, is abandoned as ill-founded and defective. Since inferential processes, involving considerations about the speaker's intentions, in a crucial way contribute to identifying what speakers explicitly convey (Wilson and Sperber 2004), the demarcation line separating the two layers of communicated meaning cannot be based on the kind of simple standard that Grice (1967/89, 1975/89) envisaged. Inevitably, as observed above, the explicit-implicit divide is subtler on the relevance-theoretic construal, but certainly much more appealing and compatible with language users' intuitions.

This chapter begins with a brief discussion of how explicatures are differentiated from implicatures in RT (Ch.3.2). The distinction between implications and implicatures is focused on next (Ch.3.3). The emphasis on the communicator's intentions in the case of the latter and their possible indeterminacy in certain cases, which is different from underdeterminacy referred to in the preceding chapter, brings to light the underdeterminacy–indeterminacy contrast, which is scrutinized in section 3.4. Section 3.5 introduces the notion of the strong-weak communication continuum. It is argued that, despite its unpromising label, weak communication has significant potential and may be sometimes preferable to strong communication. The impact of weak communication in terms of the outcomes it yields can probably be most fully appreciated when the so-called poetic effect is created: aphorisms are chosen to demonstrate how this effect originates and what it involves (Ch.3.6). Since poetic effects, like other instances of weak communication, involve interpretations that go beyond what the communicator manifestly endorses, they raise the question of the scope of communicated content, and in consequence, of meaning. This issue is addressed in the section that follows (3.7). All these considerations suggest that communicative goals are frequently geared towards what Sperber and Wilson (forthcoming) refer to as cognitive alignment and this idea is briefly considered in subchapter 3.8. The main points are summarized in concluding remarks (Ch.3.9).

3.2 Implicature: a relevance-theoretic construal

Approaching utterance comprehension in terms of non-demonstrative inference (cf. Ch.1.8), the originators of RT identify three major subtasks to be performed in recovering the speaker's meaning:

> (a) Constructing an appropriate hypothesis about explicit content (explicatures) (…).
> (b) Constructing an appropriate hypothesis about the intended contextual assumptions (implicated premises).
> (c) Constructing an appropriate hypothesis about the intended contextual implications (implicated conclusions). (Wilson and Sperber 2004: 615)

While explicatures, as a detailed discussion in the previous chapter emphasized, "are arrived at by a combination of decoding and inference" (Wilson and Sperber 2002: 620), the generation of implicatures, defined in RT as any assumptions which are "communicated, but not explicitly" (Sperber and Wilson 1986/95: 182), is wholly inferential. On the relevance-theoretic construal then, at the level of explicit import speaker-meaning is taken to be made out via the pragmatic precisification of the logical form that the language parser decodes (cf. Ch.2.2 and 2.3), whereas what is implicitly conveyed is assumed to be inferred by combining the assumption identified as explicitly communicated with a highly accessible and salient background assumption or assumptions.

This means that in recovering the implicitly communicated content, what is explicitly conveyed becomes a premise in a non-demonstrative inferential process (Carston 2004b: 639). This premise combined with another contextual assumption (or some other contextual assumptions) that the speaker evidently trusts the recipient to bring in into the interpretation process, will yield a conclusion warranted by the premise. As indicated earlier (see Ch.2.3 and 2.9), the inferential process is not taken to proceed sequentially from premises to conclusions: the idea that on-line comprehension involves parallel mutual adjustment of hypotheses about the explicitly and implicitly communicated content indicates that a conclusion as to what is being communicated, which surfaces as optimally relevant in a given context, can be accessed first and the premises (in the form of an explicature adequately warranting this conclusion) will then be constructed through backwards inferencing (Carston 2002a; Sperber and Wilson 1986/95, 2005; Wilson and

Sperber 2002, 2004; Wilson and Carston 2006, 2007; Vega Moreno 2003, 2005, 2007). As Carston (2002a: 143) underlines, "[t]he process may involve several backwards and forwards adjustments of content before an equilibrium is achieved which meets the system's current 'expectation' of relevance."

All the above suggests that, on the relevance-theoretic model, explicatures and implicatures are both generated via inferencing, as performed by a relevance-guided comprehension procedure, the cornerstone of which is the Communicative Principle of Relevance and the presumption of optimal relevance (see Ch.1.5 and Ch.2.3). The major difference between explicatures and implicatures has to do with the derivation route via which they are recovered. Assumptions communicated explicitly are inferred directly on the basis of what has been decoded, so they are framed on the logical form (or forms, in the case of ambiguous sentences) as supplied by the language module (Carston 2002a: 94). By contrast, implicatures are calculated by bringing together the explicitly communicated proposition and a highly accessible contextual assumption.[1] This suggests that implicit import embraces an implicated contextual assumption (or some such assumptions) which processed together with the explicature will yield an implicated conclusion. Thus there are two subsets within implicitly communicated assumptions. Those assumptions that are accessed as the context in which the incoming information is to be processed are identified as implicated premises, whereas the inferences derived from the contextual implications combined with the explicit content of the utterance form implicated conclusions (Wilson and Sperber 2004: 615). This explains the three comprehension subtasks (and three kinds of hypotheses about the speaker meaning that the hearer may need to construct during the interpretation process) listed above after Wilson and Sperber (2004).

At this juncture, it seems worth indicating that the contextual cognitive fix construal, postulated in the preceding chapter (see Ch. 2.6-2.7) to replace enrichment in generating explicatures in the relevance-theoretic model, points to another substantive difference between explicatures and implicatures, which refers both to the process of the recovery of the two layers of intended import[2] and to the product that gets communicated. The process of retrieving explicatures via

---

1 It seems to me that Carston's (2002a: 142) formulation: "the explicature/implicature is essentially two ways of deriving communicated assumptions: by developing the linguistically given logical form and by pragmatic inference" is not very fortunate. As a matter of fact, pragmatic inference, as frequently emphasized by Carston herself (e.g., 1988, 2004a, 2004b, 2009), in an important way contributes to generating explicatures not just implicatures.

2 In one of their most recent papers, Sperber and Wilson (forthcoming) use the term *intended import* to cover overtly intended cognitive effect of a communicative act, whether explicitly or implicitly conveyed.

contextual cognitive fix, assumed to arise in the course of relevance-guided search for meaning, is that of *zooming in* on the meaning to get a *fine-grained* speaker-intended sense. The process of computing implicatures, which likewise takes place as part of relevance-oriented comprehension procedure, involves *zooming out* beyond what has been expressed in order to get *coarser-grained* meaning, not recoverable from the logical form itself that the language parser returns.

The treatment of implicatures in RT is both simpler than in other pragmatic models and at the same time more comprehensive, in that, on the one hand, the taxonomy introduced is minimal and quite straightforward, while its undertaking to explore and elucidate quite intricate and more obscure aspects of the workings of implicit communication goes well beyond the research agenda of other theories.

The typology of implicatures is relatively simple, since the classification into implicated premises and implicated conclusions is the only systematization proposed at the level of implicit import in the relevance-theoretic framework.[3] It is recognized as a more or less natural division to be introduced in the model of verbal communication as it simply reflects the two subsets within implicit import described above which may be generated[4] in the process of utterance interpretation. The meaning conveyed explicitly and implicit contextual assumptions are taken to function as premises from which the implicated conclusion follows. This shows that the distinction between implicated premises and implicated conclusions is motivated by how the processes underlying utterance interpretation are modelled and is not a theory-internal construct introduced purely for the sake of building

---

3   Jary (2013) has recently proposed that implicatures can be divided into material, that is, those not based on a premise about the speaker's mental states (viz. her intentions), and behavioural, which are generated by taking into consideration the speaker's intention, suggesting that "the distinction is already implicit in Relevance Theory" (2013: 638), which appears a bit far-fetched. Based on the claim that not all implicatures rely on a premise about the communicator's behaviour, Jary's classification seems to complicate rather than explain the implicit layer of communication. Indeed, as the author admits, ultimately "*all* utterance interpretation involves the hearer explaining the speaker's verbal behaviour as a means of arriving at her intended meaning" (Jary 2013: 642; original emphasis), and this can hardly be viewed just as "a theoretical commitment", but seems to be an essential assumption about ostensive communication. While fully agreeing with Jary that postulating complex mental state attributions à la Grice is neither necessary nor psychologically plausible, in the first place, I do believe that RT assumes that the relevance-guided search for speaker-intended meaning is (invariably) constrained by the speaker's intention, so exempting just a part of it (related to the purported material implicature) from this constraint strikes me as odd. Secondly, I do not see any compelling reasons behind Jary's categorization, which appears a little otiose from a psycholinguistic perspective.

4   As will be pointed out below, what is communicated may be confined to the explicit layer, in which case implicit import will not be triggered by a given utterance.

up schemes of classifications, however interesting these might be from a formal perspective.

This being the case, in RT different classes of implicatures adopted in a number of pragmatic frameworks have no raison d'être. Certain types of implicatures, like the Gricean conventional implicatures or generalized conversational implicatures,[5] lose their status of implicature altogether the way they are re-analysed in the relevance-theoretic framework. What Grice (1975/89) labels as conventional implicatures[6] are regarded in RT to be linguistically encoded directions on the inferential path that the interpreter should follow, viewed as cases of the so-called *procedural meaning* (the notion introduced and to date most thoroughly explored by Blakemore 1987, 2002, 2007, 2010; for useful discussions of what is involved see also Bezuidenhout 2004; Escandell-Vidal et al. 2011; Hall 2007b, and Iten 2005). Many of the Gricean generalized conversational implicatures are approached in relevance-theoretic analyses as inferential developments at the level of explicature (Carston 1988, 2002a, 2004b, 2004c, 2010; Carston and Hall 2012; see also Gibbs and Moise 1997 for empirical findings providing evidence for the explicature rather than implicature treatment of the relevant linguistic phenomena).

In the same vein, different varieties of implicature that arise because of the application of different maxims or principles are also found not to be very relevant on the relevance-theoretic approach. A case in point is Hornian (Horn 1984, 2004, 2005, 2010) taxonomy into Q-based and R-based implicatures, assumed to be generated by exploiting the Quantity and Relation Principles. These principles are postulated by Horn (2004: 13) as "two cardinal principles regulating the economy of linguistic information", and are presumed to be responsible for upper-bounding implicatures in the case of the former principle (that is, those in which by saying p, the speaker "implicates that (for all she knows) '…at most p…'" Horn 1984: 13) and for lower-bounding conversational implicatures with reference to the latter principle (since "a speaker who says '…p…' may license the R-inference that he [sic!] meant '…more than p…'" Horn 1984:140).[7] Even though offering some

---

5   Gauker (2001: 165) makes an interesting remark about Grice's model of implicatures: Grice "defines conversational implicatures as a variety of *implicatures*, which is a concept that he apparently expected could be grasped independently. Unfortunately, where Grice explains conversational implicature, he does little to explain implicature simpliciter."

6   On an interesting discussion of the nature of Gricean conventional implicatures see Potts (2005, 2007).

7   As Horn (1984:14) goes on to explain, with R-based implicatures the "locus classicus (…) is the indirect speech act (…): if I ask you if you can pass me the salt, in the context in where your abilities to do so are not in doubt, I licence you to infer that I am doing something more than asking you whether you can pass me the salt – I am in fact asking you to do it. (If I know for a fact that you can pass me the salt, the yes-no question is pointless;

interesting insights into the semantics of scalar terms and resulting inferences (Horn 1984, 2004, 2005, 2010), these principles were shown to lead to "a strengthening or narrowing down of the encoded meaning of the utterance" (Carston 1998: 227), so they do not constitute useful basis for implicature analyses or classes in RT.

Similar objections can be raised against Levinson's (2000) treatment of implicatures. His classification of generalized conversational implicatures into Q-, I- and M-implicatures, based on the three types of heuristics designed as an elaboration and modification of the Gricean maxims, can be viewed as useful only from the internal-theory perspective. So whereas the postulated heuristics can be seen as expedient for the model of preferred (or presumptive) meanings that the researcher focuses on, they are not designed to accommodate other vital aspects of verbal communication. Undeniably, while the three kinds of implicatures postulated by Levinson (2000)[8] do contribute to making his model coherent and provide useful tools for describing a range of linguistic phenomena (among them some mechanisms of grammaticalization and lexicalization), his project focusing on utterance-type meanings rather than speaker-intended meanings (or "utterance-token-meanings" as Levinson 2000: 22 refers to them), departs from the research agenda pursued by relevance theorists (cf. Sbisà 2006).[9] As a consequence, it is only to be expected that Levinson's implicature types do not tally with the relevance-theoretic model, on which the notion of generalized conversation implicatures is dismissed.[10]

Juxtaposed against the tri-heuristic model by Levinson (2000) and the dualistic one by Horn (1984, 2004, 2010), the mono-principled RT approach to implicature[11] appears as a simpler and truly Occamistic, but at the same time much more comprehensive and psychologically more plausible.[12] As indicated above, its foundation is a uniform comprehension heuristic, which is rooted in

---

the assumption that I am obeying the Relation maxim allows you to infer that I mean something more than what I say.)" For a critical appraisal of Horn's ideas of maximizing and minimizing informativeness, see Carston (1998).

8   See Bezuidenhout (2002b) for a critique of Levinson's default inferences.

9   For a critical discussion of Levinson's proposal, see Carston (2002a, 2004b).

10 For some empirical evidence on how RT's and Levinson's predictions about the recovery of certain conversational implicatures compare, see Reboul (2004).

11 I have borrowed the labels for the three pragmatic models under consideration from Horn (2004: 24).

12 To be sure, what appears an advantage from one vantage point may be considered a disadvantage from another perspective. For instance, Łyda (2007: 119), who acknowledges that a relevance-theoretic treatment of discourse connectives "opens new possibilities for their classification", at the same time indicates that a unitary approach to the underlying inferential processes for different discourse markers is unproductive for classificatory purposes.

the Communicative Principle of Relevance and its corollary in the form of the presumption of optimal relevance (cf. Ch1.5), and is assumed to be responsible for all utterance interpretation processes. This unitary system is postulated to provide a principled means for dealing with explicit and implicit communication phenomena. This approach, with its primary goal of creating an explanatory account of ostensive communication, eschews spurious typologies and systematizations, which – although attractive from the theory-building point of view – may obfuscate and distort the reality.

While accommodating two levels of communicated import, RT does not claim that it is always the case that what is communicated goes beyond the explicit layer and must involve implicatures. The intended meaning and the expected and satisfying level of relevance may be confined to identifying the explicitly conveyed content, as example (1) shows:

(1)　(a) Peter: Have you walked the dog yet?
　　　(b) Mary: Yes, I have.

Peter's question indicates precisely what information he wants to obtain, and by answering in the positive, Mary directly satisfies his expectations of relevance, since the cognitive effects recovered fully meet his current cognitive needs. To be sure, this direct answer may carry certain crucial implications for Peter, like, for instance, that he does not have to take the dog for a walk in the nearest future and can happily spend another two hours watching a football match on TV. However, these cannot be taken to fall within the speaker's intention and are not communicated by Mary's reply in (1b): as not warranted by the informative intention made manifest in the context, they exceed the scope of actually communicated assumptions. This brings to light an important contrast between implied and implicated assumptions that I would like to turn to now.

3.3 Implications vs. implicatures

Different types of inputs that the mental systems process can give rise to various implications, that is, assumptions that can be inferred from the stimuli that the senses receive. For instance, if I can see my neighbour driving a brand new Toyota which I have not seen before, I can infer that she has bought a new car. If I hear the characteristic sound of the gate opening at around 6 p.m., I can infer that my husband is coming back home from work.

In the same way, utterances, being ostensive verbal stimuli, can prompt various inferences, some of which will be merely *implied* by what the speaker has expressed, while some others will be *implicated* by her utterance. The difference between the two, which amounts to the distinction between *implications* and *implicatures*, has to do with whether the assumptions inferred on the basis of the explicitly communicated content can be viewed as licenced by the communicator's intentions (cf. Dahlman 2013: 322). As the relevance-theoretic definition given above (Ch. 3.2) makes clear, implicatures are those assumptions which are communicated non-explicitly, so by definition they are taken to fall within the speaker's intentions, which means that "intended implications are implicatures of the utterance" (Sperber and Wilson 2008: 99).

One of the pivotal observations that the relevance-theoretic model of ostensive communication capitalizes on is that both implications and implicatures come with varying degrees of strength (Sperber and Wilson 2008). Implications, which follow from the premises available to a given individual at a certain moment and are formed on the basis of various incoming stimuli, may be stronger or weaker, depending on how well evidenced they are or, in other words, how confident an individual may be that they are true. Similarly, implicatures can be stronger or weaker, depending on the extent to which they can be considered by the recipient to be intended as "manifestly relevant implications" (Sperber and Wilson 1986/95: 275) by the communicator (cf. Kalisz 1993: 86). This means that the recovery of implicatures, constrained – as are all aspects of utterance interpretation – by the pursuit of satisfying cognitive effects that the speaker manifestly must have intended may lead to the recovery of the implicit content which is strongly or less strongly supported by the speaker's intentions. To see what is involved and how strengths of implications and implicatures may be germane to the interpretation process, let us look at the brief exchange between two friends in (2).

> (2)   (a) Peter: Have you finished the book?
>   (b) Mary: I'm three-quarters through.

Let us stipulate that it is mutually manifest to both interactants that Peter's question is about whether Mary has finished listening to the audiobook version of *The Da Vinci Code* that she borrowed from Peter three weeks earlier. In these circumstances, Mary's answer above will achieve optimal relevance by indicating whether she has or has not yet finished listening to the audiobook. By providing an indirect answer in (2b), in which she explicitly reveals that she is three-quarters through with her listening, Mary implicates that she has not finished listening to the audiobook in question, as (2c) spells out:

> (2)   (c) Mary has not finished listening to the audiobook version of *The Da Vinci Code* yet, as she still has one-quarter to listen to.

In the context specified above, (2c) is generated as an implicated conclusion: Mary's utterance in (2b) makes highly accessible to the hearer the contextual assumption, or implicit premise, that if someone is three-quarters through with their listening of a certain audiobook, then they still have one-quarter to listen to, so they have not finished the book. This implicit premise processed together with what Mary explicitly conveys leads to the implicature that Mary has not finished listening to the audiobook version of *The Da Vinci Code* yet, as she still has one-quarter of the book to go through. Thus (2c) is recovered as a strong implicature of Mary's reply in (2b), because she must intend and expect Peter to draw this implicature if her utterance is intended to be optimally relevant to him. In other words, if Mary does not have good reasons to think that by processing (2b) together with some highly accessible background assumptions Peter will generate (2c), then she cannot have produced (2b) as optimally relevant, and she would not be engaging in *bona fide* communication. It is the very high probability that the speaker intends (2c) to be part of what she means by her utterance that makes (2c) a strong implicature to be derived from (2b) (cf. Wilson 2007). At the same time, because Peter is likely to accept (2c) as true, it is a strong implication of what Mary conveys in uttering (2b).

However, by producing an indirect answer to Peter's question, Mary encourages him to go beyond (2c) and recover some further cognitive effects in this communicative situation: otherwise she would have replied with a simple and direct "No, I haven't yet" or "No, I haven't finished it yet." Her answer in (2b) does not only implicate (2c), but makes highly accessible a range of further implications which can be inferred from what she has said and some background assumptions salient to Peter, a few of which are listed in (2d)-(2h).

(2)   (d) It took Mary three weeks to listen to three-quarters of *The Da Vinci Code*.

        (e) It will take Mary another week or two to finish listening to *The Da Vinci Code*.

        (f) Mary will be ready to return the audiobook to Peter in a week or two.

        (g) There are three weeks to Christmas, so Peter will probably get the audiobook back before Christmas.

        (h) Mary will want to see the film *The Da Vinci Code*, because she is keen on watching films based on the books that she has read.

In the context of a highly salient background assumption that Mary borrowed the audiobook three weeks earlier, (2d) is very well-evidenced and may emerge as a strong implication of (2b). Can this implication be justifiably attributed as intended by the speaker? If we assume that, for instance, it is mutually manifest to both interlocutors that in asking the question in (2a) Peter is trying to obtain information about how likely it is that Mary might soon return the audiobook that she borrowed from Peter three weeks earlier, (2d) provides the basis for non-demonstrative inferences like (2e), (2f) and (2g), which appear particularly relevant in the context. These three implications differ in how well-evidenced they are: the probability that (2d) is true is very high, which follows from the assumption that she explicitly communicates in (2b) and the fact that Peter lent the audiobook to her three weeks before, so it is a strong implication of (2b). On the other hand, (2e), (2f) and (2g) are just conjectures, so they are merely weak implications of (2b). It is important to observe that even though (2d) has the status of a strong implication here, because it appears to be true in the context, it is only weakly implicated by Mary. The point is that while the relevance of Mary's utterance in (2b) depends on Peter's generating (2c), there is no obvious endorsement of Mary's manifest intention for any of a whole range of implications that follow from (2b), although this intention reaches beyond (2c) and Peter is manifestly intended to entertain some further implications as part of the overall interpretation. As noted above, by uttering (2b) Mary encourages Peter to get some further cognitive effects, but leaves it to him which implications inferable from the explicature conveyed he will actually recover. This has important consequences for the interpretation that Peter will end up with: her act of communication will be successful as long as the overall import will embrace a strong implicature in (2c) and some other weakly implicated assumptions that Peter derives. However, Mary's manifest intention does not support any particular implication(s) apart from (2c), so Peter must take some responsibility for drawing these further implications. In other words, she evidently wants Peter to draw some further implications, but it is up to him which of the implications that become manifestly salient due to his processing of the utterance in (2b) he will compute. Table 1 below provides a synopsis of the implicatures and implications featuring in the analysis of example (2b).

(2) (a) Peter: Have you finished the book?
(b) Mary: I'm three-quarters through.

| (c) Mary has not finished listening to the audiobook version of *The Da Vinci Code* yet, as she still has one-quarter to listen to. =>**strong implicature** of (2b) in the context in which it is produced as the answer to Peter's enquiry about whether Mary has finished listening to the audiobook version of *The Da Vinci Code* | (c) Mary has not finished listening to the audiobook version of *The Da Vinci Code* yet, as she still has one-quarter to listen to. =>**strong implication** of (2b) in the context in which in it is produced as the answer to Peter's enquiry about whether Mary has finished listening to the audiobook version of *The Da Vinci Code* (d) It took Mary three weeks to listen to three-quarters of *The Da Vinci Code*. =>**strong implication** that follows from the highly salient background assumption that Mary borrowed the audiobook version of *The Da Vinci Code* three weeks earlier and the explicature of (2b) |

(d) It took Mary three weeks to listen to three-quarters of *The Da Vinci Code*. (e) It will take Mary another week or two to finish listening to *The Da Vinci Code*. (f) Mary is likely to return the audiobook to Peter in a week or two. (g) There are three weeks to Christmas, so Peter will probably get the audiobook back before Christmas. (h) Mary will want to see the film *The Da Vinci Code*, because she is keen on watching films based on the books that she has read. => **weak implicatures** of (2b) recovered as part of the overall interpretation of Mary's utterance	(e) It will take Mary another week or two to finish listening to *The Da Vinci Code*. (f) Mary will be ready to return the audiobook to Peter in a week or two. (g) There are three weeks to Christmas, so Peter will probably get the audiobook back before Christmas. => **weak implications** of (2b), highly salient to Peter interested in getting back his audiobook soon (h) Mary will want to see the film *The Da Vinci Code*, because she is keen on watching films based on the books that she has read. => further **weak implication** also salient to Peter

Table 1. Varying strengths of implicatures and implications of Mary's reply in (2b).

It seems vital to observe that if exactly the same utterance were to be provided by Mary as a reply to a slightly different question by Peter, then the implicit import recovered by the addressee would be different. Let us consider what (3b) might be taken to communicate in answer to (3a).

(3)   (a) Peter: Do you think you will be ready to return the audiobook before Christmas?

(b) Mary: I'm three-quarters through.

In this communicative situation, Mary's answer will yield satisfying cognitive effects as long as it informs Peter about whether he will get the audiobook back before Christmas, so by uttering (3b) she manifestly intends Peter to draw inferences that will fulfil this expectation. Since she does not provide a direct response to (3a), as was the case with (2b), Peter will share some responsibility for how he interprets her utterance. However, by uttering (2b) she very strongly implicates a negative answer to Peter's query about whether she has completed listening to *The Da Vinci Code*, which – being very well-evidenced – is a strong implication of (2b), and therefore something that Peter can have confidence in. In contrast, there is much less confidence that Peter can have in deriving implicit import communicated by (3b). The point is that (3b) only weakly implies that Mary will return the audiobook to Peter before Christmas, because the strength of this implication depends on the strength of other background assumptions, in particular those listed in (2e)-(2g), which are only weak implications available to Peter. So Mary may be taken to strongly implicate that she thinks she will be ready to return the audiobook version of *The Da Vinci Code* to Peter before Christmas, even though this implicated conclusion has a status of only a weak implication under the circumstances. In other words, while manifestly intending the addressee to derive an implication about whether she will return the audiobook before Christmas, which is therefore strongly implicated, the speaker leaves it to the hearer to decide how likely it is that she will meet the deadline: the evidence for drawing the specific implication that would satisfy the expectation of optimal relevance rests on the beliefs that are brought to bear on the interpretation by the recipient himself. Observe that the element of indeterminacy does not undermine the success of the communicative act: Peter's accessing the most salient assumptions that Mary can have manifestly foreseen and intended, and drawing on them in the interpretation process, results in his arriving at the optimally relevant interpretation which embraces what Mary may have rationally planned.

As the originators of RT (Sperber and Wilson 2008; Wilson 2007) underscore, and as the examples in (2) and (3) above illustrate, the strengths of implications and implicatures are independent, but they are both crucial to accounting for how communication is achieved and how indeterminacy, which verbal communication often involves, both results from the underlying speaker's intentions and contributes to the interpretation formed by the hearer, who will, under the circumstances, inevitably share some responsibility for the meaning recovered in the course of utterance processing.

While it always takes at least two to dance the communication tango, the party mainly responsible for getting the intended meaning is the hearer. Comprehension always involves a risk, since even if the speaker's intention is fully transparent and determinate, the language stimulus produced as evidence for this intention inevitably underdetermines the meaning conveyed. So one way or another, in the course of utterance processing, the comprehender has to face underdeterminacy, indeterminacy or both.

3.4 Underdeterminacy vs. indeterminacy

Two apparently similar notions have been referred to in the relevance-theoretic account of how addressees arrive at the speaker-intended meaning presented so far, namely, underdeterminacy and indeterminacy, and it appears vital to give some consideration to the contrast between them.

As emphasized in the previous chapter (see in particular 2.3, 2.5 and 2.6), what speakers say unavoidably underdetermines what is intended as explicitly communicated, so the recipient necessarily needs to work out the occasion-specific contextual meaning. In other words, linguistic meaning severely underdetermines what is actually communicated (Carston 2002a: Ch.1.2), that is why interpreting the meaning that is explicitly conveyed may involve recovering the ellipted material, assigning values to indexical expressions, identifying referents, disambiguation, resolving apparent contradictions, adjusting meanings of decoded lexical items, deciding about the intended illocutionary force of a given utterance, etc.

Even though it is generally agreed that utterances, one way or another, come incomplete, there is a lot of contention over how such underdeterminacies are resolved and where the borderline between the explicit and implicit should be placed. In effect, there is no unanimous agreement as to the nature and exact processes that contribute to settling underdeterminacies at the level of explicitly communicated content (see Ch. 2.2-2.3). On the relevance-theoretic model, pinning down the meaning that the speaker is expressing is taken to involve inferencing geared towards the recovery of an interpretation manifestly intended by the speaker as optimally relevant in the communicative situation in which an utterance is used. To be precise, this amounts to pursuing a relevance-oriented interpretation path that will return a worthwhile range of cognitive effects for no gratuitous effort (see Ch. 2).

Prima facie, it may appear paradoxical that the debate over implicit import of utterances is less intense, but this can be easily explained by the very fact that what speakers implicate by definition requires inferencing, so the character of the processes at work remains indubitable (cf. Jary 2013). So, while debates over explicatures revolve around quite basic issues, the fundamentals of implicatures are accepted without much polemic.

I think there is another important reason behind a more liberal stance that is allowed in theorizing about implicatures[13] in contrast to a more rigid treatment required for explicatures. It seems to pass unnoticed that, more often than not, the meaning that is being explicitly communicated is backed up by a very specific speaker's intention which endorses a particular meaning that she manifestly wants to express in a certain situation, whereas with reference to implicitly communicated meaning there is frequently some indeterminacy of what is being implicated on a given occasion. It is in fact the indeterminacy of the underlying speaker's intention which, on the one hand, creates certain expectations of looseness of the interpretation that the recipient is intended to recover at the level of implicature (cf. Sperber and Wilson 1986/95: 56), and, on the other, encourages analysts to take a more open-mined and lenient approach towards implicatures. As observed by Grice himself, who coined the term *implicature* and laid foundation for research

---

13   In this vein, e.g., Brown and Yule (1983: 33) assume that generating implicatures involves "a rather loose form of inferencing", Bach and Harnish's (1979, in Bach 1990) Speech Act Schema involves "an inference to a plausible explanation", and is designed as a model that "merely schematizes hearers' inferences" (Bach 1990: 393), and Davis (1998: 155) argues that "implicature practices are arbitrary to some extent rather than completely determinate."

into the phenomena involved, some indeterminacy as to what is communicated implicitly is its significant feature:

> Since, to calculate a conversational implicature is to calculate what has to be supposed in order to preserve the supposition that the Cooperative Principle is being observed, and since there may be various possible explanations, a list of which may be open, the conversational implicature in such cases will be an open disjunction of such specific explanations, and if the list of these is open, the implicatum will have just the kind of indeterminacy that many actual implicata do in fact seem to possess. (Grice 1975/89: 39-40)

Indeterminacy that is thus sanctioned leaves some latitude in analysing implicit meanings, without causing a bitter disagreement among pragmaticists.

What has been written above about underdeterminacy and indeterminacy reveals the major difference between the two: while underdeterminacy invites or even calls for adequate resolution in the process of comprehension, so that the meaning conveyed by the communicator can be relevantly pinned down by the recipient, an element of indeterminacy encourages the type of interpretation which is partly tentative. Furthermore, it becomes evident that it is the speaker's intentions that are responsible for the indeterminacy of the implicitly communicated import, because it arises when these intentions are "partly precise and partly vague" (Sperber and Wilson 1986/95: 59). This is quite different from underdeterminacy in the case of explicatures, where the source of potential problems with determining the actual meaning can be identified in how language functions:[14] the tools it provides make it virtually impossible to express eternal sentences, "interpretable as expressing a definite proposition on the basis of lexicon and syntactic structure alone irrespective of the context of utterance" (Gauker 2001: 166; see also Ch. 2.5 above), and there is no failsafe mechanism that will guarantee the recovery of precisely the kind of meaning that the speaker has in mind.[15] As aptly remarked by Carston (2002a: 20-21), indeterminacy has to do with circumstances in which

---

14   As Gleitman and Papafragou (2013: 505) bluntly put it, "while speakers generally mean what they say, they do not and could not say exactly what they mean ..., [as] linguistic representations underdetermine the conceptual contents they are used to convey: Language is *sketchy* compared to the richness of our thought" (original emphasis).

15   As pointed out by Sperber and Wilson (1986/95: 172-176), the primary function of language is information-processing rather than communication: language is neither essentially just a communicative tool (there are languages not used for communication, e.g. the language of music) nor an indispensable medium of communication (after all, people can and do communicate by using non-verbal stimuli). The primary and principal form of communication, which must have preceded coded, linguistic communication, is inferential communication based on ostension: "human external languages are of adaptive value only for a species already deeply involved in inferential communication" (Sperber and Wilson 1986/95: 176). Most researchers take the communicative role of language for

there are a few hypotheses about the intended meaning and no fact of the matter about which of them is the right one, so "no conclusion can be drawn because *there is none to be drawn*. Linguistic underdeterminacy, by comparison, does not entail that there is no fact of the matter as regards the proposition expressed, but rather that it cannot be determined by linguistic meaning alone" (emphasis mine).

It needs to be added that, in spite of the fact that, generally, indeterminacy can be predicted to frequently arise at the level of implicit import, it may also be present in what the speaker communicates explicitly, as pointed out by Sperber and Wilson (forthcoming). Here is an example that the creators of RT use to illustrate how the meaning of an explicature may prove indeterminate:

(4)   (a) Mark: We can't afford La Cantina.
       (b) Pamela: I've got money.

In the context in which it is uttered, (4b) implicates that Pamela is offering to pay for the meal at La Cantina, but it is difficult to pin down the exact meaning that the lexical item *money* is supposed to have in the context. While the utterance would be literally true even if Pamela had just £1 in her pocket, it is not the kind meaning she has in mind here, assuming that she utters (4b) as a bona fide speaker: she manifestly communicates that her financial resources are sufficient to pay for the restaurant meal. The important thing is that for this implicature to get through, it must be warranted by the explicature, but this raises the question about the sense of *money* in it. A relevance-theoretic analysis suggests that the intended sense of the word emerges through mutual adjustment of the intended and expected cognitive effects (in the form of implicit import), explicit content and context as the ad hoc concept MONEY*.[16] The meaning of this ad hoc concept can roughly be taken to relate to the amount of money that a meal at La Cantina costs, whatever that might be. Inevitably then, this sense remains rather vague, and, as indicated by Sperber and Wilson (forthcoming), Mark may have no idea of how much money may actually be involved. Strictly speaking then, there is some vagueness or indeterminacy in the meaning that the speaker conveys in (4b). What is more, there is no English word or expression that would denote exactly what she wants to express, but the (partly obscure) meaning can be inferred in context to secure an optimally relevant overall interpretation. As might only be expected, the meaning of creative metaphoric expressions will be indeterminate in this kind of way (Carston 2002c, 2010a, 2010b; Sperber and Wilson 2008;

---

    granted, and treat it as primary and superior to its other functions, as does, for instance, Wittgenstein (see Chrzanowska-Kluczewska 2004: 25, 32).

16 On ad hoc concepts, see Ch. 2.9 and references therein.

Wilson and Carston 2006).[17] The ad hoc concept that is postulated in RT to be part of a metaphoric utterance is taken to provide the basis for and to warrant implications that will contribute to the overall optimally relevant interpretation of the utterance, without having a precise semantic construal in a given context. This supports and elucidates the prediction that the meaning of metaphoric utterances will be mostly unparaphrasable: the ad hoc concept used "is characterized by its inferential role and not by a definition, and moreover this inferential role, to a much greater extent than in the case of mere approximations, is left to the hearer to elaborate" (Sperber and Wilson 2005: 377-378).

As demonstrated by the example above, indeterminacies occur not just at the level of implicature but also at the level of explicit content. It is important to observe that the element of indeterminacy does by no means undermine the success of a communicative act: the indeterminacy has its source in the underlying speaker's intentions, which, as indicated above, are partly definite and partly elusive, and as a result, what the addressee recovers is necessarily fuzzy. This indicates that communication may involve deliberate indeterminacy, because a speaker's thought that gives rise to her verbal production (or, more generally, ostensive communicative performance) may itself be very complex and dense, with its contents virtually impossible to specify or itemize. Thus RT predicts that there may be an element of vagueness inherently involved in the meaning that communicators intend to convey (Sperber and Wilson 1986/95: 56) and, unlike other pragmatic theories, the model does not idealize away these aspects of human communication and language use which are difficult to handle (Sperber and Wilson 2005, forthcoming). Instead, it attempts to penetrate their nature and puts forth a plausible, coherent and explicit explanation of what may be involved. In fact, one of the important and, regrettably, underestimated assets of the framework under discussion is that it affords a model on which these vaguer aspects of communication are described in a fairly precise way. This account is rooted in the crucial distinction between strong and weak communication that Sperber and Wilson (1986/95) introduce and which will be the subject matter of the section to follow.

---

17 In a thought-provoking paper entitled "Against metaphoric meaning", Lepore and Stone (2010) deny that creative metaphors carry propositional meanings altogether and they reject the idea that there is metaphoric meaning that could be recognized on the basis of attributable speaker's intentions. The authors argue that metaphors are used to make a point, to make the audience notice and see things rather than to communicate something to the audience, concluding that "interlocutors use their metaphorical discourse not to assert and deny propositions but to develop imagery and to pursue a shared understanding" (Lepore and Stone 2010: 177).

3.5 From strong to weak communication or the other way round?

According to RT, communication is a matter of degree, because a speaker's meaning may come as a proposition (or a set of propositions) with a determinate, very precise meaning, or as a "meaning package" whose content may be largely unparaphrasable and (at least partly) indeterminate, with a continuum in between these two extremes (cf. Wilson and Sperber 1991b). This means that, by definition, human communication is assumed to result in more precise or less precise cognitive effects, which affects its strength (Sperber and Wilson 1986/95, 2008, forthcoming).

How can this be accounted for? As underlined in chapter 1, RT is designed to be a model of ostensive-inferential communication,[18] that is the type of communication in which the communicator makes it manifest to the audience that she intends to make manifest to them a set of assumptions I.[19] As pointed out earlier (see Ch.1.5), there are two layers of information that an ostensive communicative stimulus comes with: the basic information, embracing a set of assumptions I,[20] and a higher order, meta-information that the basic information is intentionally made manifest. These two are formalized in RT as the informative and communicative intention, the definitions of which were discussed in Ch.1.5 and are repeated here for the reader's convenience:

> *Informative intention:* to make manifest or more manifest to the audience a set of assumptions I. (Sperber and Wilson 1986/95: 58)
> *Communicative intention:* to make it mutually manifest to audience and communicator that the communicator has this informative intention. (Sperber and Wilson 1986/95: 61)

It must be highlighted that the set of assumptions I that falls under the informative intention need not consist of a list of specific assumptions, individually entertained by the speaker and duly replicated in the hearer's mind as the effect of his processing of a given ostensive stimulus. As Sperber and Wilson (1986/95: 68) argue, "to have a representation of a set of assumptions it is not necessary to have a representation of each assumption in the set. Any individuating description may do." In the case of communicative encounters in which the communicator entertains a complex thought which she wants to communicate, what she has in mind and what surfaces in the recipient's mind as the outcome of his interpretation

---

18   Strictly speaking, what the communicator engages in is ostension, while what the audience engage in is inferencing, hence the term ostensive-inferential (Sperber and Wilson 1986/95: 54); for a fuller description of communication as construed in the relevance-theoretic framework see Ch. 1.

19   On manifestness as a technical term used in RT see Ch.1.6 and Ch.2.6, fn. 24 .

20   For the sake of clarity, the present discussion focuses exclusively on declarative utterances, even though relevance-theoretic analyses extend to the interrogative and imperative as well.

of the presented ostensive stimulus may not be amenable to a representation in terms of a proposition or an array of propositions, as indicated above (see Ch. 3.4).

This means that while sometimes what is communicated amounts to a single proposition, which is easy to recognize, there are situations in which the communicator's meaning, though not necessarily difficult to identify, may be quite hard to spell out (Wilson and Wharton 2006: 1572). Let us look at some examples. Consider the utterance in (5), which – let us assume – is provided by a teacher in answer to the student's query about his final test score.

(5)   Your score is 49 out of 50.

Under the circumstances, (5) comes as a direct answer to the student's question, and the assumption that is made manifest, namely that the student's score is 49 points out of 50, is straightforwardly backed up by the speaker's manifest informative intention. There is a single candidate for the explicitly communicated assumption and, even though the recovered explicature may give rise to some implications that the student may further infer (e.g., that his score is one of the top scores in the group, that his performance on the test was nearly perfect, etc.), there is a definite and determinate meaning communicated by the teacher uttering (5), which does not go beyond what she explicitly expresses: her answer is evidently intended to achieve relevance conveying just this meaning. This is a case of what Sperber and Wilson (1986/95: 59) refer to as strong communication, which they characterize as follows: "[w]hen the communicator makes strongly manifest her informative intention to make some particular assumption strongly manifest, then that assumption is strongly communicated." By contrast, "[w]hen the communicator's intention is to increase simultaneously the manifestness of a wide range of assumptions, so that her intention concerning each of these assumptions is weakly manifest, then each of them is weakly communicated." The latter type could be illustrated by a loud whistle, produced by Peter on seeing his wife, Mary, in her New-Year's party outfit, disguised as an alien. While the non-verbal stimulus used by her husband can be taken by Mary to manifestly convey his bewilderment, astonishment and admiration, there may be some consternation discernible in Peter's ostensive behaviour (in particular, when the whistle is accompanied by a disconcerted facial expression), which Mary, who knows his conservative outlook and sober and conventional attitudes, may also detect. There is no single proposition that can be identified as communicated here, though there is a whole array of propositions that become manifest or more manifest to Mary on hearing the whistle.[21] Conceivably, it may happen that Mary will consider Peter's non-

---

21 So, as Wilson and Sperber (1991a: 384) put it, "the speaker has a general idea of the type of assumption to be supplied and the type of conclusion to be derived, but may not know or care which specific assumptions or conclusions of this type will be supplied."

verbal ostensive feedback on how she looks to suggest that her outfit is too bold, which may even induce her to change into something less daring. Such weakly communicated assumptions, only the gist of which can be described, but which can hardly be listed as a set of assumptions that the communicator intends to convey and the recipient is expected to recover, become part of the mutual cognitive environment of Peter and Mary as a result of Peter's ostensive act (cf. Sperber and Wilson forthcoming). Importantly though, these assumptions are identifiable – however tentative they may be – as communicated, because they satisfy the addressee's "expectations of relevance in a way the speaker [or the communicator] might manifestly have foreseen" and intended (Wilson 1992: 176; cf. also Sperber and Wilson forthcoming). As in other cases of interpreting ostensive stimuli, the recipient recognizes the array of weakly communicated assumptions, or, in other words, recovers the expected and anticipated cognitive effects by following the path of least effort and testing interpretive hypotheses in order of accessibility, stopping as soon as the satisfying level of relevance is reached (Wilson and Sperber 2004: 613).

The example with Peter's whistling used above to illustrate weak communication should not be taken to suggest that verbal communication will be of the strong type, while non-verbal communication will always be much weaker. Non-verbal stimuli may be used to make strongly manifest the speaker's informative intention to make a very specific assumption manifest: an ostensive gesture, for instance, can be used to convey a determinate, obvious and precise meaning. So, for example, if in answer to the question how I am getting to Prague, I just spread my arms and imitate aircraft's wings, there is a precise, strongly communicated meaning that I am travelling by plane. On the other hand, as indicated above (see Ch. 3.4), verbal communication may be quite weak, both at the explicit and implicit levels, with metaphoric utterances frequently adduced to to expound this point.

In fact, I have argued elsewhere (Jodłowiec 1991a, 1991b, 2008) that humour in verbal jokes can be fruitfully analysed in terms of weak communication effects. In a nutshell, the argument is that when the punchline is processed, there is a rich cognitive impact on the recipient, in which unexpectedly a plethora of assumptions become simultaneously manifest or more manifest in the joke interpreter's mind. This is postulated to result in the cognitive overload and contribute to an affective effect, released through the audience's laughter. Here is an illustration of what is hypothesized to be involved.

(6)   (a) Harry invites his old friend John home for dinner one evening. At the dinner table Harry talks to his wife using endearing terms, such as *Honey, My Love, Darling, Sweetheart, Pumpkin*, etc. The couple have been married almost 30 years and John is truly impressed. When Harry's wife is out of the room, John leans over and says, "I think it's wonderful that, after all these years,

> you still call your wife those loving pet names. What is the secret to this
> long-lasting marital happiness?"
> "Do you really want an honest answer?" Harry asks. "But of course," the
> friend replies.

(6)   (b) "To tell you the truth, I forgot this woman's name a couple of years ago and
it is a bit awkward to ask now."

The idea is that when (6b) is processed, there is a host of assumptions made manifest to the recipient, which concern husbands' (often inconsiderate) attitudes to their wives (assumptions possibly similar to those listed in (7a)-(7d)), problems with communication that married couples commonly face (e.g., (7f)-(7h)), unfeasibility of long-lasting marital happiness (e.g., (7i)-(7k)), suspiciousness with which spouses should probably approach unexpected warm affections displayed by the better half (e.g., (7l)-(7n)), etc., with obvious differences in what becomes manifest across different individuals exposed to the joke.

(7)   (a) Husbands often exhibit a careless attitude to vital detail of everyday life.
(b) Spouses get used to certain patterns of behaviour and follow routines.
(c) Husbands sometimes take it for granted that their wives are just a part of their life.
(d) Husbands and wives frequently tend to treat their spouse in an instrumental way.
(e) The lack of respect for the partner is the greatest enemy of marriage.
(f) Husbands and wives often find it difficult to talk to each other about important issues.
(g) Married couples do not spend much time sharing what they really think.
(h) Even though they spend lots of time in each other's company, spouses often wrongly interpret each other's attitudes and motives.
(i) Few marriages last decades.
(j) As the number of year together increases, true affection decreases.
(k) Frustration, hopelessness and dissatisfaction take control of the relationship with time.
(l) After a while married couples forget what affection is.
(m) Pet names that your spouse uses may be a sign of routine behaviour rather than genuine affection.

(n) If, after years spent together, your partner is too kind to you, it may be a sign of crisis.

Very few (if any) from this "constellation" of potential assumptions that become suddenly manifest (or more manifest) to him will actually be represented by the interpreter, so they can just be hypothesized to cross his mind like a comet making a pass near the Earth. Hence the idea that they create a cognitive overload: a state of mind (possibly also a brain-state) in which a vast number of assumptions become suddenly manifest (or more manifest) to the individual, with none of them, or at best very few of them,[22] being actually represented. It is their totality that creates the cognitive impact mentioned above. All the (potentially accessible) assumptions that become manifest when the punchline is processed are incompatible with those that the joke-setting (in the example above embracing text in (6a)) evokes, hence the clash and resulting incongruity which is responsible for the humorous effect.

This suggests that any attempt at explaining the humorous aspect of jokes by pinning down the meaning that is communicated seems doomed to failure, precisely because the punchline effect results in the cognitive overload of this kind and what the punchline very weakly communicates is likely to be accessed only at a subrepresentational level. Even though none of them can strictly speaking be identified as part of the intended interpretation, the whole effect involving a vast array of weakly communicated assumptions, whatever they might be for different recipients, is assumed to be intended as part of the joke interpretation, so these assumptions have the status of weak implicatures (and necessarily weak or strong implications): they make the punchline relevant in just the right way (for a fully-developed weak communication account of jokes, see Jodłowiec 1991b).[23]

As this very brief presentation of how verbal jokes might be analysed along weak communication lines brings to light, weak communication proves a very efficient communicative tool: a lot is conveyed by employing relatively modest linguistic means. This suggests a potential advantage of weak communication over strong communication, particularly over strong communication of the explicit kind.

---

22 Some of them may occasionally surface, and access to them is certainly open, since when people are asked to explain why they find a certain joke funny, they refer to these assumptions.

23 One of the advantages of this kind of weak communication account of verbal jokes is that it explains why certain themes are good (or not very good) subjects for jokes: for the punchline to unleash the required rich weak communication effect, there must be a multitude of assumptions that can potentially be activated. That is why jokes about, for instance, the Canadians are not likely to be particularly amusing for a Polish audience, in contrast to, say, Americans, because, overall, Polish recipients (unlike American audiences) have restricted access to a wide range of contextual assumptions about Canadians that the punchline could make manifest. Mothers-in-law, on the other hand, appear to be a perfect joke-topic worldwide (though, of course, cultural differences will come into play). On this model of joke comprehension, intellectual robustness, that is, the readiness of different language users to rely on an activation of a relatively vast range of cognitive resources in processing language stimuli, may be appealed to in order to account for idiosyncratic differences in response to humorous texts and suggests a vital ingredient in what we refer to as a sense of humour. (For alternative RT inspired approaches to humour, see Curcó 1995, 1996; Piskorska 2012, 2014, and Yus 2003, 2008.)

I am in total agreement with a number of researchers, among them Brożek (2014), Carston (1999, 2002a, 2005, 2009, 2012), Dascal (2003), Searle (1992) and Wilson (2014), who believe that full explicitness in verbal communication is neither achievable nor desirable. Here is how Searle (1992: 67) puts it:

> Suppose I go into the restaurant and order a meal. Suppose I say, speaking literally, "Bring me a steak with fried potatoes." Even though the utterance is meant and understood literally, the number of possible misinterpretations is strictly limitless. I take it for granted that they will not deliver the meal to my house, or to my place of work. I take it for granted that the steak will not be encased in concrete, or petrified. It will not be stuffed into my pockets or spread over my head. But none of these assumptions was made explicit in the literal utterance. The temptation is to think that I could make them fully explicit by simply adding them as further restrictions, making my original order more precise. But that is also a mistake. First, it is a mistake because there is no limit to the number of additions I would have to make to the original order to block possible misinterpretations, and second, each of the additions is itself subject to different interpretations.

In a similar vein, Carston (2005: 276) maintains that

> [e]ven if this were possible, there is just no evidence that hearers prefer a given message or meaning to be as fully encoded as possible. A good speaker, as opposed to one who is found to be tedious, pedantic, even misleading, is one who does not over-encode, judging more or less correctly what a hearer can easily infer in a particular context: when a particular referent is highly salient, a pronoun is preferable to a name or a description; when a topic is established, a phrasal utterance (e.g. 'On the table') may be preferable to a sentential one (e.g. 'Mary put the book on the table'), etc.

Inevitably then, as also argued at length earlier (see Ch. 2), people always say less than they mean, however, they sometimes say it in such a way that they mean by far much more. Paradoxically, strong communication should therefore not be recognized as the preferred and superior kind; weak communication presents itself as offering a tremendous potential. This potential is probably exploited to the full in what Sperber and Wilson (1986/95, 2008; Wilson and Sperber 2004) refer to as poetic effects.

3.6 Poetic effects: the case of aphorisms

Sperber and Wilson (1986/95, 2008; Wilson and Sperber 2004) use the label *poetic effect* in a technical sense to identify a special communicative effect of achieving relevance "through a wide array of weak implications which are themselves weakly implicated"[24] (2008: 100). As the authors explain in more detail:

---

24   See Ch.3.3 above on weakly implicated weak implicatures.

> The speaker – or writer, since this method of achieving relevance is particularly well developed in literature – has good reason to suppose that enough of a wide array of potential implications with similar import are true or probably true, although she does not know which these are (hence, they are weak implications) and is neither able to anticipate nor particularly concerned about which of them will be considered and accepted by the audience (hence, they are weakly implicated). (Sperber and Wilson 2008: 100)

Sperber and Wilson (2008: 100) go on to show how this effect can be seen at work in Japanese haiku poems, which belong to "the most effective forms of poetry in world literature,"[25] and in some poetic metaphors.[26]

I would like to present now how the relevance-theoretic model of utterance interpretation, and in particular the notion of weak communication and poetic effect, can explain the anatomy of aphorisms (a preliminary discussion along relevance-theoretic lines was offered in Jodłowiec 1991b).

As is frequently the case with literary genres, aphorism eludes a straightforward, satisfactory and rigorous definition, and, depending on the research perspective adopted and scholarly goals pursued, different researchers focus on its different characteristics, as rightly pointed out by Kuźniak (2005: 13-16; cf. also remarks by Ángel-Lara 2011; Stephenson 1980 and Wolf 1994). As is emphasized in one of the most recent surveys of aphoristic literature,

> there is no agreed-upon definition of terms such as 'aphorism', 'saying', 'apothegm', or 'maxim'. Aphorisms sometimes include all short works, sometimes just those examples that have an author, and sometimes only a small subset that may be variously identified either by tone, form, or idea. One man's aphorism is another man's maxim. Etymology rarely helps, since the meanings of terms shift radically over ages and cultures. Hippocrates' aphorisms would not be called that today. They are closer to what we might call maxims, while the works La Rochefoucauld called maxims bear little resemblance to maxims as we usually think of them. If one struggles to arrive at the true meaning of these terms, one will surely be lost in an endless labyrinth. (Morson 2012: 4)

In view of the fact that my aim here is to show how the ticking mechanism of aphorisms can be disassembled and explained with the help of the toolkit of RT rather than to solve terminological conundrums related to the notion as such, an informal

---

25 As pointed out by Chrzanowska-Kluczewska (2013: 124), the figuration in these poems operates in the "behind the scenes" way, they rely on synaesthetic imagery and are a real challenge for the translator.

26 Possible applications of RT in the investigation of literary communication, its aesthetic value and different types of stylistic effects can be found, inter alia, in Blakemore (2010), Boase-Baier (2004), Clark B. (1996), Furlong (1996), Kolaiti (2009), Pilkington (2000), and Uchida (1998).

definition of the notion will be adopted.[27] Hence, for the purposes of the present discussion, aphorisms will be defined as short, pithy mini-texts, often confined to one-sentence, "which comment on some recurrent aspect of life, couched in terms that are meant to be permanently and universally applicable" (Gross 1983: viii). This definition focuses on the most prototypical structural (related to the form) and functional (having to do with philosophical, anthropocentric meaning, cf. Geary 2005: 15, 19; Kuźniak 2005: 15) characteristics of aphorisms, revealing that there is no clear border-line between aphorisms and proverbs, maxims, wellerisms, etc. (cf. Kuźniak 2005: 33), but that, importantly, they constitute a "coherent, cognitively identifiable systematized unit of a text" (Kuźniak 2005: 53; cf. also Kośka 1999: 16).

Since, in contrast to analysts who aim at providing a systematic and exhaustive anatomy of the genre, my major focus is on *what* and *how* aphorisms communicate, I will not venture even a sketchy overview of the wealth of syntactic patterns, semantic figures, rhetorical devices, propositional attitudes and cognitive schemas underlying aphorisms,[28] and I will concentrate entirely on the interpretation process involved.

I would like to argue that in the case of aphorisms the major pragmatic meaning conveyed lies beyond the explicature and it has to do with recovering what is being conveyed implicitly. That is why the interpreter is not so much concerned with pinning down the explicature expressed, but instead immediately goes well beyond it and focuses on recovering the implicit import, even though, for instance, disambiguation and lexical modulation necessary to warrant implicatures will be carried out. This implicit import is computed on the basis of the concepts that are encoded by the words used in a given aphorism: in the relevance-theoretic framework it is assumed that concepts provide access to different kinds of information, in particular encyclopaedic information (Sperber and Wilson 1986/95: 87-88; Wilson and Sperber 1991a: 382). Encyclopaedic information includes "commonplace assumptions, scientific information, culture-specific beliefs and personal, idiosyncratic observations and experiences. Some of this information may be stored as discrete propositional representations, some of it may be in the form of integrated scripts or scenarios (…), and some may be represented in an analogue (as opposed to digital) format, perhaps as mental images of some sort" (Carston 2002a: 321). It is assumptions of this kind stored in the recipient's mind under encyclopaedic entries of the concepts encoded in

---

27 As cleverly observed by Geary (2005: 8), "[i]ronically for the world's shortest form of literature, the compact definition of the aphorism is impossible."

28 For an in-depth, extensive analysis of aphorisms couched in the framework of cognitive linguistics and for a network model of the aphoristic output by Stanisław Jerzy Lec, based on a schematic cognitive micro- and macro-topological representation see Kuźniak (2009).

the aphorism that provide the basis for the implicit import that the interpretation process yields.

Let us see how it actually works. The examples in (8)-(12) below represent a quite random selection from aphorisms by Stanisław Jerzy Lec,[29] an eminent Polish poet and satirist, who is widely recognized as one of the virtuosos of the genre,[30] used here solely as a material for pragmatic analyses.

(8)   The poet has the sixth sense, but lacks the first five.
(9)   When will man conquer the interhuman space?
(10) I'll really laugh if the world ends just before they manage to destroy it.
(11) In the beginning was the Word – at the end just the Cliché.

As hinted at above, a relevance-theoretic model predicts that, in processing (8), assumptions about POETS, THE HUMAN SENSES, THE SIXTH SENSE (as well as possibly some others that cross-referencing among the encyclopaedic entries of these concepts will bring to the fore) will be made available, and as a result, a number of implications will (at least potentially) arise. Some of the latter may not be unlike (12a)-(12e) below:

(12) (a) Poets are individuals endowed with exceptional sensitivity and insight, but down-to-earth, everyday matters may be a real be challenge to them.
       (b) They are believed to feel, hear and see about the world more than others, but they may not respond quickly to physical stimuli around them.
       (c) Their spiritual life may be richer than that of ordinary people, but at the same time poets may lack practical skills important in every-day life.
       (d) They may excel at exploring the depth of life and afterlife, but are often out of touch with reality.
       (e) They may experience the extraordinary, but may not hear, feel, see, taste and touch the ordinary.

Similarly, by evoking the accessible assumptions that the concepts in (9) and (10) make accessible, the interpreter may infer a range of implicatures that, respectively, the rhetorical question and an apparently personal confession of the aphorist bring to mind, some of which may resemble those in (13a)-(13e) and in (14a)-(14e):

(13) (a) Man ventures to explore the outer space, but seems helpless when it comes to improving human relationships.
       (b) Major progress in science and technology is not paralleled by achievements in helping people communicate with and understand their neighbour better.

---

29 Examples (8)-(11) come from an English translation of Lec's collection entitled *More Unkempt Thoughts* (1968, translated by Jacek Gałązka), available at: https://www.tsbvi. edu/braille/books/moreunkempt1.brf (accessed December 2014), and example (12) is cited after Geary (2005: 190).

30 For detailed analyses of Lec's literary output, which goes well beyond aphorisms, see Kośka (2008).

(c) While man accomplishes what seems difficult and impossible, achieving something apparently much easier, like being closer with other human beings, appears unattainable.

(d) Man is more likely to make friends with aliens than with his brothers and sisters.

(e) Love your neighbour as you love yourself proves a real challenge for humankind.

(14) (a) People's expectation that the world will end due to some cosmic disaster may turn out mistaken.

(b) It might be an ultimate irony if people manage to destroy the world before God ends it.

(c) Paradoxically, man is the worst enemy of the world he lives in.

(d) Conventional war or nuclear war is likely to bring the world to an end before people expect it.

(e) Man is the most destructive force on the planet.

In the same manner, there is a whole range of implicatures communicated by (11), this time about how words may have the power to create reality, about their rich potential and symbolism, and at the same time about how they can be empty, meaningless and trivial. The clash in implications that is very conspicuous here, and equally apparent in (13) and (14), suggests a paradox that the aphorism brings to the interpreter's attention, and is indicative of the pessimistic overtones communicated as the negative innuendoes prevail.

The weak communication effect present here seems analogous to what was postulated above about the interpretation of jokes.[31] As was hypothesized in the case of the punchline effect (see Ch.3.5), these implications may or may not surface in the reader's or hearer's mind: the mere increase in the manifestness of a number of assumptions may result in a satisfactory cognitive effect and the interpreter will stop at that, without computing (some of) the implications that become available. The elusiveness of meaning that this points to, which is one of essential qualities of aphorisms, seems typical for literary meaning in general, with the reader's or hearer's intuitions about the meaning conveyed frequently shaking "under the weight of the extremely diverse, thoroughly context-sensitive and remarkably creative facts of language use" (Kolaiti 2009: 36). It is frequently emphasized that trying to make sense of aphorisms is tantamount to endless groping through vagueness (Morson 2003: 421), because they are just "flashes that die out before we have quite made out what they reveal" (Morson 2003: 423).[32]

---

31 Close affinities between jokes and aphorisms are pointed out by a number of authors, e.g., Geary (2005), Jodłowiec (1991b), Kośka (1999), Wolf (1994).

32 This suggests an inherent paradox in the aphorism: its role is often associated with some didactic function it is supposed to serve, but it is debatable if this function can be fulfilled

This kind of weak communication approach to aphorisms throws some light both on the nature of the processes involved in understanding them and on the inherent features of the aphorism *per se*.

In the first place, as indicated above, all the implications generated in the course of processing of an aphorism, like those in (13)-(15), are postulated to be computed as weak implicatures that the interpretation process returns: the manifest intention of the communicator encourages the recipient to recover some such implications, but there is transparent indeterminacy as to which the communicator actually endorses. Evidently then, the author of the aphorism does not expect the audience to recover a certain preconceived set of implications: with the whole range of implications that are brought to bear in the interpretation process and some effects completely unforeseeable by the communicator, the audience is left a lot of latitude about which subset will be activated in their mind or which will be actually derived (cf. Sperber and Wilson 1986/95: 201). This means that the responsibility for arriving at some rather than other implications is shared with the interpreter, as is always the case with weakly communicated implicatures (cf. Wilson 2011). That is why, due to idiosyncrasies related to encyclopaedic knowledge that each person accumulates, there will certainly be differences in interpretations across different individuals.[33]

Besides, unlike in many cases of on-line communication in which interactants have fairly precise expectations of relevance, there is no established level of relevance that, on the one hand, the communicator can anticipate and, on the other, the recipient will find satisfactory. In fact, the interpreter of aphorisms may spend as much time and effort in computing the relevant implications as he deems suitable.[34] Therefore, even one and the same individual may on one occasion come up with a narrower, less elaborate interpretation, while under different circumstances he may engage in an expanded, fuller interpretation. This indicates that sometimes certain hearers or readers may spend quite a lot of time on thinking about a given aphorism, extending the initial set of assumptions and seeking further implications, while others will stop at the cognitive effect in which a simultaneous increase in the manifestness of a number of assumptions is reached. This is the poetic effect, referred to above more than once, which is brought about by the aphorism, which – if the recipient feels like it, or is asked to do explain how he understands the mini-text – can be pursued further to yield

---

if the thought of the aphorist is so hard to fathom and is characterized by open-endedness (cf. Stephenson 1980).

33 Cf. Kośka's (1999: 23) remarks about the direction and depth of individual interpretations of Lec's aphorisms that are argued to depend on the recipient's background knowledge.

34 As Wilson and Sperber (1991a: 391) emphasize, there are texts, like sacred texts or prophecies, which some readers might be ready "to devote a lifetime's effort" to interpreting.

a more concrete interpretation. This means that, having access to a great many assumptions that the encyclopaedic entries of the evoked concepts afford may motivate the recipient to engage in exploring them and considering various implications, of varying degrees of strengths, and to accept them as implicatures weakly communicated by a given aphorism.

Secondly, the analysis reveals that the aphorist may induce a rich information state in the audience: by making the interpreter access assumptions attached to a certain concept together with assumptions stored under some other concept or concepts, the author causes the interpreter to activate or compute implications that he may have never digested before, since these concepts may never have been contemplated together. In aphorisms then, words are intricately woven together to create a special cognitive effect which – as emphasized by Kośka (1999: 49) – is not supposed to be precise but comprehensive. As a result, an assemble of implications concerning the world are brought about, some of which may never have been examined before, so they will be genuinely new to the recipient (cf. Wilson 2011).

Thirdly, the relevance-theoretic approach points to the importance of words used by the aphorist: as indicated earlier, it is the concepts encoded by specific words that afford access to assumptions crucial for the interpretation process. It needs to be emphasized here that while many pragmatic theories often take the inferential mechanisms underlying implicature generation for granted, and tend to rely on some default procedures, RT offers a fairly precise account of what is going on. Specifically, RT predicts that the decoded content of a given linguistic stimulus, and in particular the concepts evoked in the course of utterance interpretation, do not just contribute to the explicature recovered, but also constrain the recovery of implicatures (cf. Carston 2002a: 95). Thus the model under discussion offers a full cognitively-motivated account of (strong and weak) implicatures. Another asset is that no special interpretive methods need to be appealed to in order to explain the comprehension of literary texts: the processes is assumed to draw "on the same basic cognitive and communicative abilities [that are] used in ordinary, face-to-face exchanges" (Wilson 2011: 70).

All that has been said above about interpreting aphorisms suggests that it is more appropriate and revealing to think of the aphorist's intention in terms of changing the cognitive environment of the addressee, "that is, their possibilities of thinking" (Wilson 2011:78). This means that rather than intending to make the audience entertain a specific proposition (or a set of these), non-propositional effects are aimed at (Wilson 2011: 78). Strictly speaking then, aphorisms just stir the mind of the audience and communicate impressions.[35] Thus they

---

35 For a relevance-theoretic account of what impressions involve, how they are communicated and what effects they give rise to see Sperber and Wilson (1986/95: 57-59, forthcoming) and Wilson (2011).

exemplify the type of discourse in which, as Sperber and Wilson (forthcoming) convincingly argue, "[t]he communicator need not intend the addressee to make this or that specific inference; her intentions may concern only the general drift of the addressee's inferences and remain quite vague, and so may the addressee's understanding, without this amounting to a failure of comprehension. What is aimed at in such cases of weak communication is a degree of cognitive alignment, not a duplication of precise contents." This seems to me a particularly important and valuable observation, which provides useful insight into how aphorisms work and defines the background against which the interpretation process unfolds.

I hope to have demonstrated that the RT-inspired analysis of how aphorisms are interpreted shows that the relevance-theoretic framework, apart from accounting for more straightforward cases of conveying meanings, affords also an explicit and precise elucidation of the subtler and vaguer aspects of verbal communication.[36] To finish this section on an aphoristic note, since – as Nietzsche observed (in *The Twilight of the Idols*, cited in Morson 2012: 1) – aphorisms "are a form of eternity", by scrutinizing them we have caught a glimpse of the reality that goes beyond down-to-earth communication.

Indeed, this last point, and, even more importantly, the nature of weak communication itself, evidently bring to the fore two problems. One has to do with the question about whether it is fully legitimate to talk about meaning in instances of weak communication. After all, weakly implicated weak implications, which the recipient arrives at partly on his own accord, cannot be treated as genuinely endorsed by the communicator's intention. The other issue has to do with the possible influence of communication on mental processes in general. The two sections that follow will focus on each of these strands.

3.7 Implicit communication: whose meaning is it?

As hinted at earlier (Ch.3.3), in communicative encounters the ultimate responsibility for resolving underdeterminacies, dealing with indeterminacies or settling both if required, lies with the comprehender. RT assumes the existence of a tacit comprehension heuristic, the cornerstone of which is the Communicative Principle of Relevance (see Ch.1.5 and Ch.2.3), which is automatically triggered by ostensive acts directed at the recipient, and which underlies his inferencing geared towards identifying the speaker-intended meaning.

---

36   There is an aspect of the aphorism, namely its wit, which has not been dealt with in the present discussion: it is a vast topic, worthy of an extensive investigation, which lies outside the scope of the present inquiry. For a relevance-theoretic discussion of wit, see Furlong (2011).

The manifest speaker's intentions and the regular search for relevance are postulated to lead to fixing underdeterminacies at the level of explicature (see Ch.2 and Ch.3.4), so speaker meaning is very much in focus. Resolving indeterminacies, though based on exactly the same relevance-guided heuristic, is a little more tricky, as the communicator's intentions, being partly vague, endorse a range of assumptions, some of which she may not even be aware of, let alone back up. So unavoidably, the control over the meaning recovered is, to some extent, handed over to the interpreter. This is an inherent feature of weak communication, as described in some detail above (Ch.3.5) and affects the recovery of both explicit and implicit import.

Thus, as indicated earlier (Ch.2.8 and 3.5), sometimes the indeterminacy of the speaker's intention will affect – but may not have very severe repercussions for – the recovery of explicatures. Generally, in such cases the cognitive effects that the speaker manifestly intends the hearer to recover belong to what is implicitly conveyed. In effect, shallow, good enough interpretations may suffice in recovering what is explicitly conveyed (see Ch.2.8). In other words, given that the major goal of the hearer is invariably "to understand the pragmatic effect that the speaker wishes to communicate" (Gibbs and Colston 2012: 6), when the major intended import is implicitly conveyed, it is enough if the explicature is only shallowly processed to warrant the expected and foreseeable inferential outcomes at the implicit level. Under the circumstances, the intended explicit import that is generated falls under the speaker's manifest intention, even though this intention is partly vague, and as a result, the explicature arrived at inherits this vagueness (see Ch.3.5). But the speaker meaning is not lost sight of.

The problem appears graver for implicit import. In this case, if the manifest speaker's intention is (at least partly) indeterminate, apart from what may be computed as a strong implicature (or implicatures), that is, one (or ones) which will satisfy the hearer's expectations of relevance in a manifestly foreseeable manner (cf. Sperber and Wilson 1990/2012: 89-92; Wilson and Sperber 1992: 73-75), some weak implicatures are also generated. The comprehender is encouraged to recover the latter, because they contribute to arriving at an interpretation that makes the utterance optimally relevant. They are weak, because in this situation "the speaker has not singled out and endorsed any particular assumptions, but has rather encouraged the hearer to explore within the range of activated assumptions. Precisely which ones the hearer does in fact derive as implicatures of the utterance is, in large measure, a matter of his own choice and responsibility" (Carston 2002a: 358). Inevitably, weak interpretations beg the question of whether they can be legitimately called *meaning*, as – under the circumstances – the status of the speaker's intentions underpinning them is dubious. What exactly is the role of speaker's intentions: is it the case that they inherently constrain utterance interpretation, or maybe, they do only in some situations but not in others? And if their capacity to control interpretation is limited, can the meaning recovered under such conditions be legitimately called *speaker meaning*?

The origins of this problem can be traced back to Grice, who is commonly taken to "explain the meaning of an utterance in terms of the intentions of the speaker who uttered it" (Thompson 2008: 284). The cornerstone of Grice's "intention-based semantics", as Schiffer (1982) dubs it, or "intentional theory of communication", as Roberts (2004) refers to it, is the well-known and often quoted Grice's (1969/89) original definition of utterer's (U) meaning, also labelled as meaning$_{nn}$, that is, non-natural meaning:

> "U meant something by uttering x" is true iff, for some audience A, U uttered x intending:
> (1) A to produce a particular response r
> (2) A to think (recognize) that U intends (1)
> (3) A to fulfil (1) on the basis of his fulfillment of (2).
> (…) And to suppose A to produce r *"on the basis of"* his thinking that U intends him to produce r is to suppose that his thinking that U intends his to produce r is at least part of his reason for producing r and not merely his cause of producing r. (Grice's 1969/89: 92)

Non-natural meaning is assumed to be inextricably bound up with the communicator's intention, the recognition of which "exhausts or realizes the intention" (Levinson 1995: 228), so it is a necessary and sufficient requirement for achieving the communicator's goal (Rooy 2004).

The above definition of speaker meaning, in which the utterer's intentionality features[37] as a constitutive aspect of the concept, has given rise to a number of counterexamples, and as a result, there have been attempts at reinterpreting and reformulating it both by Grice (1969/89, 1982/89, 1989) and other researchers (e.g., Neale 1992; Schiffer 1982; Thompson 2008; Wharton 2009),[38] with clause (3)

---

37 Levinson's (1983: 16) rendering of Gricean non-natural meaning, which is as follows:
    S *meant-nn z* by uttering U if and only if:
    (i) S intended U to cause some effect z in recipient H
    (ii) S intended (i) to be achieved simply by H recognizing that intention (i)
    points to two types of intentions that meaning embraces. The first of them (i) is the causal intention and the second (ii) is the reflexive intention, which is fulfilled simply by being recognized (Arundale 2008: 234). These intentions are also thought of as the primary and the secondary intention respectively, to the effect that Gricean speaker meaning can be identified as "including an attempt to communicate that one has this primary intention" (Doerge and Siebel 2008: 56), even though, as emphasized by Doerge and Siebel (2008:56), "Grice himself did not make use of the word 'communication'."

38 For a comprehensive discussion of the counterexamples to the Gricean definition of meaning as presented above and other amendments offered by various philosophers of

proving particularly problematic in situations involving very complex intentions, which unavoidably lead to an infinite regress (Origgi and Sperber 2000: 157).

But controversies over the Gricean approach to speaker meaning extend beyond problems with the formal definition. While it is widely recognized that Grice's idea of meaning as inherently involving intention attribution was a turning point in modern studies of verbal behaviour, not all researchers in the field are ready to read Grice in this way. Some, like Saul (2002), reject the approach to utterance comprehension as necessarily involving considerations of speaker's intentions, treating it as a major departure from Gricean thinking.

In an interesting paper devoted mainly to implicitly conveyed import, Saul (2002) strongly criticizes conceptions of implicature constrained by speaker's intentions and argues that they distort Grice's original model. Saul (2002: 230) maintains that speaker meaning and conversational implicature, as conceived of by Grice, belong to two distinct realms of the communicative space: while speaker meaning is cast "completely in terms of speaker intentions", conversational implicatures are "entirely removed from the control (or possibly even awareness) of speakers."

A point of departure for Saul's (2002) argument is the claim that utterance meaning may go beyond what is said and what is implicated. In other words, Saul contends that, to use relevance-theoretic terms, identifying the explicatures and implicatures of a given utterance may not exhaust the meaning that is conveyed by the speaker. In an effort to substantiate this claim, she refers to a situation of an unsuccessful attempt to implicate something. In her example, a tutor who is writing a testimonial for one of her students, Fred, who happens to be a poor philosopher and a petty thief, praises Fred's typing skills, which he undeniably has. The tutor hopes to be communicating that Fred should not be offered a job as a philosopher, but she fails to do so, since actually Fred is applying for a job of a typist, which the tutor is totally unaware of. The readers of the testimonial take it to mean exactly what is said, as the information about Fred's typing skills is precisely the kind of information they are looking for. Following Grice's (1969/89: 86) rather informal characterization of conversational implicature,[39] in

---

language and pragmaticists in order to save the Gricean model of speaker meaning, see Thompson (2008; cf. also remarks by Sperber and Wilson forthcoming).

39   A fuller explication of how Grice (1975/89: 30-1) approaches implicature is the following: "A man who, by (in, when) saying (or making as if to say) that p has *implicated* that q, may be said to have *conversationally implicated* that q, provided that: (1) he is to be presumed to be observing the conversational maxims, or at least the Cooperative Principle; (2) the supposition that he is aware that, or thinks that, *q* is required in order to make his saying or making as if to say p (or doing so in *those* terms) consistent with this presumption; and (3) the speaker thinks (and would expect the hearer to think that the speaker thinks) that it is

accordance with which "what is implicated is what it is required that one assume a speaker to think in order to preserve the assumption that he is following the Cooperative Principle (and perhaps some conversational maxims as well), if not at the level of what is said, at least at the level of what is implicated", Saul regards this as the case of speaker meaning that fails to be implicated. Since no breach in Gricean cooperativeness is detected, the recipients will not have a chance to see that something more needs to be read into the letter in order to assume that the communicator is fully cooperative. The failure of the implicature to go through in such communicative contexts makes Saul (2002: 230) conclude that there are cases of the speaker meaning something "which she neither says nor implicates", therefore "what a speaker means cannot be divided exhaustively into what she says and what she implicates."

Saul makes no reference here to miscommunication, which seems to have taken place, and which RT can easily explain. In the first place, there is an obvious mismatch in the relevance aimed at by the speaker, or rather writer, and the relevance expected by the addressees. The tutor intends the relevance of what she has written to be evaluated by the audience anticipating information concerning the candidate's philosophical abilities, whereas in reality the addressees are interested in the information about the candidate's typing skills. As a result, the context envisaged by the communicator as most accessible to the addressees is completely different from the context that is most accessible to and actually accessed by them. Hence, a range of implications about the irrelevance of somebody's excellence at typing for being a good philosopher that the tutor intends to covey, fails to become manifest to the addressees not concerned in the least with Fred's academic potential. In fact, the message achieves what Sperber (1994a) and Wilson (2000, 2005) call accidental relevance, since "the first interpretation the hearer finds relevant enough is not the intended one" (Wilson 2005: 1142),[40]

---

within the competence of the hearer to work out, or grasp intuitively, that the supposition mentioned in (2) is required" (emphasis mine). The introductory sentence in this definition indicates that what is conversationally implicated is taken by Grice to be a special instance of a more general case of implicating, where the term *implicate* is synonymous with "imply, suggest or mean" (Grice 1975/89: 24). As Grice himself states in his discussion the famous bank-employee example, the hearer "might well inquire, what B was implying, what he was suggesting, or even what he meant by saying that C has not yet been to prison." This makes it clear that implicature for Grice falls within the speaker-intended meaning, and as such, it is taken to be bound by the speaker's intentions. Attending in her paper to the three conditions characterizing implicature, Saul (2002: 231) views condition (2) as opening "the gap between speaker meaning and implicature" to be filled in by meaning which is neither said nor implicated (in Gricean terminology).

40   The recipient's awareness of that the first interpretation that achieves optimal relevance cannot be the one intended by the speaker will lead the former to abandon this interpretation

of which both the communicator and the addressee remain completely unaware, therefore miscommunication results. The problem is that what is taken by the audience to be the manifest speaker intention is completely at odds with her true intention but neither party is aware of this and the communicator's intention to convey information about the inadequacy of Fred as a philosopher is not mutually manifest.

As indicated above, misunderstandings which may pass unnoticed have to do with the fact that the range of contextual effects as predicted by the communicator is completely different from those actually recovered by the recipient, whose interpretation achieves a satisfying level of relevance in the fashion unexpected by the communicator. If there is no follow-up that would reveal the discrepancy, the misunderstanding will be undetected.

It seems a bit odd to postulate a category of meaning that is rooted in misunderstanding and Saul's category of speaker meaning which is communicated neither explicitly nor implicated is not very appealing. Unfortunately, the same can be said about her notions of audience-implicatures and unmeant conversational implicatures.

Audience-implicatures are supposed to be implicatures over which only the recipient has authority, so they are postulated as not falling under the communicator's intentions. To illustrate this type, Saul reverses the situation presented in the previous example. Writing a testimonial for an excellent student of philosophy, Felix, for a change, the tutor mistakenly believes that he is applying for a typist job. So she writes a letter full of praise for the student's typing skills, describing also other virtues that are invaluable for an office employee. The philosophy appointments board understands the referee to be implicating that Felix is an incompetent philosopher. A mismatch between the intended and the actual context is obvious here, as is the fact that the interpretation recovered by the addressees results from their search for cognitive effects of a completely different kind from those predicted by the communicator. Again, the differences in what the communicator and the interpreter envisage as relevant, and accidental relevance that the message achieves upset the communicative exchange. So this is just

---

in favour of a different one likely to fall within the manifest speaker's intention, which would prevent a communication breakdown. In the example under scrutiny, the manifest communicator's intention appears to endorse the first relevant interpretation. She inadvertently makes this intention manifest, since she is unaware that she is writing a reference for a typist job and not a philosopher's post. The intention that her act of ostension makes manifest, identified as such by the addressees pursuing a path of least effort in interpreting the meaning conveyed, happens to considerably diverge from her genuine intention, but, as RT rightly predicts and plausibly explains, this cannot be recognized by the audience.

another case of communication failure, which as relevance theory predicts, results from a mismatch in the speaker-expected and the actual audience-relevance that the message attains. The implicature is derived in the typical relevance-oriented interpretation process and no special mechanisms or phenomena can be identified. Again, audience-implicatures – as originating in misunderstandings – arouse suspicion. As do unmeant conversational implicatures.

The class of unmeant conversational implicatures seems a little bit paradoxical in the context of the prior (even if debatable) claims of the researcher that, in Gricean terms, implicatures should not be viewed as controlled by speaker intentions, so in Saul's interpretation, they all may be unmeant anyway. This inconsequence aside, it seems that the kind of argument that Saul advances is not very convincing. Unmeant conversational implicatures are supposed to be those which, even though the conditions for them to go through are apparently met, are not intended by the communicator. Saul (2002: 237-238) illustrates this kind of implicature with an example of a tutor who likes her student, Roland, and wishes him well, but knows that he is a poor philosopher. As a responsible scholar, she cannot write an enthusiastic letter of reference for Roland, so she writes a very long letter, full of detail about the classes Roland took and the assignments he completed, without evaluating Roland's performance in any way. This reference is intended to boost (rather than reduce) his chances of getting a philosopher's position and, at the same time, to be a truthful testimonial. The tutor believes that, pressed for time, the committee will not give the letter enough attention to figure out that what is stated implies that Roland is a poor philosopher, and instead, impressed by the length and amount of information included in the letter, his application for the job will be successful. Saul (2002: 238) concludes that under the circumstances the communicator does not mean what is implicated.

Saul makes no reference to it, but the intention of the tutor that the audience should not work out the implicature remains hidden, whereas what the testimonial (as a piece of ostensive behaviour) makes manifest is the very implicature that she hopes the audience will not compute. In fact, they will not get the implicature only if they do not process what is written in a way required to understand the message, so on condition that – to use terminology of the code-model of communication – some noise in the channel occurs and prevents adequate interpreting. A notion of unmeant conversational implicature, if not a blatant contradiction in terms (at least in accordance with mainstream Gricean, neo-Gricean and post-Gricean programmes), gives the impression of being far-fetched.

Saul's (2002) new categories of implicature, bred on various mismatches of intended and attributable (and/or actually attributed) or concealed intentions, can hardly be accepted without reservation and may lead to scepticism over the very nature of implicatures. To be sure, "[o]ften, intentional communication involves a degree of manipulation and concealment" (Wilson 1994: 35), but it is not entirely obvious that the best way to deal with these aspects of communication is by treating them as conversational implicatures. In order to accommodate Saul's implicatures, a widely accepted and useful conceptualization of the notion involving the underlying speaker intentions, which is commonly taken to be in line with Gricean account, would have to be abandoned in favour of some new definition.

More importantly for my current purposes, Saul's conversational implicatures are incompatible with ostensive-inferential communication that RT is designed to model. However, Saul's arguments are important because they powerfully demonstrate that the ability to attribute mental states to others and recognize them correctly lies at the heart of meaning and communication[41] (pace Arundale 2008). Moreover, Saul's ideas make it evident that an explanatory pragmatic model necessarily needs to illuminate the relationship between meaning and communication, and without it, confusion results as to what can be legitimately postulated as communicated and/or meant.

As Wilson and Sperber (1993) observed long ago, not all assumptions that an utterance makes manifest are ostensively communicated: for instance, some may be accidentally transmitted and some may be part of different types of covert communication.[42] As stated earlier, RT is concerned with overt intentional communication, which the originators of the theory call ostensive-inferential or ostensive in short (see Ch.1), that is, the type of communication which involves both getting the content intended "to be picked up" as well as the information that this content is intentionally "pointed out" (Sperber and Wilson 1986/95: 50). As Sperber and Wilson (1986/95: 53) argue, ostension ranges over a continuum of cases "from 'showing', where strong direct evidence for the basic layer of information is provided, to 'saying that', where all the evidence is indirect." This means that on this approach communication covers not only cases in which all the evidence for the intended content comes indirectly from what the communicator's behaviour reveals about her intention (which Grice refers to as meaning$_{nn}$, as denoted by his definition cited above, and commonly identified as speaker

---

41 Assumptions of this kind seem a common denominator for neo-Gricean and post-Gricean pragmatic analyses. Frequently recognized as belonging to the latter camp, Sperber and Wilson (2002; Wilson and Sperber 2004; Wilson 2005) explicitly argue that predicting and manipulating mental states of others is crucial for ostensive-inferential communication and it is possible because of the underlying human cognitive "tendency to maximize relevance" (Wilson and Sperber 2004: 610).

42 All kinds of covert communication just "fall short of fully overt and mutually apparent nature typical of verbal utterances" (Carston 2000: 90). For relevance-inspired comments on various aspects of covert communication phenomena, see *inter alia* Crook (2004), Durán Martínez (2005), Pop (2007), Tanaka (1992, 1994) and Wharton (2009).

meaning), but also cases of providing direct evidence for what the communicator wants to communicate, with different degrees of meaning and showing in between the two poles (Sperber and Wilson forthcoming).

To make the picture more complex, but truer to fact, meaning itself is a matter of degree. As argued above (see Ch.3.4-3.5), the underlying indeterminacy of the communicator's intention may produce a communicative outcome with no fully determinate meaning for the recipient to retrieve: under the circumstances, the latter will be partly responsible for what is recovered. The important thing is that the weakly communicated assumptions, strictly speaking unendorsed by the communicator's intentions as a specific, enumerable set, are taken to come as an *intended* (and foreseeable) part of the overall interpretation on the relevance-theoretic approach. The point is that the manifest (and at least to some extent) indeterminate speaker's intention encourages the interpreter to generate some such assumptions, as without these additional cognitive effects, the expected (and manifestly anticipated) level of relevance could not be reached. Thus RT shows that indeterminate speaker's intentions invariably constrain interpretation. It also explains in an explicit way these rather more complex and definitely less obvious communicative effects.

To recapitulate, RT assumes that the single tacit relevance-guided comprehension procedure is followed by the addressee in recovering both fully determinate, strong meanings, as well as partly indeterminate, weak meanings. Importantly, the framework predicts what kind of meaning a given recipient is likely to arrive at in the latter situation: constrained by the manifest communicator's intentions, the interpreter will access most accessible assumptions made manifest to him by the utterance that will satisfy his current expectations of relevance. In this way, RT accounts for both comprehension processes which return a fully determinate, single interpretation as well as those in which the interpretation cannot be fully determined, and because of the element of indeterminacy involved, the interpreter is merely constrained to "the intended *line* of interpretation" (Wilson 1994: 40; original emphasis). As a result, it is predicted that in understanding utterances that carry poetic effects, there will be differences in the interpretations generated by different interpreters, because of the different assumptions stored in each individual's encyclopaedic entries of the concepts recovered. However, as in all instances of processing of ostensive inputs, even in weaker types of communication, the recipient's goal is to construct "an interpretation that is relevant in the *expected* way" (Wilson 2014: 9; my emphasis). This suggests that even in the case of weak communication, the speaker's intention underlies and licenses the overall interpretation, and the inferential path followed by the comprehender, while not necessarily spotlit, is at least (even though sometimes dimly) floodlit by the communicator.

Sperber and Wilson (forthcoming) convincingly argue that the strong-weak communication continuum runs orthogonal to the showing-meaning continuum. So, as stated above more than once, apart from fully determinate meanings (e.g., "The train to Warsaw leaves from platform 5 at 16.25" announced at the train station), speakers may convey semi-determinate meanings (illustrated by the authors by the hyperbolic "I could kill for a glass of water"), for which a range of intended conclusions is not that difficult to identify, or indeterminate meanings (as conveyed by the metaphoric "Juliet is the sun"). Communicators may sometimes convey determinate meanings and at the same time show what they mean (which happens, as Sperber and Wilson indicate, e.g., when, in answer to the query who is the tallest learner in class, the teacher says "He is", pointing to the relevant person), or resort to determinate showing (when I show you a bottle of coke, in answer to the question about what I bought at the airport kiosk), or indeterminate showing (which happens when somebody is showing pictures of their children to a visitor, as Sperber and Wilson exemplify), where there is no paraphrasable content. There are also other possible categories involving various degrees of meaning and showing, which Sperber and Wilson (forthcoming) briefly discuss as well.

By showing how the determinate-indeterminate meaning and the meaning-showing[43] dimensions cross-cut each other, forming fuzzy hybrid categories, Sperber and Wilson (forthcoming) provide a brilliant and profound insight into different aspects and shades of communication. By doing that, they draw a map of a diverse and uneven communication terrain and show that the original Gricean conception of meaning (as presented above) is not fully adequate to elucidate a full spectrum of relevant cases.

With its scope reaching over strong as well as weak communication and determinate as well as indeterminate meaning and showing, the relevance-theoretic approach appears to help untie a number of tangled knots. Furthermore, it indicates that ostensive communication, even of the weakest kind, conveys (one way or another) the *speaker* meaning which the hearer seeks to recover. Communication is assumed to be successful not when (hardly attainable) thought duplication takes place (Sperber and Wilson 1986/95: 193; cf. also Blakemore 2010: 579; Carston 2002a: 47; Wharton 2001: 145), but when the addressee's state of mind is changed in the way intended by the communicator (Sperber and Wilson forthcoming). So the answer to the question asked in the title of this section, i.e. whose meaning it is, is that it is invariably speaker meaning, even without her full control over the overall interpretation. But it is also the recipient's thinking and this is the issue I would like to pass on to.

---

43 As recently emphasized by Sperber et al. (2010: 367), a clear-cut distinction between meaning and showing is completely otiose.

3.8 From communication to parallel (though diverse) thinking

One of the important ideas that Sperber and Wilson (1986/95, forthcoming) have espoused for almost three decades now is that even though communication may be vague, both as far as the presented ostensive input and generated output are concerned, this does not undermine its success. The point is that, in a broader perspective, the goal that communicators pursue should be thought of as effecting changes in the cognitive environment of the addressee (Sperber and Wilson 1986/9: 46, forthcoming), that is, "in the set of facts that are manifest to him" (Sperber and Wilson 1986/9: 39). As hinted at above, successful communication is postulated to lead to enlarging the mutual cognitive environments of the participants, that is, the set of assumptions which are mutually manifest to the interactants.

This is true of strong and weak communication alike, but is especially significant in the case of the latter. The results of weak communication in general, and in particular of poetic effects it may be used to create, can probably be best explained in terms of producing a certain scope of "cognitive alignment" between the communicator and the recipient (Sperber and Wilson forthcoming). If cognitive alignment is achieved, a change in manifestness of an array of assumptions occurs, which transpires as a communicative effect intended by the speaker and becomes the main recognizable outcome of communication. This is precisely what it was like in the case of aphorisms. As the above analysis of aphorisms hopefully showed (Ch. 3.6), all the aphorist can hope for is to make a range of implications manifest or more manifest to the audience, inciting "hearers or readers to search (...) for interpretations most relevant to them" (Sperber 1985: 53). This means that the author is chiefly concerned with sharing with the hearer or reader a mental experience of exploring a certain cognitive zone by drawing a number of implications which become accessible via concepts activated due to processing some carefully crafted language input.

More generally, RT predicts that the communicator who wants to convey a whole array of assumptions but cannot and does not anticipate that she will achieve a predetermined and clearly identifiable range of cognitive effects will often just aim at "steer[ing] the thoughts of the audience in a certain direction" (Sperber and Wilson 1986/95: 60). To put it simply, rational speakers[44] whose manifest intentions remain party vague in acts of ostension cannot expect to attain more but

---

44 One of the important contributions of Grice to the study of verbal exchanges was drawing researchers' attention to the fact that interactants behave as rational agents and "conversation is a rational cooperative activity" (Sperber and Wilson 2005: 355), so there are certain standards that govern the use of language in such exchanges and they are exploited by speakers and provide guidelines for hearers.

to launch the interpreter on a certain inferential path and this really seems quite a lot and enough for the current communicative purposes they want to accomplish.

This brings us directly to some hypotheses about how thoughts are affected by communication, which the relevance-theoretic account affords. As Sperber and Wilson (1998: 190) contend, "inferential communication involves a communicator ostensively engaging in some behaviour (e.g. a piece of miming or the production of a coded signal) likely to activate in the addressee (via recognition or decoding) some specific conceptual structure or idea." This conceptual structure or idea triggers inferencing, which ultimately leads to the recovery of a set of assumptions that will make the ostensive act optimally relevant to the addressee in a way that the communicator may manifestly have foreseen. Since an assumption "is a structured set of concepts" (Sperber and Wilson 1986/95: 85), each concept in the assumptions recovered as explicitly and/or implicitly communicated import provides access to further assumptions representing encyclopaedic knowledge stored under a given conceptual address (cf. 3.6 above). In this way different assumptions stored under the concepts accessed in the process of utterance interpretation can give rise to various implications that the individual can draw,[45] with idiosyncrasy being the hallmark of the flow and content of what is *brought to mind* (cf. Wilson 2007). A snowballing effect is implicit in the mental process which is being described: the assumptions recovered as a result of utterance interpretation evoke concepts, which in turn enable access to further assumptions composed of some other concepts, with various possibilities of cross-referencing facilitated in this was. Nevertheless, this kind of effect is a mere potentiality, since on-line mental processes are conditioned by a great number of factors of different kinds. Which implications will actually be formed, how many of them will emerge, whether any of them will actually surface and what direction the train of thought initiated as a result of utterance interpretation will take, depends on a range of conditions. The most decisive ones among them appear to embrace: an individual's current short-term cognitive goals, the saliency of specific bits of encyclopaedic knowledge (which is related to the co-presence of some other concepts in on-line processing) at a given point, other stimuli coming in from the environment and their relevance, the person's earlier thoughts, his or her physical and psychological state, etc.

This suggests that while it cannot be exactly predicted how the line of thought will actually develop, RT makes it possible to identify some general guiding principles and factors that affect thinking patterns at a certain point, and to delineate underlying schemes of thought sequences potentially open to an individual who has just processed a certain verbal input. The crux of the matter is that if

---

45 Recall that all kinds of stimuli available to an individual at a given moment can give rise to various kinds of implications (see Ch. 3.3).

communication is approached as ultimately geared to achieving a certain level of cognitive alignment between the communicator and the addressee (Sperber and Wilson forthcoming), as hinted at above, on processing the ostensive input the latter will be in a certain state of mind initiated by the former, and probably ready to explore further the set of assumptions that have been made accessible. A mental state intentionally activated through communication may then become direct food for thought.

It is worth pointing out at this juncture that cognitive alignment accomplished through successful communication has significant social consequences, since, as underscored by Sperber and Wilson (1986/95: 61-62), "[a] change in the mutual cognitive environment of two people is a change in their possibilities of interaction (and, in particular, in their possibilities of further communication)."

While there is nothing surprising about the idea that communication influences thinking (Bloom and Keil 2001: 364), the conceptual apparatus of RT highlights and elucidates the intersubjectivity involved, showing how ostensive stimuli in general, and language in particular, contribute to bringing about certain mental states in others.

3.9 Concluding remarks

In RT the division into explicit-implicit import does not tally with decoded vs. inferred communicated content, and a subtler though intuitively more plausible demarcation line is drawn, which takes into account the nature of the processes involved: decoding together with inferencing is taken to underlie the recovery of explicatures while only inferencing is employed in the case of implicatures. With just two categories of implicatures distinguished, that is, implicated premises and implicated conclusions, the model offers a parsimonious taxonomy of implicit import, however, this is the only distinction that appears externally motivated, as it reflects two natural sets among implications brought to bear in the interpretation process. All other classifications that are proposed in the literature appear to be important for theory-building purposes rather than for shedding light on the psycholinguistic processes that are going on.

Like explicatures, implicatures are approached in the relevance-theoretic framework as a species of speaker meaning, so they are treated as falling under the speaker's intentions. However, speaker's intentions, as RT acknowledges, may be more or less determinate, and the notion of weak communication, unique to this pragmatic model, provides an important theoretic construct to explore how less determinate meanings, which are often aimed at by communicators, may be actually recovered. The full spectrum of strong and weak communication phenomena, sometimes underlain by determinate and on other occasions by (partly) indeterminate speaker's intentions, as well as acts of showing and meaning that ostensive communication may involve, are all embraced by and accounted for within the relevance-theoretic model. So the model under scrutiny, on the one hand, supplies a systematic and principled pragmatic procedure for calculating implicatures and, on the other, predicts and accounts for indeterminacy inevitably involved in the recovery of what is communicated implicitly. Thus it fully meets the postulate that an adequate pragmatic model "has to avoid specifying any implicature as fully determinate, yet has to capture the relative certainty and reliability with which most implicatures are inferred, as well as the basis for variations in how close versus open-ended, certain versus uncertain, they are" (Cooren and Sanders 2002: 1046).

As I was trying to show in the present chapter, one of the clear and unprecedented advantages of RT seems to be that it penetrates these rarely explored expanses of communication, and provides a relatively detailed and precise account of complex, subtle and vague aspects of human interactions. Furthermore, it shows that weak communication is by no means a less preferred kind; on the contrary, its effects may be richer and more satisfying, in that more meaning can be conveyed by saying less: "minus dicimus et plus significamus", as is emphasized by Horn (2005: 191). This kind of efficiency, culminating in what Sperber and Wilson refer to as poetic effects, may suggest that weak communication, even if yielding less precise interpretations, is a cognitively more stimulating and rewarding undertaking, inviting the addressee to be an active participant in the comprehension process, not just a receptacle which takes meanings in.

Chapter 4
Relevance and the miracle of communication

4.1 Introduction

It is absolutely phenomenal that humans process linguistic signals extremely fast, practically effortlessly and, as we tend to strongly believe, successfully, at least most of the time. This might be taken as a truism, except that there has been some serious debate revolving around this alleged miracle of communication. The perennial question: how do we manage to communicate, appears to be waiting for an exhaustive and precise answer which would take into account the (enormous) complexity and (at least partial) unpredictability of the enterprise.

My aim in this chapter is to argue that RT provides a gripping albeit coarse-grained answer to this fundamental and pertinent question. Thus, while not pretending to be solving all the problems and spelling out all the detail, the relevance-theoretic venture in this respect is definitely an interesting, plausible and worthwhile proposal. It is probably the best one we can hope to come up with right now. It might be that, considering the largely subpersonal nature of the explanations involved (see Ch.4.7), there is a limit to how far they can be penetrated, so a fully-fledged and complete answer – at least of the type we are seeking to get in accordance with the present pragmatic agenda – may be beyond reach altogether. But let us not give in to undue pessimism before the problem has been adequately framed.

This chapter begins with the idea that, contrary to prevailing beliefs, RT represents radical pragmaticism rather than radical contextualism, since its fundamental programmatic motivations and theoretical biases are principally pragmatic (Ch.4.2). So the relevance-theoretic foundation and perspective are first and foremost cognitive and pragmatic, even if context-sensitivity remains a pivotal factor in the comprehension model advanced by RT. This means that speaker-intended occasion-specific meanings are identified on this approach as the target of utterance processing. And this is what makes the model *prima facie* vulnerable to the miracle of communication argument as mounted by Cappelen and Lepore (2005), which is focussed on in section 4.3. Even though Cappelen and Lepore's conception of Insensitive Semantics seems not to have endured the heavy storm of criticism it provoked, the miracle of communication argument they have brought to light can hardly be obliterated, as it is related to the principal question about how all the immensely complex and open-texture processes underpinning verbal communication can proceed so fast and effectively. As hinted at above, the relevance-theoretic answer to the Master Question helps, at least to some extent, to come to grips with the knotty problem. Before a relevance-theoretic solution can be presented, some stage setting is required, so first the issue of reasoning processes vis-à-vis the hypothesized modular composition of the mind will be briefly discussed (Ch.4.4). Ostensive-inferential communication depends on mind-reading abilities, which are focused on next (Ch.4.5). This will lead on to the characterization of the comprehension module, as postulated in the relevance-theoretic framework. Its characteristics and workings, it will be argued, are directly relevant to answering the Master Question (Ch. 4.6). As will be shown next (Ch.4.7), the subpersonal nature of some of the processes underlying communication may be one of the important reasons for which communication eludes fully-fledged explanation. The contextual cognitive fix mechanism, introduced earlier (Ch.2.6) as an innovation in the relevance-theoretic procedure of generating explicatures, seems to account better for communicative efficiency than free enrichment, which the former mechanism is postulated to replace, as will be emphasized in section 4.8. The chapter ends with concluding remarks.

4.2 RT, contextualism and pragmaticism

As argued in chapter 1, RT is par excellence a cognitive model of communication: its theoretical tenets and conceptual tools are set against a broad frame of reference of human cognition. Even more importantly, its central claims and assumptions concerning human overt intentional communication stem from certain pivotal observations and empirical evidence about how cognition works and they substantiate the modular outlook of the human mind by corroborating its key hypotheses about the human mental architecture (see Ch.1.3).

In the relevance-theoretic framework, pragmatics is approached as "a capacity of the mind" (Carston 2002b: 128), that is, a special system which takes as input ostensive stimuli produced by communicators and returns as output their interpretations in the form of occasion-specific communicator-intended meanings. These meanings, underwritten by the mutually manifest communicator's intentions, are arrived at by the interpreter seeking a fair return of cognitive effects for the effort required to process the input in the way that will make it optimally relevant. This happens, as RT posits, thanks to a tacit comprehension heuristic, rooted in the Communicative Principle of Relevance and a presumption of optimal relevance as its corollary, which entitles the addressee to follow a path of least effort to compute the manifestly foreseeable and intended cognitive effects and to stop processing as soon as the recipient's expectations of relevance are satisfied (see Ch.1.5 and Ch.2.3).

Defining optimal relevance in terms of the intended (by the communicator) and expected (by the recipient) cognitive effects balanced against the cognitive effort necessarily expended (by the recipient) in achieving them reinforces the idea that this model of pragmatics is inherently cognitive. Crucially, as Carston (2002b) underscores, there is a single pragmatic system postulated in the relevance-theoretic framework: as explicitly discussed in the above-presented accounts (Ch.2 and Ch.3) of how explicit and implicit import is taken to be generated and as shown in all the analyses in the preceding chapters, there is one pragmatic strategy responsible for settling different aspects of communicated meaning.[1] In this way RT is a genuinely unitary pragmatic model, with a broad scope of application over a range of different phenomena.[2]

As argued in chapters 2 and 3 above, in contrast to other pragmatic models, RT assumes that utterance comprehension is inferential through and through. Thus, not just the generation of implicatures, as is universally assumed, but also the recovery of content that is explicitly communicated is posited to rely heavily on inferencing (see Ch. 2). Furthermore, the meanings generated by the relevance-theoretic comprehension heuristic are all speaker-intended context-sensitive meanings. This results from the fact that in his processing of a certain verbal input, the hearer is by definition interested in arriving at the speaker-intended meaning, which tends to be highly context-dependent (cf. Sperber

---

1 As argued by Carston (2002b: 141-142), this is one of the three most common approaches to how many pragmatic systems it might be useful to postulate. The other two involve:

   (a) a multi-system pragmatics, with a distinct pragmatic scheme for each of the specific pragmatic tasks to be performed, such as resolving ambiguities, setting values for indexicals, ascribing a relevant propositional attitude to a given utterance, etc.; and

   (b) a dual system, with processes underlying the generation of explicatures treated as separate from (and often conceived of as chronologically prior to) those responsible for computing implicatures.

   Approach (a) is, for instance, employed for the purposes of AI analysis (cf. Kasher 1991a, 1991b, as cited in Carston 2002b), while (b) is favoured, among others, by Levinson (2000) and Recanati (2002a, 2004). Carston (2002b) presents a thorough critique of Recanati's view in this respect.

2 As remarked earlier, RT has been successfully applied to investigating an extraordinary range of very diverse areas, going well beyond proper verbal and non-verbal communication phenomena and extending to translation studies (see, e.g., Díaz-Pérez 2014; Gutt 1991, 1998), first language acquisition (e.g., Ryder and Leinonen 2003; Wałaszewska 2011) and second language acquisition research (e.g., Foster-Cohen 2004; Ifantidou 2013, 2014; Jodłowiec 2010; Liszka 2004; Niżegorodcew 2004, 2007; Paiva and Foster-Cohen 2004).

2000: 122). This noticeable feature underlying the relevance-theoretic utterance comprehension process has led a number of researchers (e.g., Bianchi 2011; Borg 2010; Cappelen and Lepore 2005) to classify RT as belonging to the so-called radical contextualist faction (Carston 2010c: 265). However, as Carston (2010c) rightly points out, its contextualist slant follows from the primary aims of RT, designed as a model of verbal and non-verbal ostensive communication. The point is that even though context-sensitive meanings are inevitably returned as a result of the processing of ostensive stimuli, context-sensitivity is not one of the motivations or theoretical tenets of the model, so, in other words, it is not one of its programmatic assumptions. As Carston (2010c: 264) puts it, the relevance-theoretic pragmatic processing is "motivated by the aim of providing an account of how it is that speakers can succeed in communicating contents that diverge in a range of ways from the meaning encoded in the linguistic expressions they employ." Therefore the typical contextualistic context shift arguments and incompleteness arguments,[3] while supported by relevance-theoretic analyses, naturally follow from rather than provide the basis for RT.

According to Carston (2010c: 266), instead of supporting a claim about massive context-sensitivity of linguistic expressions as used in communicative contexts, relevance theorists would consider it more adequate to talk about pervasive "'*pragmatic susceptibility*' (or perhaps 'pragmatic amenability')" (original italics). So while, without doubt, there exist a range of genuinely context-sensitive words and expressions (e.g., personal pronouns, demonstratives, adjectives like *actual* and *present*, common nouns like *enemy*, *foreigner*, etc.; see Cappelen and Lepore 2005: 1 for their Basic Set list), most content words should not be treated as context-sensitive, but rather as language forms whose meaning gets pragmatically adjusted for the purposes of realizing a concrete speaker-intention and conveying occasion-specific meaning. As Carston (2010c: 266) argues,

> virtually every linguistic element can be used by us to express/communicate meaning that departs in certain ways from the meaning that it encodes (its expression type meaning) and this is because of our pragmatic interpretive capacities (which include

---

3   In accordance with the context shift argument, it is assumed that a theory of meaning should account for the fact that the meanings of linguistic expressions, or to be more exact "semantic features of utterances containing" them (Pagin and Pelletier 2007: 31), change across contexts in which they are used. The incompleteness argument in turn, adduced by contextualists, suggests that, roughly, since sentences uttered by speakers express semantically incomplete propositions, the context must complete them somehow to turn them into truth-evaluable fully-fledged propositions (Pagin and Pelletier 2007: 34). Observe that in view of the arguments advanced in Ch.2 above, a relevance-theoretic comprehension process may not always lead to the recovery of a complete proposition, which indicates a divergence between mainstream contextualistic and relevance-theoretic thinking.

an acute sensitivity to relevant contextual factors). Linguistic expressions are tools with certain inherent properties (phonological, syntactic and semantic) that we, as normally functioning adult humans, can employ very flexibly for our communicative purposes by virtue of certain characteristics of our psychological makeup (specifically, our 'theory of mind' capacities, and, in particular, our attunement to each other's communicative intentions and our expectations of each other as rational speakers and hearers). Thus, while there is a limited degree of context-sensitivity built into linguistic systems, pragmatic susceptibility is a pervasive feature of language as employed by us in ostensive communication.

All this leads her to conclude that it is more appropriate to think of RT as adhering to radical pragmaticism rather than radical contextualism. I think this is perfectly justifiable not only in view of the fact that RT primarily attempts to explain how "rational communicating/interpreting agents" exploit language resources to accomplish their respective goals, as emphasized by Carston (2010c: 266), but also because of its heavy reliance on inferential processes and their non-demonstrative nature (see Ch.1). Additionally, it seems important to highlight that, on this approach, context itself does not have a power to determine meaning:[4] in the first place, context emerges in utterance processing as a set of assumptions that, can interact with the incoming information to secure that the utterance achieves predictable and satisfying level of relevance. This suggests that the manifest speaker's intentions contribute to what is chosen by the hearer as the context in which the utterance is being processed. It is then intentionality, and not context, that comes out as a mover and shaker behind utterance production and comprehension. Consequently, the pragmatic focus on the speaker's intentions appears overriding. For these reasons, it is fitting to think of RT as taking a radically pragmaticist rather than a radically contextualist turn on the speaker-intended meaning.

Even though there are thus perfectly good reasons to abandon the idea that RT be placed with radical contextualists,[5] it should not be forgotten that occasion-specific speaker-intended meanings are its principal focus. Inescapably then, the miracle of communication argument mounted mainly against radical contextualism, but essentially targeting a multitude of assumptions that are taken to have impact on utterance comprehension, cannot be conveniently swept under the carpet and needs to be given due consideration.

---

4   This is different on Recanati's (2004: 17) approach, in which primary pragmatic processes, "involved in the determination of what is said", are taken to be context-driven, unreflective and non-inferential (cf. also Carston 2010c: 266-267). See Carston (2007) for a critique of Recanati's non-inferential pragmatic processes.

5   Searle (1978/79, 1983) and Travis (1985, 1996, in Pagin and Pelletier 2007: 29) can be mentioned as true representatives of radical contextualism (Pagin and Pelletier 2007).

4.3 The miracle of communication argument

In their trenchant and, what the authors surely think of as, devastating critique of contextualism, in three successive chapters of their book *Insensitive Semantics*, Cappelen and Lepore (2005) advance three types of argument against the contextualist approach. The authors' main goal is to argue that due to severe inadequacy, imperfection and implausibility of both moderate and radical contextualism, their own model of "Semantic Minimalism is the only game in town at the end of the day" (2005: 151).

To this end, Cappelen and Lepore (2005: Ch.7) first strive to demonstrate how the rival approaches are empirically flawed, since they fail a number of context sensitivity tests that the authors devise. As Bezuidenhout (2006) and Reimer (2009) show, Cappelen and Lepore's tests when applied to a relevant set of data can be interpreted rather differently, and in effect, they do not undermine a contextualist construal the way that the creators of Insensitive Semantics want them to.

The second serious objection lodged by Cappelen and Lepore (2005: Ch. 8) is related to the amount of information that is posited to be brought to bear on utterance interpretation. Their charge is that contextualism puts impossible demands on interactants, which renders it psychologically unrealistic if not utterly absurd. This argumentation will be the bulk of the discussion in what follows, so more on that below.

The authors try to put the final nail in the contextualist coffin by allegedly exposing its internal inconsistency (Cappelen and Lepore 2005: Ch.9). The basic idea is that contextualism leads to contradictions, because the way contextualists apply different terms in their analyses appears to defeat the assumed context-sensitivity of the terms used.[6] As Bezuidenhout's (2006: 9) brief remarks make it clear, and as Travis's (2006: 46-47) apposite retort to the incoherence argument deployed by Cappelen and Lepore highlights, there is no contradiction of the type that the critics impute to contextualism.[7]

As hinted at above, my major focus here is the objection to radical contextualism raised by Cappelen and Lepore which has to do with its purported excessive demands imposed on interactants, which turn communication into a

---

6   Here is Iacono's (2008: 168-169) succinct and helpful summary of Cappelen and Lepore's inconsistency argument against contextualism: it is claimed to be inconsistent "on the ground that if radical contextualism is true, then (S8) is context-sensitive: (S8) *Radical contextualism is true*. If (S8) is context-sensitive (…) then there are false utterances of (S8) in some contexts. So there are true utterances of (S9) *Radical contextualism is false*. The thrust of the argument is that radical contextualism is internally inconsistent because its truth entails its falsity."

7   For an overall strident (not to say steamroller) critique of Cappelen and Lepore's argument by elimination, see Doerge (2010).

feat virtually beyond the bounds of human capacity. The authors' grave concerns are referred to by Maitra (2007) as the *miracle of communication argument* and are known under this label. They have their source in Bezuidenhout's (2002) inventory of background knowledge areas, posited as crucial for the production and comprehension of utterances, which calls for "a systematic account (…) of what is understood (the truth-conditional content of utterances) and how it is we are able to know this (what our semantic knowledge consists in and how this knowledge is used in context to understand what is said)" (2002: 106). Indicating that the list is not quite complete, Bezuidenhout enumerates the following aspects of background knowledge relevant to communication:

(i)   knowledge that has already been activated from the prior discourse context (if any)

(ii)   knowledge that is available based on who one's conversational partner is and on what community memberships one shares with that person

(iii)   knowledge that is available through observation of the mutual perceptual environment

(iv)   any stereotypical knowledge or scripts or frames that are associatively triggered by accessing the semantic potential of any of the expressions currently being used

(v)   knowledge of the purposes and abilities of one's conversational partner (e.g., whether the person is being deceitful or sincere, whether the person tends to verbosity or is a person of few words, etc.)

(vi)   knowledge one has of the general principles governing conversational exchanges (perhaps including Grice's conversational maxims, culturally specific norms of politeness, etc.)   (Bezuidenhout 2002: 117)

Using as an example a simple utterance in (1) below, Cappelen and Lepore (2005: 121) try to argue that if all this knowledge were to be available for utterance comprehension, communication would simply be impossible.

(1)   Philosophy is fun.

As the authors indicate, in order to understand the meaning conveyed by (1) in a certain context, they would need to have available the knowledge activated by earlier parts of the discourse, know who the addressee of (1) is and what the speaker knows about this person, be aware of what knowledge is treated as shared by the interactants, etc., and – although only items (i)-(iii) above have been covered – knowing just this appears a tall order. "When the full RC [radical contextualist] story is told, it will turn out to be a miracle every time anyone manages to figure out what someone had said. But there are no miracles. People do not need to access all of this knowledge in order to figure out what has been said. So, RC is false" (Cappelen and Lepore 2005: 124).

As they go on to show, there is more to it, since the whole process of generating the explicitly communicated meaning is assumed to be based on an intricate psychological procedure, involving access to a range of shared beliefs against which the utterance should be processed. So, in the case of a third person listening to (1) who happens to disbelieve a relevant range of background asumptions shared by the speaker and the audience, this person should anyway be able to adequately fix the mind on the (wrong, in this person's estimation) beliefs. This leads Cappelen and Lepore (2005: 124) to conclude that "[i]f RC were true, it would be a miracle if speakers in different contexts were ever able to agree, disagree, or more generally, share contents."

It needs to be pointed out that there seems to be a glaring contradiction in what Cappelen and Lepore are critical about and what they themselves write and believe is essential for the production and reception of utterances in communicative contexts (cf. Leslie 2007: 162-163). As the miracle of communication argument above spells out, they consider it implausible that speakers and hearers might be able to deal with the burden and scope of background knowledge appealed to on the contexualist account of meaning. On the other hand, in presenting their thesis of Speech Act Pluralism, they openly declare that "[n]o one thing is said (or asserted, or claimed, or . . .) by any utterance: rather, indefinitely many propositions are said, asserted, claimed, stated. What is said (asserted, claimed, etc.) depends on a wide range of facts other than the proposition semantically expressed. It depends on a potentially indefinite number of features of the context of utterance and of the context of those who report on (or think about) what was said by the utterance" (Cappelen and Lepore 2005: 4). And they proceed to summarize a number of factors that affect utterance comprehension, among which the most important seem to be: assumptions about the speaker's beliefs and intentions, information about the context in which the conversation is taking place and its theme, relevant background knowledge about the world, logical inferences that follow from what is said, etc. (Cappelen and Lepore 2005: 193-194). Having proclaimed that and substantiating the aforementioned ideas with a chapter-length elaboration, Cappelen and Lepore (2005: 190, 200) express extreme scepticism about any systematic study of communicated meanings, which they refer to as the "nontheory theory of speech act content." Is this all in any way reconcilable with the miracle of communication argument, earlier presented by Cappelen and Lepore as fatal for contextualism?

Probably aware that even if their ideas are not taken to be downright schizophrenic, there can be a conspicuous clash detected between what they preach and what they practice, the authors themselves bring out the question: "*how is communication nonmiraculous?*" (Cappelen and Lepore 2005: 204; original italics). According to the two researchers, it is only what they characterize as the minimal semantic content, viz. the context-invariant meaning that can be identified as fully understood and communicated across the different contexts in which it is used. Beyond this, there can be no guarantee whatsoever as to what and how will be comprehended. This causes Cappelen and Lepore (2005: 205) to end on a rather pessimistic note:

> We don't think successful communication is easy. On our view, any utterance succeeds in expressing an indefinite number of propositions. One of these, the proposition semantically expressed, is easy to grasp. Others are extremely hard to access and there is no reason to think that any *one* person can ever grasp all that was said by an utterance, not even the speaker. This is how Semantic Minimalism combined with Speech Act Pluralism can account for both the sense in which communication is easy and the sense in which it is impossibly difficult.

Apparently, human communication is essentially overwhelmingly difficult for Capellen and Lepore. On their approach, it seems, there is no miracle of communication because most meaning will not get communicated, so it would be more adequate to talk of minimal communication in this context.

Cappelen and Lepore's semantic project has never really taken off, and instead, it has attracted a lot of criticism. Neither Insensitive Semantics as a programmatic study of meaning nor its creators' defeatist attitudes have proved very captivating. But the questions underpinning the miracle of communication argument seem not to have lost their significance. Neale's (forthcoming) Master Question appears both relevant and important:

> How are we able to accomplish so much, so efficiently—so quickly, systematically and consistently—by making various noises or marks, for example, how are we able to express our thoughts, to convey to others information about the world, about our beliefs, desires, plans, hopes, fears, and feelings?
>
> Things often go horribly wrong, of course, but the striking fact is just how often they *don't*, and this is a big part of what needs explaining.

As hinted at earlier, RT has got something to offer with respect to how this question should be approached. But because trying to launch an answer takes us back to the sphere of cognition and the mind, it is important to take a few steps back and take up the modularity issue again (see also Ch.1.3).

4.4 Inferencing and modularity

As indicated in chapter 1, RT endorses the massive modularity view of the human mind. In very general terms, according to the modularity thesis, the human mind's architecture is computational. This means that the mind is hypothesized to embrace a (great) number of modules of different kinds, responsible for processing various types of inputs and for managing the mind's internal resources (see Ch.1.3). These modules, posited to have developed through various evolutionary adaptations, are believed to have a phylogenetic basis, but also to be ontogenetically shaped to some extent.

The possibility of a multimodular structure of the mind has far-reaching implications for understanding human cognitive functioning as such. In particular, it appears crucial for theorizing about quotidian reasoning. Accepting that everyday reasoning relies on inferencing performed by many domain-specific modules, massive modularists hypothesize that the inferential procedures followed by each module are highly specialized (so in this way are marked by encapsulation, cf. Ch. 1.3) in that they "take advantage of the peculiar regularities of their specific domains to apply inferential procedures that would be inappropriate in other domains" (Mercier and Sperber 2009: 150).

At first blush, this suggestion appears hard to reconcile with the observation that reasoning necessarily draws on premises that are supplied by different domains: it is rather obvious that people must and do integrate information from different modules. To use Sperber's (1994b, 1996) example, seeing and hearing a mastiff Goliath effects an identification of a certain familiar dog, so there must be cross-feeding of outputs from different perceptual modules. Pursuing it further, it seems plausible to assume that a person might develop a rule in accordance with which, for instance, a sighting of three potentially dangerous dogs calls for taking a flight. This points to some kind of information sharing between, say, a relevant numerical module and a living-kind module, so extensive networking across the various modules appears to be an absolute necessity (Sperber 1994b, 1996).

Fodor (2001, in Mercier and Sperber 2009) raises another serious challenge for conceptual modularity. Since modules are believed to be automatically set in operation whenever a given input meets relevant input conditions, regardless of context, the same stimulus should unleash the same process of inferencing, which should result in the same output. This kind of stimulus-driven, context-insensitive conceptual processing is utterly incompatible with ever-present context-sensitivity of human inferencing, which appears to be its inherent feature (Mercier and Sperber 2009: 151).

The question then is: do these discordances between, on the one hand, the internal organization and dedicated mission of the different modules and, on the other, the inferential operations necessary for cognitive functioning render massive modularity unfit to account for how the mind actually works? The answer is: not necessarily, which Mercier and Sperber (2009) convincingly argue for. In the first place, there is empirical evidence indicating that it is not adequate to regard cognitive processes to be mandatory in the Fodorian sense. As experimentally demonstrated by Simons and Chabris (1999, in Mercier and Sperber 2009), people fail to see certain conspicuous developments in the scene they are surveying as long as their attention is directed at something else in the scene. So, for instance, when they are asked to count the passes of a basketball for a certain team of players while watching them play on a video, a number of subjects fail to see a man dressed as a gorilla or a woman with an umbrella walking across a basketball court. As many as 73% did not report seeing anything odd if the "the intruder" was displayed as semi-transparent, and 23% denied noticing any incidents in the case of "alien entity" being fully opaque (Ludwig 2006: 261).[8]

Secondly, even those inferential processes that seem to be genuinely universal in the sense of applying in an unchanged manner to all kinds of inputs of a certain representational form (like, say, rules of the modus ponens type) appear domain-specific on closer examination (Mercier and Sperber 2009: 152). The point is that these inferences are carried out on conceptual representations of a certain form. This means that they are sensitive to the conceptual composition of a certain type and are put into operation if the specific input conditions are met, however, that alone does not make them domain-general. Since they apply only to inputs with specific properties within a particular domain, they are domain-specific and modular: they are dedicated to deal with the data within this very module and they supply outputs of a certain domain-specific variety (Mercier and Sperber 2009: 152).

To recapitulate, a number of arguments have been advanced to show that there is no incompatibility between the massive modularity view of the mind and inferential processes which manipulate cognitive representations. As Mercier and Sperber (2009: 151) point out, it is reasonable to "assume that the same premise can be processed successively or in parallel by several modules, just as the same food can be decomposed successively or in parallel by several enzymes (…). Multi-domain inferences can be the joint work of several domain-specific modules."[9] With this potential obstacle out of the way, we can go back to issues directly related to communication and its relevance-theoretic model, which not only assumes massive modularity, but capitalizes on it to explain high operational human communicative efficiency.

---

8   As both Ludwig (2006) and Viger (2006) argue, these cases should not be viewed as providing evidence for perceptual flaws, even though they seem to be perceptual inaccuracies. The point is that in order to be cognitively relevant, perceptual experiences need to be subservient to the current cognitive goals of the organism. So "there are at least some cases in which abstracting away from the particular perceptual circumstances to produce conceptual representations that can be used by more central cognitive processes results in inaccurate representations" (Viger 2006: 285). Thus prioritizing the immediate cognitive aims may in certain situations result in what prima facie is inaccurate perception, but as a matter of fact what makes these representations efficacious is precisely that "they are *not* accurate" (Viger 2006: 285; emphasis mine).

9   This view contrasts sharply with Prinz's (2006) ideas on domain-specificity.

4.5 Communication and mind-reading

As indicated earlier (see in particular, Ch.1.6, Ch.3.7), relevance theorists assume that predicting and manipulating the mental states of others in an important way contributes to how communication works. As demonstrated in Ch.1.6, identifying the speaker-intended meaning has to do with recognizing a particular informative intention behind a given ostensive act, which as Wilson (2005: 1132) rightly emphasizes, "is a special case of the more general problem of explaining an individual's behaviour in terms of attributed mental states. On this approach, utterance interpretation is a variety of mind-reading" (see also Wilson 2009).

In very general terms, mind-reading (also known as Theory of Mind) is a kind of metapsychological ability that has to do with predictions that people are capable of making about what their conspecifics are feeling, thinking, desiring, etc. (Sperber 2000).[10] This suggests that mind-reading is crucial in managing human social contacts and helps in predicting and understanding (or at least rationalizing) other people's behaviour. The term itself appears a bit misleading: as a matter of fact we cannot read other people's minds, but we can reason about the contents of their thoughts, beliefs, etc. (cf. footnote 10), or, in the case of certain types of behaviour, automatically access assumptions about their mental states. Therefore, for instance, if we are trying to identify somebody's intention in doing something, all we can do is to examine their behaviour, think about its desired outcomes and in this way infer the intention behind their actions (see Ch.1.6).[11]

As argued above (Ch.1.7), understanding what the communicator wants to convey via an ostensive act involves the application of mind-reading abilities, in that the recipient needs to work out the communicator's informative intention on the basis of an ostensive stimulus addressed at him. Comprehension amounts to a formulation and evaluation of a hypothesis (or hypotheses, as the case may be) about the communicator-intended meaning from a piece of evidence provided by her for precisely this purpose.

At the production end, communicators do not only attract their addressee's attention, but have certain expectations about the kind of background information that a given stimulus is likely to make most accessible to the recipient. They can also predict what kind of inferences the latter is likely to make in the specific communicative circumstances. At the receiving end, getting the speaker-intended meaning is the obvious goal of the addressee. It might appear that the

---

10   As underscored by Leslie et al. (2004: 528), this ability "does not initially develop as a theory but as a mechanism. The 'theory of mind mechanism' (ToMM) is part of the core architecture of the human mind, and is specialized for learning about mental states."

11   Of course, with certain everyday, typical behaviours, intention attribution may be to a large extent routinized and automatic.

comprehender's task is somewhat easier in the case of verbal communication than in situations in which non-coded signals are used for communicative purposes: the obvious presupposition is that his language competence will in an important way help in understanding what the speaker has said. But it is by no means so: utterances (as emphasized in a number of places in chapters 2 and 3) tend to be gappy and the specific meaning endorsed by the informative intention made mutually manifest through ostension needs to be inferentially worked out by the hearer. This suggest that, as highlighted by Wilson (2005: 1132), "[t]he inferential approach to pragmatics treats understanding an utterance as a special case of understanding intentional behaviour."

Formerly thought of as a Fodorian central cognitive process, nowadays mind-reading is approached in terms of a domain-specific module (Sperber and Wilson 2002; Wilson 2005). Different empirical findings, such as very early sensitivity (of two-year-old children) to mental states of others (Papafragou 2002), infants' ability to adjust conversation depending on whether they talk to their mothers or a stranger (Tomasello, Farrar and Dines 1983, in Papafragou 2002),[12] failure of people with autistic spectrum disorder on first- and second-order mind-reading abilities (Wilson 2005), etc., provide a rationale for a modularized basis of mind-reading. This kind of approach hypothesizes the recruitment of "special-purpose inferential procedures which work reliably in the domain of intentional behaviour, yielding the same conclusions derivable by general-purpose reasoning mechanisms, but in a less effort-demanding way" (Wilson 2005: 1136).

As Wilson (2005: 1136) convincingly argues, taking into account the scope and range of mind-reading tasks performed by individuals on a daily basis as well as some conspicuous categories of "theory of mind" tasks, it appears "reasonable to assume that mind-reading is not a single, relatively homogeneous system but a collection of autonomous mechanisms or sub-modules articulated together in some way." An Eye Direction Detector, an Intentionality Detector (Sperber and Wilson 2002; Wilson 2005; Wilson and Sperber 2004; Wilson and Wharton 2006) and a Shared Attention Mechanism (Murphy and Stich 2000) seem to be plausible candidates for such sub-modules, each sensitive to distinct types of data and fine-tuned to deliver outcomes of a specific type.

Observing that, in a similar manner, verbal comprehension involves managing distinctive kinds of input and employs special kinds of procedures, Sperber and Wilson (2002) posit the existence of a dedicated comprehension module, being a subpart of the mind-reading module.

---

12 The body of research pointing to the availability of theory of mind mechanisms in very early childhood is growing fast (see, e.g., Carruthers 2013; Csibra 2010; Thompson 2014).

4.6 The miracle worker: the relevance-theoretic comprehension module

In the introductory chapter of their fascinating book *Simple Heuristics That Make Us Smart*, Gigerenzer and Todd (1999) argue for a bounded rationality model of human reasoning and decision making (originally put forth by Simon 1987, in Gigerenzer and Todd 1999). From the evolutionary psychology vantage point, the mind can be viewed as a toolbox,[13] which being a biological adaptation, has developed a range of "fast and frugal heuristics that make inferences within limited time and knowledge" (Gigerenzer and Todd 1999: 6). Since different domains of decision-making may require different types of constraints and control over different criteria, different heuristics will have evolved for each.

As indicated earlier (see in particular Ch.1.5-1.6), Sperber and Wilson's model is based on the idea that ostensive communication, in which the communicator overtly claims the addressee's attention, is characterized by a unique feature: it creates specific expectations of relevance in the recipient. This triggers an automatic inferential interpretation pattern in the addressee, who – in his search for the manifestly intended speaker-meaning – follows a least-effort interpretation path and stops as soon as he gets a satisfying range of cognitive effects for the effort expended.[14] In the relevance-theoretic framework this kind of comprehension heuristic (see Ch. 1.5 and Ch.2.3 for a discussion) is posited to have evolved as an evolutionary adaptation, and functions as a comprehension module, calibrated to deal with ostensive stimuli in general, and with verbal utterances in particular (Sperber 2000).

The comprehension module is a highly specialized idiosyncratic system, dedicated to dealing with ostensive inputs, both non-coded and coded ones (Carston and Powell 2005). Non-coded signals can be used to convey a much more limited range of meanings than coded, verbal signals, as the latter additionally "achieve a degree of explicitness not available in non-verbal communication" (Wilson and Sperber 2004: 614).[15]

---

13 A "Swiss army knife" metaphor is used side by side with the "adaptive toolbox" one, and both are considered very misleading by Carruthers (2006a: 21) because of the object portrayal that they carry.

14 As Carston (2002a: 45) helpfully elaborates on the above, "[t]he least-effort strategy follows from the presumption of optimal relevance in that the speaker is expected to have found a vehicle for the communication of her thoughts which minimizes the hearer's effort (within the parameters set by the speaker's own abilities and goals/preferences); the justification for the addressee stopping processing as soon as an interpretation satisfies his expectation of relevance follows similarly, in that any other interpretation that might also achieve the requisite level of effects will be less accessible and so incur greater processing costs."

15 Carston (2002a: 47) expresses a similar idea by saying that "[a] linguistic system is undeniably enabling."

As indicated above, the comprehension module is triggered automatically. Besides, it is most probably (at least to a certain extent) innate. It is also fast and frugal. As Wilson (2005: 1146) emphasizes, "regularities in the relations between mental states and behaviour need not be represented and used as explicit premises in an inference process, as in standard belief-desire psychology (…), but function merely as tacit underpinnings for the working of the device. The result should be an intuitive ability to draw valid conclusions in the domain of intentional behaviour, but without any reflective awareness of how these conclusions are drawn."

This means that all that the interpreter needs to do is go ahead and, using the assumptions that the relevance-guided processing of the stimulus makes most accessible, compute the cognitive effects that come most cheap and are endorsed by the mutually manifest communicator's intention. This indicates that, in contrast to what the miracle of communication argument proclaims (see Ch.4.3), interpretation embraces only the background assumptions which can be combined with the incoming input to yield manifestly relevant inferences. In effect, Cappelen and Lepore's (2005) claims about a mass of information that necessarily needs to be brought to bear in utterance comprehension to get context sensitive meanings appear grossly exaggerated. As Reimer (2009: 246) rightly points out, it is only the features which are *"actually exploited* by the speaker in her effort to be understood as intended"* (original emphasis) that will come into play.

The comprehension process is definitely global, in that background assumptions which become salient during utterance interpretation may be quite remote from either previous discourse or the immediate physical environment in which communication is taking place, but as long as the search for an optimally relevant interpretation makes them directly accessible in the interpreter's mind, they will be instantly activated and ready to use. There is nothing miraculous about it: this is how the relevance-driven comprehension procedure works.

Carruthers (2006: 56-57) describes the modular nature of the comprehension process as follows:

> we are dealing here with a briefly existing encapsulated system, created out of the resources of a longer-lasting comprehension system by facts about the recent environment. Given the previous history of the conversation, then some items of information are much more accessible than others. So a search process that operates on principles of accessibility can only look at that information, and other information in the mind cannot influence the comprehension process. Granted, if the earlier facts about the conversation had been different, then other information could have had an influence on the comprehension of the sentence in question. But this doesn't alter the fact that, the previous history of the conversation having been what it was, that information cannot now have an influence.

In this way, the modularized, automatic, fast, and frugal relevance-oriented comprehension procedure is the answer to questions about how the alleged miracle of communication works. It does not require extraordinary feats; it relies on an in-built mechanism within the mind-reading sub-module. The search for optimal relevance underlying utterance interpretation and the overall tendency of human cognition to maximize relevance help to explain how communication functions.

To be sure, as made explicit by the analyses in chapters 2 and 3 above, more often than not, the final result of comprehension will not be "a single, sharp-edged propositional meaning" (Wedgwood 2011: 521). However, again as argued above, this is how communication works, and it is often by being less explicit and vague that the speaker may communicate more than by being, prima facie, more explicit and lucid. And it is here that an important strength of RT manifests itself: the theory does not just focus on meanings that are rather straightforward and relatively easy to pin down, but offers an account of the more subtle aspects of communication as well (see Ch.3).

RT is not formalized in the mathematical or formal logic sense, because communication does not follow algorithmic patterns which could be recorded as symbolic rules. Communication is not infallible and there is no failsafe procedure "by which the hearer can reconstruct the speaker's exact meaning" (Sperber and Wilson 1986/94: 44). It is an asset of RT that it naturally accommodates this aspect of communication, and that it can predict and explain why and how communication can fail.[16] RT can also explain that on certain occasions the meaning that the hearer gets, while carefully crafted by the speaker, will embrace more than what her manifest intentions endorse. The responsibility for the interpretation recovered will then be shared between the speaker and the hearer. This is the case, for instance, with utterances whose processing generates poetic effects (see the discussion on weak communication effects in Ch. 3.5 and 3.6).[17]

Less determinate aspects of communication are challenging to account for and may prove unamenable to scrutiny that would result in their full explication. Another reason why verbal communication may be notoriously difficult (or maybe impossible?) to describe in very precise terms has to do with its subpersonal aspects. This issue will be briefly addressed in the section that follows.

---

16   For a relevance-theoretic analysis of what may happen when communication goes wrong, see, e.g., Jodłowiec (2009a) and Padilla Cruz (2014).

17   A slightly different example of how speakers cleverly control what they say and communicate appears in Dan Brown's *The Da Vinci Code* (p. 36). The protagonist, Langdon, when asked about what he thought about the Louvre Pyramid was not sure what to answer. "The French, it seemed, loved to ask American this. It was a loaded question, of course. Admitting you like the pyramid made you a tasteless American, and expressing dislike, was an insult to the French. 'Mitterrand was a bold man, Langdon replied, splitting the difference." Langdon simply left it to the interpreter to access context that his utterance made most accessible to him.

4.7 Personal vs. subpersonal levels in pragmatics

The distinction "between the personal and subpersonal levels of explanation" is due to Dennett (1969: 95), who traces it back to Ryle's and Wittgenstein's ideas. Deliberating over how people experience and talk about pain on the one hand, and the neurophysiological processes behind pain sensations, on the other, Dennett comes to the realization that there are two levels of examining pain. The *personal* level, at which "[p]ains or painful sensations are 'things' discriminated *by people*, not, for example, by brains" (Dennett 1969: 92; original emphasis). The other level, the *subpersonal* one, is that "of brains and events in the nervous system" (Dennett 1986: 95). There are then mechanical processes at the neurophysiological (subpersonal) level, and non-mechanical (personal) processes that have to do with how people experience pain (Dennett 1969: 92-95).

As a number of researchers have observed, for instance, Recanati (2002a) and Carston (2002a), the contrast can be usefully applied in investigating cognitive, and in particular, pragmatic processes. Both levels of explanation seem to be relevant for pragmatic analyses. People can, and sometimes do reflect on different aspects of communication (for instance, if explicitly asked to do it). However, the major bulk of what communication involves takes place at the subpersonal level, with "the machinery itself being largely beyond any threshold of awareness", as Seuren (2009: 25) rightly emphasizes.

The subpersonal level of explanation prevails in pragmatics, and relevance theorists treat it as something natural. While admitting that repairs of interpretations may sometimes rely on conscious processes, for example, when the initial hypothesis about the speaker-intended meaning is disconfirmed, Sperber and Wilson consider such developments to be special- rather than normal-case phenomena. As they underline, "[w]hile reflective inferences of this type do occur when spontaneous inference fails to yield a satisfactory interpretation, inferential comprehension is in general an intuitive, unreflective process which takes place below the level of consciousness" (Sperber and Wilson 2002: 9). This makes comprehension a subpersonal process par excellence.

All of this inevitably suggests that pragmatic analyses will necessarily be affected by the subpersonal nature of the processes scrutinized, and pragmatic theories will inevitably inherit some impenetrability of these processes. RT, designed to tap the complex mechanisms underlying ostensive communication, which remain unconscious and spontaneous, "aims at a causal mechanistic account, an account in terms of sub-personal systems" (Carston 2002b: 132). This explains why certain aspects of interpretation, like, for instance, a *precise* delimitation of contextual assumptions or the explication of the conclusive interpretation of weakly communicated meanings, remain tentative in RT. In other words, there are certain aspects of utterance interpretation that elude a fully-fledged determinate explication. This does not constitute a weakness of the theory: on the contrary, it is its strength, because this model can account for the open texture of human inferencing. It seems that, at least at this stage of the development of cognitive sciences, any attempt to model inferencing that underpins comprehension in a more rigid, formalized and accurate way may be counterproductive. The point is that – as far as we are know them today – the underlying processes are fuzzy and messy. Pretending that they are neat and determinate means idealizing away their true nature.

As emphasized above more than once, the relevance-theoretic framework, which postulates that pragmatic comprehension is enabled by the comprehension module with an in-built relevance-guided heuristic, provides a useful conceptual apparatus to deal with straightforward as well as vaguer aspects of verbal communication. On-line verbal communication is fast, frugal and efficient, just like the heuristic, and sometimes yields a vague interpretation.

Before closing, I would like to go back again to a minor amendment in the workings of the relevance-theoretic interpretation procedure suggested in chapter 2 (see Ch.2.6-2.7), and show that it is a small but non-trivial contribution to making the comprehension model even a little bit more efficacious than what free enrichment provides for.

4.8 Contextual cognitive fix: comprehension efficiency revisited

One of the important assets of RT is that, as argued above, it does offer an elucidation of the extraordinary efficiency of verbal communication, in particular at the comprehension end. I would like to point out that a minor adjustment in the theoretical apparatus of the model which has to do with replacing the so-called free enrichment process with a contextual cognitive fix mechanism, as introduced in Ch.2.6, helps to account for this efficiency in a convincing way.

Recall that contextual cognitive fix was postulated earlier as an inferential mechanism responsible for zeroing in on the explicitly expressed meaning: by anchoring the interpretation in the mutually manifest cognitive environment of the interactants, the interpreter is assumed to fix on the speaker-intended meaning in the course of a relevance-guided search for satisfying cognitive effects. Posited to be a mental tool in the relevance-theoretic comprehension heuristic, the mechanism ensures that the meaning gets inferentially fixed by the manifest speaker intentions controlling relevant contextual features in order to return the expected and intended range of cognitive effects. It is postulated that this is how, for instance, the speaker-intended referents are identified and predicated meanings get zoomed in in the context in order to secure that a given utterance meets the foreseeable and expected level of optimal relevance.

Unlike free enrichment, which adds some conceptual material to adequately enhance the decoded meaning, and in this way, return the speaker-intended content, contextual cognitive fix is much more frugal and less cognitively strenuous for the interpreter. In effect, it seems that the contextual cognitive fix procedure relieves explicature generation of the cognitive burden that free enrichment imposes on it, and makes the whole process simpler and more plausible. Thus the contextual cognitive fix mechanism is posited as a simpler and psychologically more feasible way of resolving underdeterminacies.

On this construal, the ultimate cognitive effects which make the utterance optimally relevant emerge as the major goal, hallmark and focus of the interpretation process. This kind of approach both predicts and explains that shallow comprehension of the explicitly expressed meaning may not only be fully *sufficient*, but also more *efficient* than the recovery of a fully-fledged explicature. The point is that if it is the implicit import that carries the major bulk of meaning that the addressee is intended to recover, the explicitly conveyed content is just a springboard for making it possible for the interpreter to leap and grasp the implicitly communicated meaning. And just as a springboard's role is to give impetus to a gymnast to jump high, what the speaker explicitly expresses may simply set the recipient on an interpretation path, which – initiated by the concepts inferred from the decoded linguistic signal – will result in a rich and complex meaning, not necessarily reducible to a set of assumptions individually represented in the interpreter's mind.

By and large, in instances of weak communication, and especially in the case of highly effective, impressive poetic effects, the interpreter may *experience* the meaning potential that a given expression or utterance carries. By definition then, this type of communicated meaning, even though yielded by ever the same relevance-driven comprehension heuristic, will elude full explication: the cognitive effect created consists in and depends on delineating a semantic region for the interpreter to explore. This suggests that any attempt to extract and spell out what is conveyed, in the first place, destroys the effect and deprives it of its force, and secondly, is difficult because of the idiosyncratic nature of the background assumptions activated. So one way or another, pinning down what is conveyed is doomed to failure. All this suggests that communication can be successful, or – as truly creative poets convince us all the time – very successful, if the meaning is left partly vague and indeterminate. RT is singularly adept at providing an explanation how it is possible (see chapter 3).

It is worth pointing out once again that the notion of weak communication, underpinned by not fully determinate speaker's intentions, which is unique to relevance theory, provides interesting and original insight into how recipients may share responsibility for the meaning recovered. As argued in Ch.3.4, the indeterminacy of speaker's intentions may affect not just the recovery of the implicit import that is communicated, but also the explicit layer of meaning, and the relevance-guided comprehension procedure employing the contextual cognitive fix mechanism can adequately account for what is involved.

4.9 Concluding remarks

In the present chapter my major goal was to argue that the comprehension module postulated in RT, with its fast, frugal and efficient – though not failsafe – relevance-guided interpretation heuristic, helps to provide an interesting and psychologically feasible answer to the question how to explain the alleged wonder of communication. As a cognitive pragmatic framework, the model is rooted in fundamental assumptions about the human mental architecture and is powered by considerations of cognitive efficiency. With respect to ostensive-inferential communication, these considerations centre on communicator's intentionality which underpins and constrains the interpretation process. On this model, mind-reading, one of the key abilities enabling human social functioning, is taken to channel comprehension processes. Therefore, it is hypothesized that the comprehension module is a subpart of the mind-reading module. The comprehension module, posited to be adapted to deal with ostensive data, with the relevance comprehension heuristic at its heart, is a dedicated, domain-specific module which secures a fast and automatic interpretation of ostensive stimuli. This module is the relevance-theoretic answer to the question how the miracle of communication is possible. There are no magic tricks there: the alleged miracle of communication is due to human biological endowment and its extremely complex but well adapted machinery, as are in fact all other aspects of our "miraculous" cognitive and non-cognitive functioning. To be sure, the hypothesis about the existence of the comprehension module as a sub-module of the theory of mind and its workings needs substantiation and support from empirical research. Taking into consideration unprecedented progress in cognitive sciences, and especially in neuroscience, the solid backing may come earlier than expected.

Conclusion

As a pragmatic model of ostensive-inferential communication, RT offers a complex theoretical apparatus designed to explore and explain its nature and workings. It is a framework rooted in certain fundamental observations about how human cognition works. Its cornerstone is the idea that when processing incoming data of all kinds, human cognitive resources are allocated to information that is most likely to be relevant; the context for processing the incoming data is chosen in such a way that their relevance is maximized; and the overall cognitive effects searched for are expected to return (what can be informally referred to as) an improved information state of the organism. The Cognitive Principle of Relevance is a formal embodiment of these assumptions.

Against the backdrop of these considerations about cognition, Sperber and Wilson have developed a model of ostensive-inferential communication, that is, communication in which, by claiming the addressee's attention, the communicator creates in the recipient specific expectations of relevance. The Communicative Principle of Relevance, based on this claim, together with its corollary in the form of a presumption of optimal relevance, is a powerful tacit law that explains the different mechanisms at work in the production and comprehension of ostensive stimuli. As Sperber and Wilson (1991b: 544) emphasize, it is not a pragmatic maxim or rule "that people have to know, let alone learn, in order to communicate effectively; it is not something that they obey or might disobey: it is an exceptionless generalization about human communicative behaviour." A more detailed description of the relevance-theoretic framework as a cognitive model of communication is provided in chapter 1.

The conceptual tools developed by RT elucidate various aspects of ostensive-inferential communication of the non-coded as well as the coded type. In particular, the model affords credible and coherent explanation of various aspects of verbal communication. As I have tried to show in chapters 2 and 3, illuminating insights into both the explicit and implicit level of communication can be gained from relevance-theoretic analyses. On this model, the recovery of the explicit and implicit import is taken to be inferential through and through. As a result, a new way of dealing with the explicit-implicit distinction is proposed.

My contribution to the theory has to do with a minor refinement I suggest. The notion of contextual cognitive fix (introduced in Ch.2.5 and discussed further in Ch.2.7-2.9), which is postulated as a mechanism underlying the relevance-driven generation of explicatures, is quite a new idea. It is put forth as a replacement for free enrichment, a controversial, and as I tried to show, cognitively burdensome and unnecessary pragmatic procedure. I hope my suggestions will provoke discussion in relevance-theoretic circles and not only, as the implications of this innovation go beyond the relevance-theoretic framework. The whole idea certainly requires further exploration and application over a wider range of examples than could be tackled within the confines of this book. In particular, the issue of the relationship between contextual cognitive fix and ad hoc concepts construction calls for further theoretical and practical examination. At this stage, I believe there is a sound division of labour between the two, with ad hoc concepts not well suited, for instance, to account for reference resolution. Maybe contextual cognitive fix can be viewed as a basic procedure that returns adequately fixed occasion-specific meanings, some of which happen to surface as ad hoc concepts? This is an idea which requires very serious exploration and I would like to pursue it in my future research.

With respect to the implicit layer of communication, RT seems to offer more than other pragmatic theories. Extremely parsimonious in its formal classifications, the model introduces the concept of weak communication, which allows the penetration and explanation of vaguer aspects of communicated meanings. As I tried to argue in chapter 3, it throws light on notoriously shadowy and often ignored facts related to verbal comprehension, which I consider a great asset of RT.

Psychological plausibility has always been high on the relevance-theoretic agenda. It comes as no surprise then, that this model offers an answer to the perennial question about how communication – being so complex, relying on virtually unrestricted context database, involving interactants who sometimes know next to nothing about each other and happening under severe time constrains – can be achieved at all. Is it not all due to a miracle? RT suggests it is not, and the hypothesis concerning the fast, frugal and dedicated comprehension module dispels all the miracle talk. The interesting issue about the miracle of communication argument is explored in chapter 4. Pragmatic processes, as is emphasized, belong mainly to the subpersonal level of explanation, which makes them particularly difficult to scrutinize.

The complexity and richness of RT never cease to amaze me. Its predictive power is impressive, and some of the ideas advanced by Sperber and Wilson neatly dovetail with some non-relevance-theoretic conceptions. A case in point is the approach to language. Recall that in the relevance-theoretic framework, the primary role of language is that of information processing, and its use in communication is treated only as a secondary function. With a widespread underdeterminacy of meaning pervading utterances, language cannot be viewed as a perfect communicative tool. Within the relevance-theoretic framework it is the mind-reading capacity that is assumed to compensate for the apparent inadequacies of language. In fact, on this approach, full explicitness is taken to be neither possible nor desirable: efficient inferencing carried out by the comprehension module seems a very economical strategy, excellently suited for the goals communication serves. Language with one-to-one form-meaning units will not only be totally impractical, but also cognitively unmanageable and unworkable.

Interestingly, this kind of construal ties in with the thesis about structural stability of natural language and structural instability of the language of science, advanced by Heller (2002), an eminent Polish philosopher of science, astrophysicist and theologian. As Heller (2002) points out in one of his popular science books about cosmology (I owe this reference to Brożek 2014: 42-44), a language of science must necessarily be very precise and accurate, with all its terms and definitions fully explicit and unambiguous, since otherwise contradictions would arise and the theory relying on imprecise language would prove invalid. Thus the language of science is characterized by structural instability: each minute change in the meaning of an expression renders it completely inadequate and undermines its use in scientific discourse. The situation is completely different with natural languages, which have an in-built structural stability. Thanks to this mechanism, minor meaning modifications do not lead to any major disturbances and language retains its communicative power and efficiency. As Heller (2002: 37) explains, the point is that if lexical items have clear-cut and sharply distinct meanings, the system is structurally instable, and a slight semantic modification may bar successful communication. Human languages tend to be structurally stable: paradoxically, vagueness, polysemy, ambiguity, etc., which result in semantic underdeterminacy, contribute to the structural stability of language and make communication less cognitively demanding.

RT views language in a similar way: as indicated above, apparent imperfections of the linguistic system create no major obstacles for verbal communication. The cognitive hardware and software we are endowed with, and especially the underlying drive to maximize (or in the case of communication, to optimize) relevance, provide a means of overcoming these imperfections. With our general cognitive relevance-orientation everything appears to fall into place.

Unlike in Fodor's (1983) image of scholarship, which supposedly is a process of transmuting a butterfly into a caterpillar, RT appears to help us see and understand the wonder of caterpillars becoming butterflies. The model seems to rise to an even more daunting challenge: in contrast to what happens in the caterpillar transformation, which is gradual and physiological and can be watched, recorded, and studied in a stage by stage fashion, in the case of utterance interpretation, which takes place mainly at the subpersonal level, no observation is possible of what is actually going on when verbal inputs are being processed. In a nutshell, on the relevance-theoretic account, incomplete linguistic meanings

put through the magic box of relevance-driven interpretation emerge as concrete
speaker-intended pragmatic meanings. Except that the magic box is neither magic
nor a box: it is well-developed and complex conceptual apparatus of Relevance
Theory.

References

Allott, Nicholas
  2007 *Pragmatics and Rationality.* London: University of London Ph.D. thesis.
Alvarez, Maria
  2010 *Kinds of Reason. An Essay in the Philosophy of Action.* Oxford: Oxford University Press.
Ángel-Lara, Marco
  2011 "Aphorisms: Problems of 'Empirically-Based Research'." *Orbis Literatum* 63(3). 194-214.
Anscombe, Elizabeth
  1957 *Intention.* Cambridge, MA: Harvard University Press.
Ariel, Mira
  2002 "Privileged Interactional Interpretations." *Journal of Pragmatics* 34. 1003-1044.
  2010 *Defining Pragmatics.* Cambridge: Cambridge University Press.
  2012 "Research paradigms in pragmatics." *The Cambridge Handbook of Pragmatics.* Eds. Keith Allan and Kasia Jaszczolt. Cambridge: Cambridge University Press. 23-45.
Arundale, Robert
  2008 "Against (Gricean) Intentions at the Heart of Human Interaction." *Intercultural Pragmatics* 5(2). 229-258.
Assimakopoulos, Stavros
  2008 "Intention, Common Ground and the Availability of Semantic Content: A Relevance-Theoretic Perspective." *Intention, Common Ground and the Egocentric Speaker-Hearer.* Eds. Istvan Kecskes and Jacob Mey. Berlin: Mouton de Gruyter. 105-126.
Bach, Kent
  1990 "Communicative Intentions, Plan Recognition: Comments on Thomason, and on Litman and Allen." *Intentions in Communication.* Eds. Philip Cohen, Jerry Morgan and Martha Pollack. Cambridge, MA: MIT Press. 389-400.
  1994 "Semantic Slack: What Is Said and More." *Foundations of Speech Act Theory: Philosophical and Linguistic Perspectives.* Ed. Savas Tsohatzidis. London: Routledge. 267-291.
  1999 "The Myth of Conventional Implicature." *Linguistics and Philosophy* 22. 327-366.
  2001 "You Don't Say." *Synthese* 128. 15-44.

2004   "Pragmatics and the Philosophy of Language." *The Handbook of Pragmatics.* Eds. Laurence Horn and Gregory Ward. Oxford: Blackwell. 463-487.

2006a "The Excluded Middle: Semantic Minimalism Without Minimal Propositions." *Philosophy and Phenomenological Research* 73. 435-442.

2006b "Speech Acts and Pragmatics." *The Blackwell Guide to the Philosophy of Language.* Eds. Michael Devitt and Richard Hanley. Malden, MA: Blackwell. 147-167.

2007   "Regression in Pragmatics (and Semantics)." *Pragmatics.* Ed. Noel Burton-Roberts. Basingstoke: Palgrave Macmillan. 24-44.

2010   "Impliciture vs. Explicature: What's the Difference?" *Explicit Communication: Robyn Carston's Pragmatics.* Eds. Esther Romero and Belén Soria. Basingstoke: Palgrave Macmillan. 126-137.

2012   "Saying, Meaning, and Implicating." *The Cambridge Handbook of Pragmatics.* Eds. Keith Allan and Kasia Jaszczolt. Cambridge: Cambridge University Press. 47-67.

2014   "Consulting *The Reference Book.*" *Mind & Language* 28(4). 445-474.

Baptista, Luca
2011   "Say What? On Grice on What is Said." *European Journal of Philosophy* 21(1). 1-19.

Barsalou, Lawrence
1982   "Context-Independent and Context-Dependent Information in Context." *Memory & Cognition* 10(1). 82-93.

1983   "Ad Hoc Categories." *Memory & Cognition* 11(3). 217-227.

Barton, Stephen – Anthony Sanford
1993   "A Case Study of Anomaly Detection: Shallow Semantic Processing and Cohesion Establishment." *Memory & Cognition* 21(4). 477-487.

Barwise, Jon – John Perry
2004   "Situations and Attitudes." *Semantics: A Reader.* Eds. Steven Davis and Brendan Gillon. Oxford: Oxford University Press. 305-321.

Barz, Wolfgang
2008   "The Real Trouble with Intentionality." *Philosophical Explorations* 11(2). 79-92.

Benga, Oana
2009   "Intentional Communication and the Anterior Cingulate Cortex." *In Vocalize to Localize.* Eds. Christian Abry, Anne Vilain and Jean-Luc Schwartz. Amsterdam: John Benjamins. 159-177.

Bezuidenhout, Anne
2002a "Truth Conditional Pragmatics." *Philosophical Perspectives* 16. 105-134.

2002b "Generalized Conversational Implicatures and Default Pragmatic Inferences." *Meaning and Truth: Investigations in Philosophical Semantics*. Eds. Joseph Campbell, Michael O'Rourke and David Shier. New York: Seven Bridges Press. 257-283.

2006 "The Coherence of Contextualism." *Mind & Language* 21(1). 1-10.

Bezuidenhout, Anne – Cooper Cutting

2002 "Literal Mining, Minimal Propositions and Pragmatic Processing." *Journal of Pragmatics* 34. 433-456.

2004 "Procedural Meaning and the Semantics/Pragmatics Interface." *The Semantics/Pragmatics Distinction*. Ed. Claudia Bianchi. Stanford: Center for the Study of Language and Information. 101-131.

Bianchi, Claudia

2004 "Semantics and Pragmatics: The Distinction Reloaded." *The Semantics/ Pragmatics Distinction*. Ed. Claudia Bianchi. Stanford, CA: CSLI Publications. 1-11.

2011 "Contextualism." *Philosophical Perspectives for Pragmatics*. Eds. Marina Sbisà, Jan-Ola Östman and Jef Verschueren. Amsterdam: John Benjamins. 53-70.

Blakemore, Diane

1987 *Semantic Constraints on Relevance*. Oxford: Blackwell.

2002 *Relevance and Linguistic Meaning: The Semantics and Pragmatics of Discourse Markers*. Cambridge: Cambridge University Press.

2007 "Constraints, Concepts and Procedural Encoding." *Pragmatics*. Ed. Noel Burton-Roberts. Basingstoke: Palgrave Macmillan. 45-66.

2010 "Communication and the Representation of Thought." *Journal of Linguistics* 46. 575-599.

Blaye, Agnes – Edith Ackermann – Paul Light

1999 "The Relevance of Relevance in Children's Cognition." *Social and Technological Resources for Learning*. Eds. Joan Bliss, Roger Säljö and Paul Light. Oxford: Elsevier. 120-132.

Bloom, Paul – Frank Keil

2001 "Thinking Through Language." *Mind & Language* 16(4). 351-367.

Boase-Baier, Jean

2004 "Saying What Someone Else Meant: Style, Relevance and Translation." *International Journal of Applied Linguistics* 14(2). 276-287.

Borg, Emma

2010 "Semantics and the Place of Psychological Evidence." *New Waves in Philosophy of Language*. Ed. Sarah Sawyer. Basingstoke: Palgrave Macmillan. 24-40.

Bredart, Serge – Karin Modolo
    1988   "Moses Strikes Again: Focalization Effect on a Semantic Illusion."
           Acta Psychologica 67. 135-144.
Brown, Gillian – George Yule
    1983   *Discourse Analysis.* Cambridge: Cambrideg University Press.
Brożek, Bartosz
    2014   *Granice interpretacji.* Kraków: Copernicus Center Press.
Buchanan, Ray
    2010   "A Puzzle about Meaning and Communication. *Nous* 44(2). 340-371.
Burton-Roberts, Noel
    2010   "Cancellation and Intention." *Explicit Communication: Robyn Carston's
           Pragmatics.* Eds. Esther Romero and Belén Soria. Basingstoke:
           Palgrave Macmillan. 138-155.
Capone, Alessandro
    2006   "On Grice's Circle (a Theory-Internal Problem in Linguistic Theories
           of the Gricean Type)." *Journal of Pragmatics* 38. 645-669.
    2011   "Knowing How and Pragmatic Intrusion." *Intercultural Pragmatics*
           8(4). 55-83.
Cappelen, Herman
    2007   "Semantics and Pragmatics: Some Central Issues." *Context-Sensitivity
           and Semantic Minimalism: New Essays on Semantics and Pragmatics.*
           Eds. Gerhard Preyer and Georg Peter. Oxford: Oxford University
           Press. 3-22.
Cappelen, Herman – Ernie Lepore
    2005   *Insensitive Semantics: A Defense of Semantic Minimalism and Speech
           Act Pluralism.* Oxford: Blackwell.
    2007a "The Myth of Unarticulated Constituents." *Situating Semantics:
           Essays on the Philosophy of John Perry.* Eds. Michael O'Rourke and
           Corey Washington. Cambridge, MA: The MIT Press. 199-214.
    2007b "Relevance Theory and Shared Content." *Pragmatics.* Ed. Noel
           Burton-Roberts. Basingstoke: Palgrave Macmillan. 115-135.
Carruthers, Peter
    2003   "On Fodor's Problem." *Mind & Language* 18(5). 502-523.
    2006a *The Architecture of the Mind: Massive Modularity and the Flexibility
           of Thought.* Oxford: Clarendon Press.
    2006b "The Case for Massively Modular Models of Mind." *Contemporary
           Debates in Cognitive Science.* Ed. Robert Stainton. Malden, MA:
           Blackwell. 3-21.
    2013   "Mindreading in Infancy." *Mind & Language* 28(2). 141-172

Carruthers, Peter – Andrew Chamberlain
    2000 "Introduction." *Evolution and the Human Mind: Modularity, Language and Meta-Cognition*. Eds. Peter Carruthers and Andrew Chamberlain. Cambridge: Cambridge University Press. 1-12.

Carston, Robyn
    1988 "Implicature, Explicature, and Truth-Theoretic Semantics." *Mental Representations: The Interface between Language and Reality*. Ed. Ruth Kempson. Cambridge: Cambridge University Press. 155-181.
    1997 "Relevance-Theoretic Pragmatics and Modularity." *UCL Working Papers in Linguistics* 9. 29-53.
    1998 "Informativeness, Relevance and Scalar Implicature." *Relevance Theory: Applications and Implications*. Eds. Robyn Carston and Seiji Uchida. Amsterdam: John Benjamins. 179-236.
    1999 "The Semantics/Pragmatics Distinction: A View from Relevance Theory." *The Semantics/Pragmatics Interface from Different Points of View*. Ed. Ken Turner. Oxford: Elsevier Science. 85-125.
    2000 "The Relationship Between Generative Grammar and (Relevance-Theoretic) Pragmatics." *Language and Communication* 20. 87-103.
    2002a *Thoughts and Utterances. The Pragmatics of Explicit Communication*. Malden, MA: Blackwell.
    2002b "Linguistic Meaning, Communicated Meaning and Cognitive Pragmatics." *Mind & Language* 17(1-2). 127-148.
    2002c "Metaphor, Ad Hoc Concepts and Word Meaning - More Questions than Answers." *UCL Working Papers in Linguistics* 14. 83-105.
    2004a "Explicature and Semantics." *Semantics: A Reader*. Eds. Steven Davis and Brendan Gillon. Oxford: Oxford University Press. 817-845.
    2004b "Relevance Theory and the Saying/Implicating Distinction." *The Handbook of Pragmatics*. Eds. Laurence Horn and Gregory Ward. Oxford: Blackwell. 633-656.
    2004c "Truth-Conditional Content and Conversational Implicature." *The Semantics/Pragmatics Distinction*. Ed. Claudia Bianchi. Stanford, CA: CSLI Publications. 65-100.
    2005 "A Note on Pragmatic Principles of Least Effort." *UCL Working Papers in Linguistics* 17. 271-278.
    2007 "How Many Pragmatic Systems Are There?" *Saying, Meaning, Referring: Essays on the Philosophy of François Récanati*. Ed. Maria Jose Frapolli. Basingstoke: Palgrave Macmillan. 18-48.
    2008 "Linguistic Communication and the Semantics/Pragmatics Distinction." *Synthese* 165(3). 321-345.

2009 "The Explicit/Implicit Distinction in Pragmatics and the Limits of Explicit Communication." *International Review of Pragmatics* 1(1). 35-62.

2010a "Lexical Pragmatics, Ad Hoc Concepts and Metaphor: From a Relevance Theory Perspective." *Italian Journal of Linguistics* 22(1). 153-180.

2010b "Metaphor, Ad Hoc Concepts, Literal Meaning and Mental Images." *Proceedings of the Aristotelian Society* 110(3). 295-321.

2010c "Explicit Communication and 'Free' Pragmatic Enrichment." *Explicit Communication: Robyn Carston's Pragmatics.* Eds. Esther Romero and Belén Soria. Basingstoke: Palgrave Macmillan. 217-287.

2012 "Relevance Theory." *Routledge Companion to the Philosophy of Language.* Eds. Gillian Russell and Delia Graff Fara. London: Routledge. 163-176.

Carston, Robyn – Alison Hall

2012 "Implicature and Explicature." *Cognitive Pragmatics* (Vol. 4). Ed. Hans-Jörg Schmid. Berlin: Walter de Gruyter. 47-84.

Carston, Robyn – Eun-Ju Noh

1996 "A Truth-Functional Account of Metalinguistic Negation, with Evidence from Korean." *Language Sciences* 18(1-2). 1553-1570.

Carston, Robyn – George Powell

2005 "Relevance Theory – New Directions and Developments." *UCL Working Papers in Linguistics* 17. 279-299.

Chapman, Siobhan

2001 "In Defence of a Code: Linguistic Meaning and Propositionality in Verbal Communication." *Journal of Pragmatics* 33. 699-720.

Chaves, José

2010 "Explicature, What Is Said, and Gricean Factorization Criteria." *Explicit Communication: Robyn Carston's Pragmatics.* Eds. Esther Romero and Belén Soria. Basingstoke: Palgrave Macmillan. 109-125.

Chrzanowska-Kluczewska, Elżbieta

2004 *Language Games: Pro and Against.* Kraków: Universitas.

2013 *Much More than Metaphor: Master Tropes of Artistic Language and Imagination.* Frankfurt am Main: Peter Lang.

Churchland, Paul

1988 "Perceptual Plasticity and Theoretical Neutrality: A Reply to Jerry Fodor." *Philosophy of Science* 55. 167-187.

Clark, Billy

1996 "Stylistic Analysis and Relevance Theory." *Language and Literature* 5. 163-178.

Clark, Herbert
    1996   *Using Language.* Cambridge: Cambridge University Press.

Cooren, Françoise – Robert Sanders
    2002   "Implicatures: A Schematic Approach." *Journal of Pragmatics* 34.
         1045-1067.

Corazza, Eros – Jérôme Dokic
    2007   "Sense and Insensibility Or Where Minimalism Meets Contextualism."
         Context-Sensitivity and Semantic Minimalism: New Essays on
         Semantics and Pragmatics. Eds. Gerhard Preyer and Georg Peter.
         Oxford: Oxford University Press. 169-193.
    2012   "Situated Minimalism Versus Free Enrichment." *Synthese* 184.
         179-198.

Cosmides, Leda – John Tooby
    1994   "Origins of Domain Specificity: The Evolution of Functional
         Organization." *Mapping the Mind: Domain Specificity in Cognition*
         and Culture. Eds. Lawrence Hirschfeld and Susan Gelman. Cambridge:
         Cambridge University Press. 85-116.

Cova, Florian – Emmanuel Dupoux – Pierre Jacob
    2012   "On Doing Things Intentionally" *Mind & Language* 27(4). 378-409.

Cresswell, Max
    1978/2004 "Prepositions and Points of View." *Linguistics and Philosophy*
         2. 1-42. Reprinted in *Semantics: A Reader.* Eds. Steven Davis and
         Brendan Gillon. Oxford: Oxford University Press. 563-592.

Crook, John
    2004   "On Covert Communication in Advertising." *Journal of Pragmatics*
         36. 715-738.

Csibra, Gergely
    2010   "Recognizing Communicative Intentions in Infancy." *Mind &*
         Language 25(2). 141-168.

Curcó, Carmen
    1995   "Some Observations on the Pragmatics of Humorous Interpretations:
         A Relevance-Theoretic Approach." *UCL Working Papers in Linguistics*
         7. 27-47.
    1996   "The Implicit Expression of Attitudes, Mutual Manifestness and Verbal
         Humour." *UCL Working Papers in Linguistics* 8. 89-99.

Dahlman, R. Colonna
    2013   "Conversational Implicatures are Still Cancellable." *Acta Analytica*
         28. 321-327.

Dascal, Marcelo
    2003   *Interpretation and Understanding.* Amsterdam: John Benjamins.

Davies, Martin
   2006   "Foundational Issues in the Philosophy of Language." *The Blackwell Guide to the Philosophy of Language*. Eds. Michael Devitt and Richard Hanley. Oxford: Blackwell. 19-40.
Davis, Wayne
   1998   *Implicature, Intention, Convention and Principle in the Failure of Gricean Theory*. Cambridge: Cambridge University Press.
Dennett, Daniel
   1969   *Content and Consciousness*. London: Routledge.
Díaz-Pérez, Francisco Javier
   2014   "Relevance Theory and Translation: Translating Puns in Spanish Film Titles into English." *Journal of Pragmatics* 70. 108-129.
Doerge, Friedrich
   2010   "The Collapse of Insensitive Semantics." *Linguistics and Philosophy* 33(2). 117-140.
Doerge, Friedrich – Mark Siebel
   2008   "Gricean Communication and Transmission of Thoughts." *Erkenntnis* 6. 55-67.
Durán Martínez, Ramiro
   2005   "Covert Communication in the Promotion of Alcohol and Tobacco in Spanish Press Advertisements." *Revista Electrónica de Lingüística Aplicada* 4. 82-102.
Elugardo, Reinaldo
   2007   "Minimal Propositions, Cognitive Safety Mechanisms, and Psychological Reality." *Context-Sensitivity and Semantic Minimalism: New Essays on Semantics and Pragmatics*. Oxford: Oxford University Press. 278-302.
Escandell-Vidal, Victoria – Manuel Leonetti – Aoife Ahern (eds.)
   2011   *Procedural Meaning: Problems and Perspectives*. Bingley: Emerald Group Publishing.
Ferreira, Fernanda – Karl G. Bailey – Vittoria Ferraro
   2002   "Good-Enough Representations in Language Comprehension." *Current Directions in Psychological Science* 11(1). 1-15.
Ferreira, Fernanda – Nikole Patson
   2007   "The 'Good Enough' Approach to Language Comprehension." *Language and Linguistics Compass* 1(1-2). 71-83.
Floridi, Luciano
   2008   "Understanding Epistemic Relevance." *Erkenntnis* 69. 69-92.
Fodor, Jerry
   1983   *The Modularity of Mind*. Cambridge, MA: The MIT Press.

2003   *Hume Variations*. Oxford: Oxford University Press.

2008   *LOT 2: The Language of Thought Revisited*. New York: Oxford University Press.

Foster-Cohen, Susan

2004   "Relevance Theory, Action Theory and Second Language Communication Strategies." *Second Language Research* 20(3). 289-302.

Fretheim, Thornstein

2006   "English then and Norwegian da/sa Compared: A Relevance-Theoretic Account." *Nordic Journal of Linguistics* 29(1). 45-93.

Fuller, Tim – Richard Samuels

2014   "Scientific Inference and Ordinary Cognition: Fodor on Holism and Cognitive Architecture." *Mind & Language* 29(2). 201-237.

Furlong, Anne

1996   *Relevance Theory and Literary Interpretation*. London: University of London Ph.D. thesis.

2011   "The Soul of Wit: A Relevance Theoretic Discussion." *Language and Literature* 20(2). 136-150.

Gauker, Christopher

2001   "Situated Inference Versus Conversational Implicature." *Nous* 35(2). 163-189.

Geary, James

2005   *The World in a Phrase: A Brief History of the Aphorism*. New York: Bloomsbury.

Gibbs, Raymond – Herbert Colston

2012   *Interpreting Figurative Meaning*. Cambridge: Cambridge University Press.

Gibbs, Raymond – Jessica Moise

1997   "Pragmatics in Understanding What is Said." *Cognition* 62. 51-74.

Gigerenzer, Gerd – Peter Todd

1999   "The Research Agenda." *Simple Heuristics That Make Us Smart*. Gerd Gigerenzer, Peter Todd and the ABC Research Group. Oxford: Oxford University Press. 3-34.

Girotto, Vittorio – Markus Kemmelmeier – Dan Sperber – Jean-Baptiste Van der Henst

2001   "Inept Reasoners or Pragmatic Virtuosos? Relevance and the Deontic Selection Task." *Cognition* 81. 69-76.

Gleitman, Lila – Anna Papafragou

2005   "Language and Thought." *The Cambridge Handbook of Thinking and Reasoning*. Eds. Keith Holyak and Robert Morrison. Cambridge: Cambridge University Press. 633-661.

2013   "Relations Between Language and Thought." *The Oxford Handbook of Cognitive Psychology*. Ed. Daniel Reisberg. Oxford: Oxford University Press. 503-523.

Glock, Hans-Johann
2001   "Intentionality and Language." *Language and Communication* 21. 105-118.

Grice, H. Paul
1957/89 "Meaning." *Philosophical Review* 66. 377-88. Reprinted in *Studies in the Way of Words*. H. Paul Grice. 1989. Cambridge, MA: Harvard University Press. 213-223.

1967/89 *Logic and Conversation. William James Lectures*. Reprinted in *Studies in the Way of Words*. H. Paul Grice. 1989. Cambridge, MA: Harvard University Press. 3-143.

1968/89 "Utterer's Meaning, Sentence Meaning and Word-Meaning." *Foundations of Language* 4. 225-242. Reprinted in *Studies in the Way of Words*. H. Paul Grice. 1989. Cambridge, MA: Harvard University Press. 117-137.

1969/89 "Utterer's Meaning and Intentions." *Philosophical Review* 78. 147-17. Reprinted in *Studies in the Way of Words*. H. Paul Grice. 1989. Cambridge, MA: Harvard University Press. 86-116.

1975/89 "Logic and Conversation." *Syntax and Semantics 3: Speech Acts*. Eds. Peter Cole and Jerry Morgan. New York: Academic Press. 41-58. Reprinted in *Studies in the Way of Words*. H. Paul Grice. 1989. Cambridge, MA: Harvard University Press. 22-40.

1978/89 "Further Notes on Logic and Conversation." *Syntax and Semantics 9: Pragmatics*. Ed. Peter Cole. New York: Academic Press. 113-127. Reprinted in *Studies in the Way of Words*. H. Paul Grice. 1989. Cambridge, MA: Harvard University Press. 41-57.

1982/89 "Meaning Revisited." *Mutual Knowledge*. Ed. Neil Smith. New York: Academic Press. 223-243. Reprinted in *Studies in the Way of Words*. H. Paul Grice. 1989. Cambridge, MA: Harvard University Press. 283-303.

1989   "Retrospective Epilogue." *Studies in the Way of Words*. Paul Grice. 1989. Cambridge, MA: Harvard University Press. 339-385.

Gross, John (ed.)
1983   *The Oxford Book of Aphorism*. Oxford: Oxford University Press.

Grundy, Peter
2007   "Language Evolution, Pragmatic Inference, and the Use of English as Lingua Franca." *Explorations in Pragmatics: Linguistic, Cognitive*

and Intercultural Aspects. Eds. Istvan Kecskes and Laurence R. Horn. Berlin: Mouton de Gruyter. 219-256.

Gutt, Ernst-August
> 1991 *Translation and Relevance: Cognition and Context.* Oxford: Blackwell.
> 1998 "Pragmatic Aspects of Translation: Some Relevance-Theory Observations." *The Pragmatics of Translation.* Ed. Leo Hickey. Clevedon: Multilingual Matters. 41-53.

Hacker, Peter
> 2001 "An Orrery of Intentionality." *Language and Communication* 21. 119-141.

Hall, Alison
> 2007a "Subsentential Utterances, Ellipsis and Pragmatic Enrichment." *UCL Working Papers in Linguistics* 19. 235-259.
> 2007b "Do Discourse Connectives Encode Concepts or Procedures?" *Lingua* 117. 149-174.
> 2008a "Free Enrichment or Hidden Indexicals?" *Mind & Language* 23. 426-456.
> 2008b *Free Pragmatic Processes and Explicit Utterance Content.* London: University of London Ph.D. thesis.
> 2009 "Semantic Compositionality and Truth-Conditional Content." *Proceedings of the Aristotelian Society* 109(3). 353-364.

Hamblin, Jennifer L. – Raymond W. Gibbs
> 2003 "Processing the Meanings of What Speakers Say and Implicate." *Discourse Processes* 35(1). 59-80.

Haugh, Michael – Kasia Jaszczolt
> 2012 "Speaker Intentions and Intentionality." *The Cambridge Handbook of Pragmatics.* Eds. Keith Allan and Kasia Jaszczolt. Cambridge: Cambridge University Press. 87-112.

Heller, Michał
> 2002 *Początek jest wszędzie.* Warszawa: Prószyński i S-ka.

Holtgraves, Thomas
> 2008 "Automatic Intention Recognition in Conversation Processing." *Journal of Memory and Language* 58. 627-645.

Horn, Laurence
> 1984 "Toward a New Taxonomy for Pragmatic Inference: Q-Based and R-Based Implicature." *Meaning, Form, and Use in Context: Linguistic Applications.* Ed. Deborah Schiffrin. Washington: Georgetown University Press. 11-42.
> 2004 "Implicature." *The Handbook of Pragmatics.* Eds. Laurence Horn and Gregory Ward. Oxford: Blackwell. 3-28.

2005   "Current Issues in Neo-Gricean Pragmatics." *Intercultural Pragmatics* 2(2). 191-204.

2006   "The Border Wars: A Neo-Gricean Perspective." *Where Pragmatics Meets Semantics*. Eds. Klaus von Heusinger and Ken Turner. Amsterdam: Elsevier. 21-48.

2010   "WJ-40: Issues in the Investigation of Implicarure." *Meaning and Analysis. New Essays on Grice*. Ed. Klaus Petrus. Basingstoke: Palgrave Macmillan. 310-340.

Iacono, Leo

2008   *A Defense of Moderate Invariantism*. Lincoln: University of Nebraska Ph.D. thesis. Available at: http://digitalcommons.unl.edu/cgi/viewcontent.cgi?article=1000&context=philosophydiss (last access: December 2014).

Ifantidou, Elly

2001   *Evidentials and Relevance*. Amsterdam: John Benjamins.

2013   "Pragmatic Competence and Explicit Instruction." *Journal of Pragmatics* Special Issue 59 (Part A). 93-116.

2014   *Pragmatic Competence and Relevance*. Amsterdam: John Benjamins.

Iten, Corinne

2005   *Linguistic Meaning, Truth Conditions and Relevance: The Case of Concessives*. Basingstoke: Palgrave Macmillan.

Jary, Mark

2013   "Two Types of Implicature: Material and Behavioural." *Mind & Language* 28(5). 638-660.

Jaszczolt, Katarzyna

2002   "Against Ambiguity and Underspecification: Evidence from Presupposition as Anaphora." *Journal of Pragmatics* 34. 829-849.

2008   "Psychological Explanation in Gricean Pragmatics and Frege's Legacy." *Intention, Common Ground and the Egocentric Speaker-Hearer*. Eds. Istvan Kecskes and Jacob Mey. Berlin: Mouton de Gruyter. 9-44.

2012   "Semantics/Pragmatics Boundary Disputes." *Semantics: An International Handbook of Natural Language Meaning*. Vol. 3. Eds. Claudia Maienbom, Klaus von Heusinger and Paul Portner. Berlin: Mouton de Gruyter. 2333-2360.

Jodłowiec, Maria

1991a   "What Makes Jokes Tick?" *UCL Working Papers in Linguistics* 3. 241-253.

1991b   *The Role of Relevance in the Interpretation of Verbal Jokes: A Pragmatic Analysis*. Kraków: Jagiellonian University Ph.D. thesis.

2008   "What's in the Punchline?" *Relevant Worlds: Current Perspectives on Language, Translation and Relevance Theory*. Eds. Ewa Wałaszewska, Marta Kisielewska-Krysiuk, Aniela Korzeniowska and Małgorzata Grzegorzewska. Newcastle upon Tyne: Cambridge Scholars. 67-86.

2009a   "Relevance and Misunderstanding." *Communication: Understanding/ Misunderstanding. Proceedings of the 9th Congress of the IASS/ AIS – Helsinki-Imatra: 11-17 June, 2007.* Vol.1. Eds. Eero Tarasti, Paul Forsell and Richard Littlefield. Imatra: International Semiotics Institute. 651-661.

2009b   "Relevance and context." *The Contextuality of Language and Culture.* Eds. Elżbieta Chrzanowska-Kluczewska and Agnieszka Gołda-Derejczyk. Bielsko-Biała: Wydawnictwo WSEH. 35-49.

2010   "The Role of Relevance Theory in SLA Studies." *Cognitive Processing in Second Language Acquisition. Inside the Learner's Mind.* Eds. Martin Pütz and Laura Sicola. Amsterdam: John Benjamins. 49-66.

Jucker, Andreas – Sara Smith – Tanja Ludge
2003   "Interactive Aspects of Vagueness in Conversation." *Journal of Pragmatics* 35. 1737-1769.

Kalisz, Roman
1993   *Pragmatyka językowa.* Gdańsk: Wydawnictwo Uniwersytetu Gdańskiego.

Kecskes, Istvan
2013   "Why Do We Say What We Say the Way We Say It?" *Journal of Pragmatics* 48. 71-83.

Kecskes, Istvan – Jacob Mey
2008   "Introduction." *Intention, Common Ground and the Egocentric Speaker-Hearer.* Eds. Istvan Kecskes and Jacob Mey. Berlin: Mouton de Gruyter. 1-8.

King, Jeffrey – Stanley Jason
2005   "Semantics, Pragmatics and the Role of Semantic Content." *Semanitics vs. Pragmatics.* Ed. Zoltán Gendler Szabó. Oxford: Clarendon Press. 111-164.

Kolaiti, Patricia
2009   *The Limits of Expression: Language, Poetry, Thought.* London: University of London Ph.D. thesis.

Korta, Kepa
2013   "Grice's Requirements on *What is Said.*" *What is Said and What is Not.* Eds. Carlo Penco and Filippo Domaneschi. Stanford: CSLI Publications. 209-221.

Korta, Kepa – John Perry
2007 "Radical Minimalism, Moderate Contexualism." *Context-Sensitivity and Semantic Minimalism: New Essays on Semantics and Pragmatics.* Eds. Gerhard Preyer and Georg Peter. Oxford: Oxford University Press. 94-111.

Kośka, Lidia
1999 "O aforyzmach i aforyście (Preface)" Stanisław J. Lec *Myśli nieuczesane.* Kraków: Universitas. 5-66.
2008 *Autobiografia Słowa: Twórczość Stanisława Jerzego Leca.* Kraków: Jagiellonian University Ph.D. thesis.

Kuźniak, Marek
2005 *Combing 'Unkempt Thoughts'. The Aphorism: A Cognitive-Axiological Study of Myśli Nieuczesane by St. J. Lec.* Wrocław: Oficyna Wydawnicza ATUT. Wrocławskie Wydawnictwo Oświatowe.

Lepore, Ernie – Matthew Stone
2010 "Against Metaphorical Meaning." *Topoi* 29(2). 165-180.

Leslie, Alan – Orie Friedman – Tim German
2004 "Core Mechanisms in 'Theory of mind'." *Trends in Gognitive Sciences* 8(12). 529-533.

Leslie, Sarah-Jane
2007 "Moderately Sensitive Semantics." *Context-Sensitivity and Semantic Minimalism: New Essays on Semantics and Pragmatics.* Eds. Gerhard Preyer and Georg Peter. Oxford: Oxford University Press. 133-168.

Levinson, Stephen
1983 *Pragmatics.* Cambridge: Cambridge University Press.
1995 "Interactional Biases in Human Thinking." *Social Intelligence and Interaction.* Ed. Esther Goody. Cambridge: Cambridge University Press. 221-260.
2000 *Presumptive Meanings: The Theory of Generalized Conversational Implicature Language, Speech, and Communication.* Cambridge, MA: MIT Press.

Liszka, Sarah
2004 "Exploring the Effects of First Language Influence on Second Language Pragmatic Processes from a Syntactic Deficit Perspective." *Second Language Research* 20(3). 213-231.

Ludwig, Kirk
2006 "Is the Aim of Perception to Provide Accurate Representations?" *Contemporary Debates in Philosophy of Science.* Ed. Christopher Hitchcock. Malden, MA: Blackwell Publishing. 259-274.

Lyons, William
    1995   *Approaches to Intentionality.* Oxford: Oxford University Press.
Łyda, Andrzej
    2007   *Concessive Relations in Spoken Discourse: A Study into Academic Spoken English.* Katowice: Wydawnictwo Uniwersyetu Śląskiego.
MacFarlane, John
    2007   "Semantic Minimalism and Nonindexical Contextualism." *Context-Sensitivity and Semantic Minimalism: New Essays on Semantics and Pragmatics.* Eds. Gerhard Preyer and Georg Peter. Oxford: Oxford University Press. 169-193.
Maitra, Ishani
    2007   "How and Why to be a Moderate Contextualist." *Context-Sensitivity and Semantic Minimalism: New Essays on Semantics and Pragmatics.* Eds. Gerhard Preyer and Georg Peter. Oxford: Oxford University Press. 112-132.
Martí, Luisa
    2006   "Unarticulated Constituents Revisited." *Linguistics and Philosophy* 29. 135-166.
Mazzarella, Diana
    2011   "Accessibility and Relevance: A Fork in the Road." *UCL Working Papers in Linguistics* 23. 11-20.
    2013   "Associative and Inferential Approaches to Pragmatics: The State of the Art of Empirical Investigation." *Methode – Analytic Perspective*s (Special Issue on "New Perspectives for the Philosophy of Cognitive Science") 2(2). 172-194.
Mercier, Hugo – Dan Sperber
    2009   "Intuitive and Reflective Inferences." *In Two Minds: Dual Processing and Beyond.* Eds. Jonathan Evans and Keith Frankish. Oxford: Oxford University Press. 149-170.
Mioduszewska, Ewa
    2002   "Some General Remarks on the Explicature/Implicature Distinction in the Theory of Relevance." *Anglica: An International Journal of English Studies* 12. 125-133.
    2004   "On the Limits of Free Enrichment: A Voice in the Discussion." *Perspectives on Language.* Eds. Henryk Kardela, William Sullivan, and Adam Głaz. Lublin: Wydawnictwa UMCS. 161-167.
    forthcoming (a) "(Inter)subjectivity of Explicit Content in Relevance Theory." *Anglica: An International Journal of English Studies* 23.
    forthcoming (b) "Ad Hoc Concepts, Linguistically Encoded Meaning and Explicit Content: Some Remarks on Relevance Theoretic Perspective."

Within Language, Beyond Theories: Discourse Analysis, Pragmatics and Corpus-Based Studies.

Morson, Gary
2003   "The Aphorism: Fragments from the Breakdown of Reason." *New Literary History* 34(3). 409-429.
2012   *The Long and Short of It: From Aphorism to Novel.* Stanford: Stanford University Press.

Murphy, Dominic – Stephen Stich
2000   "Darwin in the Madhouse: Evolutionary Psychology and the Classification of Mental Disorders. *Evolution and the Human Mind: Modularity, Language and Meta-Cognition.* Eds. Peter Carruthers and Andrew Chamberlain. Cambridge: Cambridge University Press. 62-92.

Natsopoulos, Dimitris
1985   "A Verbal Illusion in Two Languages." *Journal of Psycholinguistic Research* 14(4). 385-398.

Neale, Stephen
1992   "Paul Grice and the Philosophy of Language." *Linguistics and Philosophy* 15. 509-559.
1993   *Descriptions.* Cambridge, MA: MIT Press.
2004   "This, That and the Other." *Descriptions and Beyond.* Eds. Marga Reimer and Anne Bezuidenhout. Oxford: Oxford University Press. 68-182.
forthcoming   "Implicit Reference." *Meanings and Other Things: Essays on Stephen Schiffer.* Ed. Gary Ostertag. Cambridge, MA: MIT Press.

Nerlich, Brigitte – David Clarke
2001   "Ambiguities We Live by: Towards a Pragmatics of Polysemy." *Journal of Pragmatics* 33. 1-20.

Nishiyama, Yuji – Koji Mineshima
2010   "Free Enrichment and the Overgeneration Problem." *In the Mind and Across Minds: A Relevance-Theoretic Perspective on Communication and Translation.* Eds. Ewa Wałaszewska, Marta Kisielewska-Krysiuk and Agnieszka Piskorska. Newcastle upon Tyne: Cambridge Scholars. 31-52.

Niżegorodcew, Anna
2004   "L2 Classroom Discourse in the Light of Input Theory and Relevance Theory." *Relevance Studies in Poland.* Vol. 1. Ed. Ewa Mioduszewska. Warsaw: Warsaw University Press. 307-315.
2007   *Input for Instructed L2 Learners: The Relevance of Relevance.* Clevedon: Multilingual Matters.

Noveck, Ira – Dan Sperber
2007   "The Why and How of Experimental Pragmatics: The Case of 'Scalar Inferences'." *Pragmatics*. Ed. Noel Burton-Roberts. Basingstoke: Palgrave Macmillan. 184-212.

Orrigi, Gloria – Dan Sperber
2000   "Evolution, Communication and the Proper Function of Language." *Evolution and the Human Mind*. Eds. Peter Carruthers and Andrew Chamberlain. Cambridge: Cambridge University Press. 140-169.

Padilla Cruz, Manuel
2012   "Epistemic Vigilance, Cautious Optimism and Sophisticated Understanding." *Research in Language* 10(4). 365-385.

Pagin, Peter – Francis Jeffry Pelletier
2007   "Content, Context, and Composition." *Context-Sensitivity and Semantic Minimalism: New Essays on Semantics and Pragmatics*. Eds. Gerhard Preyer and Georg Peter. Oxford: Oxford University Press. 25-62.

Paiva, Beatriz Mariz de – Susan Foster-Cohen
2004   "Exploring the Relationships Between Theories of Second Language Acquisition and Relevance Theory." *Second Language Research* 20(3). 281-288.

Papafragou, Anna
2002   "Mindreading and Verbal Communication." *Mind & Language* 17(1-2). 55-67.

Park, Heekyeong – Lynne Reder
2004   "Moses Illusion: Implications for Human Cognition." *Cognitive Illusions: A Handbook on Fallacies and Biases in Thinking, Judgement and Memory*. Ed. Rüdiger Phol. Hove: Psychology Press. 275-291.

Perner, Josef – Alan Garnham
1988   "Conditions for Mutuality." *Journal of Semantics* 6(1). 369-385.

Perry, John
1986/93 "Thoughts Without Representation." *Supplementary Proceedings of the Aristotelian Society* 60. 137-152. Reprinted in *The Problem of the Essential Indexical and Other Essays*. John Perry. 1993. New York: Oxford University Press. 205-225.

Petrus, Klaus
2010   "Paul Grice, Philosopher of Language, But More Than That." *Meaning and Analysis: New Essays on Grice*. Ed. Klaus Petrus. Basingstoke: Palgrave Macmillan. 1-30.

Pilkington, Adrian
  2000 *Poetic Effects: A Relevance Theory Perspective.* Amsterdam: John Benjamins.
Pinker, Steven
  2005 "So How *Does* the Mind Work?" *Mind & Language* 20(1). 1-24.
Piskorska, Anieszka
  2012 "Humour or Horror? On Propositional Attitudes in Humorous Discourse." *Relevance Theory: More than Understanding* Eds. Ewa Walaszewska and Agnieszka Piskorska. New Castle upon Tyne: Cambridge Scholars Publishing. 183-197.
  2014 "A Relevance-Theoretic Perspective on Humorous Irony and Its Failure." *Humor* 27(4). 661-685.
Pop, Anisoara
  2007 "Covert Communication in Advertising: A Case Study." *The Proceedings of the European Integration – between Tradition and Modernity Congress.* Vol. 2, nr 2. 404-410. Available at: http://www.upm.ro/facultati_departamente/stiinte_litere/conferinte/situl_integrare_europeana/Lucrari2/Anisoara%20Pop.pdf (last access: December 2014).
Potts, Christopher
  2005 *The Logic of Conventional Implicature.* Oxford: Oxford University Press.
  2007 "Into the Conventional-Implicature Dimension." *Philosophy Compass* 2(4). 665-679.
Prinz, Jesse
  2006 "Is the Mind Really Modular?" *Contemporary Debates in Cognitive Science.* Ed. Robert Stainton. Malden, MA: Blackwell. 22-36.
Reboul, Anne
  2004 "Conversational Implicatures: Nonce or Generalized?" *Experimental Pragmatics.* Eds. Ira Noveck and Dan Sperber. Basingstoke: Palgrave Macmillan. 322-333.
Recanati, Françoise
  1993 *Direct Reference: From Language to Thought.* Oxford: Blackwell.
  1995 "The Alleged Priority of Literal Interpretation." *Cognitive Science* 19. 207-232.
  2002a "Does Linguistic Communication Rest on Inference? *Mind & Language* 17. 105-126.
  2002b "Unarticulated Constituents." *Linguistics and Philosophy* 25. 299-345.
  2004 *Literal Meaning.* Cambridge: Cambridge University Press.

2007 *Perspectival Thought: A Plea for (Moderate) Relativism.* Oxford: Oxford University Press.

2010 *Truth-Conditional Pragmatics.* Oxford: Oxford University Press.

Reder, Lynne – Gail Kusbit
1991 "Locus of the Moses Illusion: Imperfect Encoding, Retrieval or Match?" *Journal of Memory and Language* 30. 385-406.

Reimer, Marga
2009 "The Direct Expression of Metaphorical Content." *Compositionality, Context and Semantic Values: Essays in Honour of Enrie Lepore.* Eds. Robert Staiton and Christopher Viger. Dordrecht: Springer. 237-253.

Roberts, Craige
2004 "Context in Dynamic Interpretation." *The Handbook of Pragmatics.* Eds. Laurence Horn and Gregory Ward. Oxford: Blackwell. 197-220.

Romero, Esther – Belén Soria
2010 "Introduction: Explicit Communication and Relevance Theory Pragmatics." *Explicit Communication: Robyn Carston's Pragmatics.* Eds. Esther Romero and Belén Soria. Basingstoke: Palgrave Macmillan. 1-24.

Rooy, Robert van
2004 "Evolution of Conventional Meaning and Conversational Principles." *Synthese* 139(2). 331-366.

Rubio-Fernández, Paula
2013 "Associative and Inferential Processes in Pragmatic Enrichment: The Case of Emergent Properties." *Language and Cognitive Processes* 28(6). 723-745.

Ryder, Nuala – Eeva Leinonen
2003 "Use of Context in Question Answering by 3-, 4- and 5-Year-Old Children." *Journal of Psycholinguistic Research* 32(4). 397-415.

Samuels, Richard
2000 "Massive Modular Minds: Evolutionary Psychology and Cognitive Architecture." *Evolution and the Human Mind: Modularity, Language and Meta-Cognition.* Eds. Peter Carruthers and Andrew Chamberlain. Cambridge: Cambridge University Press. 13-46.

2005 "The Complexity of Cognition: Tractability Arguments for Massive Modularity." *The Innate Mind: Structure and Contents.* Eds. Peter Carruthers, Stephen Lawrence and Stephen Stich. Oxford: Oxford University Press. 107-121.

Sanford, Anthony
2002 "Context, Attention and Depth of Processing During Interpretation." *Mind & Language* 17(1-2). 188-206.

Sanford, Anthony – Arthur Graesser
    2006   "Shallow Processing and Underspecification." *Discourse Processes* 42(2). 99-108.
Saul, Jennifer
    2002   "Speaker Meaning, What Is Said and What Is Implicated." *Nous* 36(2). 228-248.
Sbisà, Marina
    2006   "After Grice: Neo- and Post-Perspectives: Review of Stephen Levinson, *Presumptive Meanings The Theory of Generalized Conversational Implicature* and of Robyn Carston, *Thoughts and Utterances: The Pragmatics of Explicit Communication.*" *Journal of Pragmatics* 38. 2223-2234.
Schiffer, Stephen
    1982   "Intention-Based Semantics." *Notre Dame Journal of Formal Logic* 23(2). 119-156.
Searle, John
    1969   *Speech Acts.* Cambridge: Cambridge University Press.
    1978/79 "Literal Meaning." *Erkenntnis* 13. 207-224. Reprinted in *Expression and Meaning.* John Searle. 1979. Cambridge: Cambridge University Press. 117-136.
    1983   *Intentionality.* Cambridge: Cambridge University Press.
    1992   *The Rediscovery of the Mind.* Cambridge, MA: MIT Press.
    1996   "Contemporary Philosophy in the United States." *The Blackwell Companion to Philosophy.* Eds. Nicholas Bunnin and Eric Tsui-James. Malden, MA: Blackwell. 1-22.
    2007   "What is Language: Some Preliminary Remarks." *Explorations in Pragmatics: Linguistic, Cognitive and Intercultural Aspects.* Eds. Istvan Kecskes and Laurence Horn. Berlin: Mouton de Gruyter. 7-37.
Segal, Gabriel
    2005   "Intentionality." *The Oxford Handbook of Contemporary Philosophy.* Eds. Frank Jackson and Michael Smith. Oxford: Oxford University Press. 283-309.
Seuren, Pieter
    2009   *Language in Cognition: Language from Within.* Oxford: Oxford University Press.
Soames, Scott
    2002   *The Unfinished Semantic Agenda of Naming and Necessity.* Oxford: Oxford University Press.

Solska, Agnieszka

2012a "On the Notion of Pragmatic Ambiguity: Accessing Multiple Meanings in Free Indirect Discourse." *Relevance Studies in Poland.* Vol. 4. *Essays on Language and Communication.* Ed. Agnieszka Piskorska. Warsaw: Warsaw University Press. 54-63.

2012b "Relevance-Theoretic Comprehension Procedure and Processing Multiple Meanings in Paradigmatic Puns." *Relevance Theory: More than Understanding.* Eds. Ewa Wałaszewska and Agnieszka Piskorska. Newcastle upon Tyne: Cambridge Scholars Publishing. 167-182.

2012c "The Relevance of the Juxtaposition of Meanings in Puns." *Exploring Language through Contrast.* Eds. Waldemar Skrzypczak, Tomasz Fojt, and Sławomir Wacewicz. Newcastle upon Tyne: Cambridge Scholars Publishing. 184-200.

2012d "The Relevance-Based Model of Context in Processing Puns." *Research in Language* 10(4). 387-404.

Sperber, Dan

1985 *On Anthropological Knowledge.* Cambridge: Cambridge University Press.

1994a "Understanding Verbal Understanding." *What is Intelligence?* Ed. Jean Kahlfa. Cambridge: Cambridge University Press. 179-198.

1994b "The Modularity of Thought and the Epidemiology of Representations." *Mapping the Mind: Domain Specificity in Cognition and Culture.* Eds. Lawrence Hirschfeld and Susan Gelman. Cambridge: Cambridge University Press. 39-67.

1996 *Explaining Culture: A Naturalistic Approach.* Oxford: Blackwell.

2000 "Metarepresentations in an Evolutionary Perspective." *Metarepresentations: An Interdisciplinary Perspective.* Ed. Dan Sperber. Oxford: Oxford University Press. 117-137.

2001 "In Defense of Massive Modularity." *Language, Brain and Cognitive Development: Essays in Honor of Jacques Mehler.* Ed. Emmanuel Dupoux. Cambridge, MA: MIT Press. 47-57.

2005 "Modularity and Relevance: How Can a Massively Modular Mind Be Flexible and Context-Sensitive." *The Innate Mind: Structure and Contents.* Eds. Peter Carruthers, Stephen Lawrence and Stephen Stich. Oxford: Oxford University Press. 53-68.

Sperber, Dan – Deirdre Wilson

1986/95 *Relevance: Communication and Cognition.* Oxford: Blackwell.

1987 "Précis of *Relevance: Communication and Cognition.*" *Behavioral and Brain Sciences* 10. 697-754.

1990/2012 "Rhetoric and Relevance." *The Ends of Rhetoric: History, Theory and Practice*. Eds. David Wellbery and John Bender. Stanford: Stanford University Press. 140-155. Reprinted in *Meaning and Relevance*. Dan Sperber and Deirdre Wilson. 2012. Cambridge: Cambridge University Press. 84-96.

1991a "Irony and the Use-Mention Distinction." *Pragmatics: A Reader*. Ed. Steven Davis. Oxford: Oxford University Press. 550-564.

1991b "Loose Talk." *Pragmatics: A Reader*. Ed. Steven Davis. Oxford: Oxford University Press. 540-549.

1998 "The Mapping Between the Mental and the Public Lexicon." *Language and Thought: Interdisciplinary Themes*. Eds. Peter Carruthers and Jill Boucher. Cambridge, UK: Cambridge University Press. 184-200.

2002 "Pragmatics, Modularity and Mind-Reading." *Mind & Language* 17. 3-23.

2005 "Pragmatics." *UCL Working Papers in Linguistics* 17. 353-388. Reprinted in *Oxford Handbook of Contemporary Philosophy*. Eds. Frank Jackson and Michael Smith. 2005. Oxford: Oxford University Press. 468-501.

2008 "A Deflationary Account of Metaphors." *The Cambridge Handbook of Metaphor and Thought*. Ed. Raymond Gibbs. Cambridge: Cambridge University Press. 84-105.

forthcoming "Beyond the Speaker's Meaning."

Sperber, Dan – Fabrice Clement – Christophe Heintz – Olivier Mascaro – Hugo Mercier Gloria Origgi – Deirdre Wilson

2010 "Epistemic Vigilance." *Mind & Language* 25(4). 359-393.

Sperber, Dan – Francesco Cara – Vittorio Girotto

1995 "Relevance Theory Explains the Selection Task." *Cognition* 57. 31-95.

Sperber, Dan – Lawrence Hirschfeld

1999 "Culture, Cognition, and Evolution." *MIT Encyclopedia of the Cognitive Sciences*. Eds. Robert Wilson and Frank Keil. Cambridge, MA: MIT Press. cxi-cxxxii.

Stainton, Robert

1994 "Using Non-Sentences: An Application of Relevance Theory." *Pragmatics and Cognition* 2(2). 269-284.

Stanley, Jason

2000 "Context and Logical Form." *Linguistics and Philosophy* 23. 391-434.

2002a "Modality and What is Said." *Philosophical Perspectives* 16. 321-344.

2002b "Making It Articulated." *Mind & Language* 17(1-2). 149-168.

2005 "Semantics in Context." *Contextualism in Philosophy: Knowledge, Meaning and Truth.* Eds. Gerhad Preyer and Georg Peter. Oxford: Clarendon Press. 221-253.

Stanley, Jason – Zoltán Gendler Szabó
2000 "On Quantifier Domain Restriction." *Mind & Language* 15(2-3). 219-261.

Stephenson, R.H.
1980 "On the Widespread Use of an Inappropriate and Restricted Model of the Literary Aphorism." *Modern Language Review* 75. 1-17.

Tanaka, Keiko
1992 "The Pun in Adverting: A Pragmatic Approach." *Lingua* 87. 91-102.
1994 *Advertising Language: A Pragmatic Approach to Advertisements in Britain and Japan.* London: Routledge.

Taylor, Kenneth
2001 "Sex, Breakfast, and Descriptus Interruptus." *Synthese* 128. 45-61.

Thompson, Robert
2008 "Grades of Meaning." *Synthese* 161. 238-308.
2014 "Meaning and Mindreading." *Mind & Language* 29(2). 167-200.

Travis, Charles
2006 "Insensitive Semantics." *Mind & Language* 21(1). 39-49.

Tsimply, Ianthi-Maria – Neil Smith
1998 "Modules and Quasi-Modules: Language and Theory of Mind in a Polyglot Savant." *Learning and Individual Differences* 10(3). 193-215.

Uchida, Seiji
1998 "Text and Relevance." *Relevance Theory: Applications and Implications.* Eds. Robyn Carston and Seiji Uchida. Amsterdam: John Benjamins. 161-178.

Van der Henst, Jean-Baptiste – Dan Sperber
2004 "Testing the Cognitive and Communicative Principles of Relevance." *Experimental Pragmatics.* Eds. Ira Noveck and Dan Sperber. Basingstoke: Palgrave Macmillan. 141-171.

Van der Henst, Jean-Baptiste – Dan Sperber – Guy Politzer
2002 "When Is a Conclusion Not Worth Deriving?" *Thinking and Reasoning* 8(1). 1-20.

Van Mulken, Margot – Renske van Enschot-van Dijk – Hans Hoeken
2005 "Puns, Relevance and Appreciation in Advertisements." *Journal of Pragmatics* 37. 707-721.

Van Oostendorp, Herre – Sjaak de Mul
1990 "Moses Beats Adam: A Semantic Relatedness Effect on a Semantic Illusion." *Acta Psychologica* 74. 35-46.

Vega Moreno, Rosa
    2003   "Relevance Theory and the Construction of Idiom Meaning." *UCL Working Papers in Linguistics* 15. 83-104.
    2005   "Idioms, Transparency and Pragmatic Inference." *UCL Working Papers in Linguistics* 17. 389-426.
    2007   *Creativity and Convention: The Pragmatics of Everyday Figurative Speech*. Amsterdam: John Benjamins.

Viger, Christopher
    2006   "Is the Aim of Perception to Provide Accurate Representations? A Case for the 'No' Side." *Contemporary Debates in Philosophy of Science*. Ed. Christopher Hitchcock. Malden, MA: Blackwell Publishing. 275-288.

Viscente, Augustín – Fernando Martínez-Manrique
    2005   "Semantic Underdetermination and the Cognitive Uses of Language." *Mind & Language* 20(5). 537-558.

Wałaszewska, Ewa
    2011   "Broadening and Narrowing in Lexical Development: How Relevance Theory Can Account for Children's Overextensions and Underextensions." *Journal of Pragmatics* 43. 314-326.

Wedgwood, Daniel
    2007   "Shared Assumptions: Semantic Minimalism and Relevance Theory." *Journal of Linguistics* 43(3). 647-681.
    2011   "The Individual in Interaction: Why Cognitive and Discourse-Level Pragmatics Need Not Conflict." *Intercultural Pragmatics* 8(4). 517-542.

Wettstein, Howard
    1979   "Indexical Reference and Propositional Content." *Philosophical Studies* 36. 91-100.

Wharton, Tim
    2001   "Natural Pragmatics and Natural Codes." *UCL Working Papers in Linguistics* 13. 109-158.
    2002   "Paul Grice, Saying and Meaning." *UCL Working Papers in Linguistics* 14. 207-248.
    2009   *Pragmatics and Non-Verbal Communication*. Cambridge: Cambridge University Press.

Wilson, Deirdre
    1992   "Reference and Relevance." *UCL Working Papers in Linguistics* 4. 167-191.

1994   "Relevance and Understanding." *Language and Understanding*. Eds. Gillian Brown, Kirsten Malmkjaer, Alastair Pollitt and John Williams. Oxford: Oxford University Press. 35-58.

1998   "Discourse, Coherence and Relevance: A Reply to Rachel Giora." *Journal of Pragmatics* 29. 57-74.

2000   "Metarepresentation in Linguistic Communication." *Metarepresentations: A Multidisciplinary Perspective*. Ed. Dan Sperber. Oxford: Oxford University Press. 411-448.

2004   "Relevance and Lexical Pragmatics." *UCL Working Papers in Linguistics* 16. 343-360.

2005   "New Directions for Research on Pragmatics and Modularity." *Lingua* 115. 1129-1146.

2007   "Inference, Implication and Implicature." Paper presented at the Shared Content Workshop: Implicatures, the Centre for the Study of Mind in Nature, University of Oslo, 3-4 November.

2009   "Irony and metarepresentation." *UCL Working Papers in Linguistics* 21. 183-226.

2011   "Relevance and the Interpretation of Literary Works." *UCL Working Papers in Linguistics* 23. 69-80.

2014   "Relevance theory." *UCL Working Papers in Linguistics* 26. http://www.ucl.ac.uk/pals/research/linguistics/publications/wpl/14papers/wilson. (last access: January, 2015).

Wilson, Deirdre – Dan Sperber

1981   "On Grice's Theory of Conversation." *Conversation and Discourse*. Ed. Paul Werth. London: Croom Helm. 155-178.

1991a   "Inference and Implicature." *Pragmatics: A Reader*. Ed. Steven Davis. Oxford: Oxford University Press. 377-393.

1991b   "Pragmatics and Modularity." *Pragmatics: A Reader*. Ed. Steven Davis. Oxford: Oxford University Press. 583-595.

1992   "On Verbal Irony." *Lingua* 87(1). 53-76.

1993   "Linguistic Form and Relevance." *Lingua* 90(2). 1-25.

1998   "Pragmatics and Time." *Relevance Theory: Applications and Implications*. Eds. Robyn Carston and Seiji Uchida. Amsterdam: John Benjamins. 1-22.

2002   "Truthfulness and Relevance." *Mind* 111. 583-632.

2004   "Relevance Theory." *The Handbook of Pragmatics*. Eds. Laurence Horn and Gregory Ward. Oxford: Blackwell. 607-632.

Wilson, Deirdre – Robyn Carston

2006   "Metaphor, Relevance and the 'Emergent Property' Issue." *Mind & Language* 21. 404-433.

2007   "A Unitary Approach to Lexical Pragmatics: Relevance, Inference and Ad Hoc Concepts." *Pragmatics*. Ed. Noel Burton-Roberts. Basingstoke: Palgrave Macmillan. 230-259.

Wilson, Deirdre – Tim Wharton
2006   "Relevance and Prosody." *Journal of Pragmatics* 38. 1559-1579.

Wilson, Robert
2004   "What Computations (Still, Still) Can't Do: Jerry Fodor on Computation and Modularity." *New Essays in the Philosophy of Language and Mind*. Eds. Maite Ezcurdia, Robert Stainton and Christopher Viger. Calgary: University of Calgary Press. 407-425.

Wolf, Manfred
1994   "The Aphorism." *Et Cetera: A Review of General Semantics* 51(4). 432-439.

Woodward, James – Fiona Cowie
2006   "The Mind is Not (Just) a System of Modules Shaped (Just) by Natural Selection." *Contemporary Debates in Philosophy of Science*. Ed. Christopher Hitchcock. Malden, MA: Blackwell Publishing. 312-334.

Yus, Francisco
2003   "Humour and the Search for Relevance." *Journal of Pragmatics* 35. 1295-1331.
2006   "Relevance Theory." *Encyclopedia of Language and Linguistics* (2nd edition). Ed. Keith Brown. Oxford: Elsevier. 512-519.
2008   "A Relevance-Theoretic Classification of Jokes." *Lodz Papers in Pragmatics* 4(1). 131-157.

Žegarac, Vladimir
2006   "*Believing in:* A Pragmatic Account." *Lingua* 116. 1703-1721.

Index